Kingdom of the Seashell

In each caption in this book, magnification is indicated as follows: X 3—magnified three times, etc.

Kingdom of the Seashell

by R. Tucker Abbott, Ph.D.

Former du Pont Chair of Malacology
Delaware Museum of Natural History

Bonanza Books
New York

This 1982 edition is published by Bonanza Books,
distributed by Crown Publishers, Inc.,
by arrangement with Crown Publishers, Inc.

Manufactured in Hong Kong

Library of Congress Cataloging in Publication Data
Abbott, R. Tucker (Robert Tucker), 1919-
   Kingdom of the seashell.
   Reprint. Originally published: New York,
N.Y. : Crown, c1972.
   Includes index.
   1. Shells.   2. Mollusks.   I. Title.
QL403.A22   1982   594'.047   82-9644

ISBN: 0-517-166089
h   g   f   e

PRECEDING PAGES: The Elegant Feather Snail, *Cyerce*, from
Australia. × 15. THIS PAGE: Recently discovered
Latiaxis santacruzensis Emerson and D'Attilio, 1970,
from deep water off the Galápagos Islands. × 10.

Contents

OPPOSITE: Australian trochids swarm over marine vegetation. × 3.

Dedicated to my wife, Sue

Introduction

Shells, and the creatures they contain, have fascinated man since the dawn of civilization, and he has made them part of his life in a hundred ways —as food, as trade goods, as money, as medicine, as tools, as ornaments and as objects of art, design and scientific investigation. Shells are produced as outer skeletons by soft-bodied creatures called *mollusks*. They are found in great abundance in almost every part of the world, as testified to by the many beds of oysters, clams and scallops in our shallow seas and by the myriads of garden snails and slugs found throughout most countries. Other mollusks, such as the conchs, whelks, squids and octopuses, are familiar to men of the sea and marine biologists.

The study of shells is an ancient one, going back to the Dark Ages and taking its place beside the studies of alchemy and primitive medicine. Aristotle and Pliny, the scientists of the Ancient World, wrote thousands of words upon the subject. The English of the Victorian era called it *conchology,* and the French dubbed it *malacology.* It was known as "the queen of natural history studies" in nineteenth-century Europe and as "the emperor's science" in Japan.

Unlike almost any other hobby, conchology weds a wide spectrum of activities, ranging from the rigorous sport of scuba diving and reef searching to the placid satisfaction of naming and classifying the 70,000 kinds of shells. Physicians are intrigued by the fatal bites inflicted by cones and octopuses. Parasitologists spend lifetimes studying fatal diseases carried by certain tropical freshwater snails. Biochemists attempt to analyze the antiviral and antibacterial powers of the juices of clams and abalone snails. Mathematicians study the progressive chambers of the nautilus shells, and artists use the scallop motif in a hundred ways.

Many trade routes of ancient peoples and primitive tribes have been worked out by archaeologists' identifying the sources of the shells found in graves and kitchen dumps. The climates of New England and Greenland a thousand years ago have been verified by the types of temperature-sensitive shells unearthed from recent digs. Paleontologists can predict the presence of oil by studying the mollusks and other invertebrates found fossilized in the various layers of ancient rocks.

Primarily, this book is for those who have been recently exposed to molluscan shells and want to know more about their habits, uses and beauty. But it is also designed to challenge the amateur conchologist by offering many little-known facts about the way in which mollusks live. I believe that this book will expose more basic mollusk biology to shell collectors than has any other popular presentation. If this proves to be true, even in small measure, conchology has been served and I shall know that perhaps a few persons will have had the doors opened to a rewarding study.

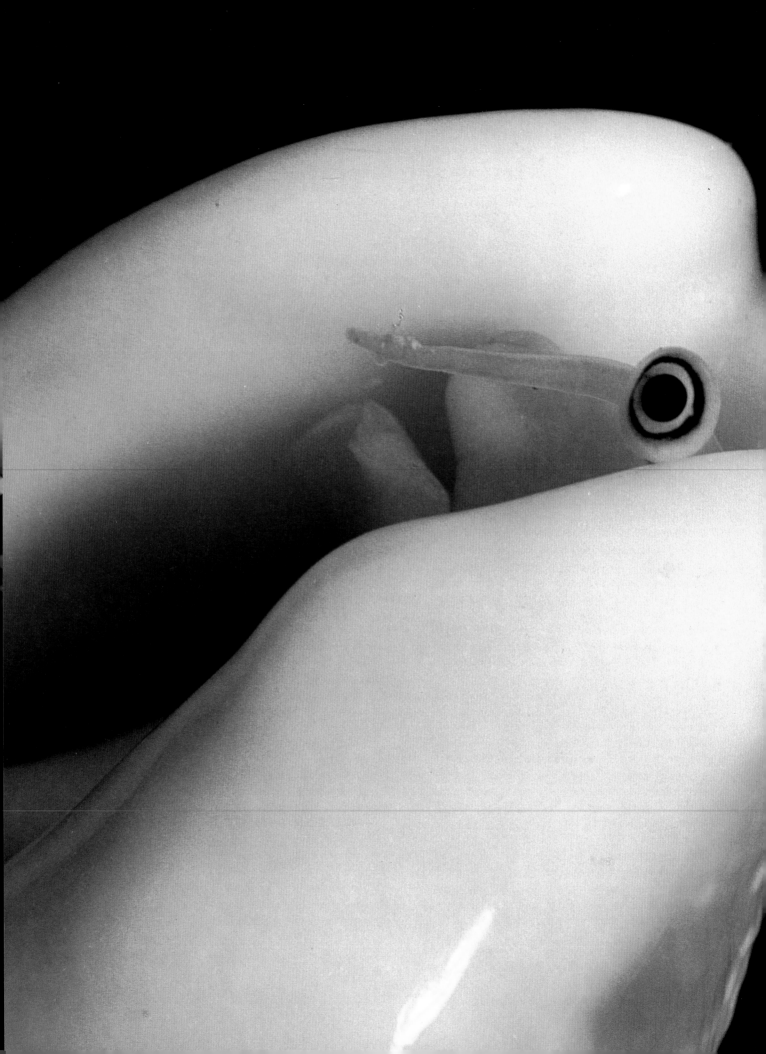

Molluscan seashells 1

What is a mollusk?

Although it is not absolutely necessary to define a mollusk in order for one to enjoy a book about shells, it does seem advisable to outline the basic attributes and limits of this group, if for no other reason than that a person who becomes interested in a subject usually wants to know exactly what is being discussed.

Based on internal structure and patterns of function, animals may be grouped into *phyla*. Mollusks comprise one such group. It includes such well-known creatures as snails, clams, oysters, periwinkles, scallops, squid and octopuses, slugs and whelks. Novices to biology often believe that the mollusk group also includes such seashore life as barnacles and crabs (they are crustaceans) and sand dollars (they are echinoderms, closely related to the starfish). Although, like the mollusks, these creatures have external shells and no internal backbone, they lack the biological makeup necessary to qualify them as mollusks.

In general, mollusks are soft-bodied animals that usually produce an external shell composed of a limy material, calcium carbonate. The one feature unique to all mollusks is the presence of a fleshy mantle—a fold or lobe or pair of lobes lining the shell—that secretes this shell-building material. Other anatomical characteristics, however, differ within the phylum. Consequently, the mollusks are further divided into classes. Three of the classes are well known to many people—the univalves (Gastropoda), which includes the snails, conchs and periwinkles; the bivalves (Bivalvia), which includes the clams, oysters and scallops; the cephalopods (Cephalopoda), which embraces the squids, nautiluses and octopuses. There are three minor, although peculiarly distinctive, groups—the chitons (Amphineura), the tooth shells (Scaphopoda) and the gastroverms (Monoplacophora).

Members of all the classes except for the bivalves possess a ribbonlike set of hooked teeth, or *radula,* that they rasp back and forth over food, using it much as a cat uses its tongue to lap milk. Most mollusks also have a well-defined nervous system with a primitive brain; a circulatory system that has a full-fledged, two-chambered heart; a complicated digestive system that includes jaws, pharynx, esophagus, stomach, intestine and anus; and a reproductive system that produces eggs in the water either as single floating objects or in protective capsules. Most snails and all cephalopods have eyes and tentacles.

The embryological development of most mollusks includes a larval stage known as the trochophore. This is a multicellular larval form that is surrounded by numerous, hairlike cilia. The trochophore sometimes completes its development within the egg and, in many marine species, hatches out into a more complicated larval creature called a veliger. The veliger swims freely through the water to new living grounds and then changes into a miniature adult snail or clam or whatever the case may be.

There are about 70,000 kinds of living mollusks, although other estimates by specialists range from 50,000 to 100,000. There may have been twice this number of species in previous geological times, but their fossil numbers are shrouded in rocky mystery. Mollusks have a wide variety of habitats. There are clams and snails living in lakes and ponds, at the seashore, in the deepest parts of the oceans, in hot springs and at the tops of high mountains. There are clams that burrow in wood and limestone rock and others that attach themselves to the undersides of sea urchins or suck on to the gills of fish. Some snails live in high trees; others, within the intestines of sea puddings or within the arms of starfish. And squids, by jetting out of the water and using their side fins to glide in the wind, can "fly" for several hundred feet.

PRECEDING PAGES: Peering out at the watery world, a conch, *Strombus bulla* (Röding), displays its agatelike eyes. × 10.
OPPOSITE: The Great Scallop, *Pecten maximus* (Linné), has a ribbed shell and fleshy interior. × 1.

The univalves

Of the six classes of mollusks, the largest, and certainly the best known from many standpoints, is the class Gastropoda, which contains such univalves (one-shelled creatures) as the conchs, whelks and snails. It is the only class to contain species that have ventured permanently onto land. The evolutionary process has enabled these snaillike members to make such a move by giving them an efficient gliding foot with which to travel across land, eyes with which to see, an aggressive eating mechanism and a pulmonary system with which to acquire oxygen from the air. Those of the univalves that remained in the sea kept their original gill structure for breathing.

There are at least 30,000 species of univalves.

Although most of them bear a single, coiled shell, many, such as the limpets and abalones, have a flat saucerlike shell while others do not have a shell at all, as is the case with the garden slugs and many sea slugs. Most also have a radula.

Many snails have an operculum, or trapdoor, that is grown on top of the back part of the foot. When the snail withdraws into its shell, the operculum seals the mouth of the shell. Many families of marine snails, such as the nerites and turbans, have a heavy, shelly operculum while other families, such as the whelks and tulip shells, have thin, brown, horny opercula. Some groups, such as the glossy cowries and the figshells, do not have this trapdoor.

Although most marine univalves have separate sexes, the females usually having shells slightly larger than those of the males, a large number of families, particularly among the land pulmonate snails and the marine bubble snails and sea hares, are hermaphroditic—that is, the organs of both sexes are housed within the same individual.

During the long evolutionary development of the univalves, beginning at least 500 million years ago in the Cambrian period, several basically different stocks arose. This has resulted today in their being divided into three main subclasses.

1. The subclass Prosobranchia includes the gill-bearing snails that have one or two gills in a mantle cavity that is found at the front of the animal instead of the back. Most of them are aquatic, and the majority have an operculum of some sort. The limpets, periwinkles, conchs, whelks, cones and volutes, to mention but a few major families, belong to this subclass.

2. The subclass Opisthobranchia contains only marine species, most of which have either a much-reduced shell, such as found inside the sea hares, or no shell at all, as is the case with the nudibranchian sea slugs. A few, such as the bubble shells, have a copious, hard shell. The gills are generally posterior to the heart and are usually on the outside of the animal in the form of plumes. Most are herbivorous, but many, such as the pyramidellids, are parasitic on bivalves and other sea creatures.

3. The subclass Pulmonata contains most of the woodland and garden snails. They are all air-breathers equipped with pulmonary sacs. Both sexes are present in each individual. The garden slugs are merely pulmonate snails that evolved over many millions of years without developing shells. Many freshwater pond snails, such as *Physa, Planorbis* and *Lymnaea*, are also pulmonates.

OPPOSITE: The Australian Acorn Snail, *Nassarius glans* (Linné), crawls on a flat, speckled foot; in front is a long siphon and two pointed tentacles. × 3.
TOP RIGHT: Chitinous operculum, or trapdoor, of a *Cittarium* snail. × 2. LOWER RIGHT: Radular ribbon of teeth removed from a *Urosalpinx* oyster drill. × 200.

The bivalves

Perhaps more important economically to man than the other mollusks, at least from the standpoint of food, the class Bivalvia has always commanded attention because of its wide variety of forms, including the oysters, clams and scallops. Although the pelecypods, as they are sometimes called, form the second largest of the molluscan classes, containing about 10,000 species, not one of the species has ventured onto land or taken to the air.

The bivalves, as the name suggests, have two shelly valves into which the animal can withdraw for protection. These valves are brought together by one or two strong adductor muscles and forced ajar by a rubberlike wedge, or *resilium*, which acts much the same way as a rubber wedge placed in the hinged side of a closing door.

Their mode of progression is usually by means of a muscular, wedge-shaped foot that protrudes in front of the shell. Using the tip of the foot to anchor itself, the bivalve pulls itself up to the anchored foot. Those bivalves, such as the oysters and mussels, that do not inch along in the sand or mud are usually solidly attached to rocks by means of a byssus, a clump of chitinous, or horny, threads secreted by a gland in the foot.

All members of this class differ from the other mollusks in that they lack the radular feeding mechanism. Bivalves are mainly herbivorous, feeding either by drawing in seawater containing plankton or by sucking up detritus, which is debris resulting from the decomposition of animal, mineral and vegetable matter in the sea. The fine food particles are drawn in through a spout-shaped siphon and passed over the gills, where they are entrapped in sticky mucus. Thousands of microscopic hairs, or cilia, beat the food and mucus toward the mouth. Small flaps, or *palps,* then push the collected food into the mouth.

Although many mollusks lay their eggs in compact capsules of horny material, most bivalves simply shed their eggs into the open water, where they are fertilized by wandering sperm. In some cases, the eggs—internally fertilized—are kept inside the mother and incubated within the gills. Strangest of the reproductive cycles is that of the freshwater pearly mussels of the rivers of North America. After the eggs have been laid within the mantle cavity and fertilized by sperm, the larvae hatch into a brood chamber of the mother. There the young develop special shelly hooks. At an appropriate moment, the female clam expels these tiny, spined clams, or glochidia, into the river water, usually in the vicinity of a particular species of passing fish. These specialized glochidia, as they are called, snap furiously through the water until, by chance, they latch onto the gills of these fish. Once clamped upon the gill, the glochidium acts as a parasite and for the next few weeks sucks vital blood juices from its fish host. When grown to a respectable size, the heavy young clam drops off the fish to the bottom of the pond or stream and there begins its adult life.

There are many evolutionary avenues that the bivalves have taken. Among the major groups that have resulted are the iridescent nut clams with their numerous comblike teeth, the blue mussels that attach themselves to wharves and rocks with threadlike byssal anchors, the sturdy venus clams that make their way through sand with a hatchet-shaped foot and the specialized teredo shipworms that look more like long, shell-encased worms than bivalves.

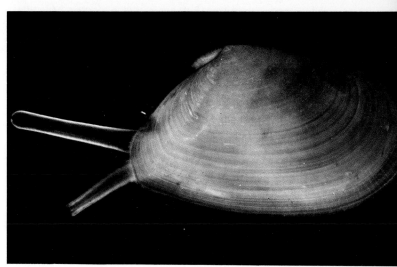

ABOVE: Some bivalves, such as this *Spondylus americanus* Hermann, sport
long spines. × 1. LOWER LEFT: The Sunray Clam, *Macrocallista
nimbosa* (Lightfoot), of Florida is smooth shelled. × 1. LOWER RIGHT:
This *Tellina agilis* Stimpson uses siphons to inhale and exhale water. × 3.

The squids, octopuses and nautiluses

It is most surprising to the average person that the squids, octopuses and chambered nautiluses should be considered members of the molluscan clan. These creatures appear to be far more advanced in their construction and habits than the sluggish snail and lazy oyster. But, again, the biologists have discovered that the embryological development, the structural aspects of the mantle and the presence of classical radular teeth leave no doubt that the class Cephalopoda belongs within the molluscan phylum.

The cephalopods are the most active of all the invertebrates and demonstrate a remarkable intelligence for such lowly creatures. All are marine, and all have a long, noble history stretching back through geological time to the Ordovician period, some 400 million years ago. They have a cartilaginous brain case and a well-developed nervous system that permits great speed, strength and agility. The eyes of the squid reach a size and perfection found nowhere else among the invertebrates.

The squids and octopuses are rapacious feeders, usually attacking fish and crustacea. A series of prehensile tentacles, or arms, surrounds the mouth, which is furnished with a parrotlike, chitinous beak and, within the pharynx, with a strong set of radular teeth.

The octopus has eight arms, each of which is studded with numerous small suction disks. Squids have, in addition to the eight arms, a pair of much longer tentacles, thus giving them ten appendages. Most species of living cephalopods have a sac that produces a brown or purple-black ink used to ward off attacking fish or to serve as a protective smoke screen.

Squids have been known to reach a length of seventy-three feet. These monsters of the depths off Newfoundland and New Zealand are relatively sluggish and seldom come to the surface. On occasion they are attacked by whales whose diet includes squid. The beaks of the latter sometimes become entangled in the intestine of the whale and cause the formation of ambergris, the valuable

paraffinlike substance used as a fixative in the manufacture of perfume.

There are several hundred species of living cephalopods—about 150 kinds of octopods and nearly 350 squid species. Some small squids are so abundant that they have supported commercial fisheries for centuries in Japan and Newfoundland, where they are caught for food and fish bait. In the Ancient World of the Mediterranean, the Sepia Squid, or Cuttlefish, was the chief source of the dark brown sepia ink. Today this species is still the chief source of the chalky cuttlefish bone that is used in making toothpaste and for supplying pet birds with calcium.

The chambered nautilus produces a beautiful chambered shell. Externally, it is creamy white with broad rusty brown stripes; within, it is a brilliant iridescent mother-of-pearl. The pearly nautiluses are the last of a vanishing line of cephalopods once abundant 400 million years ago. Today, they are limited to three or four kinds, inhabiting deep water off the islands of the southwest Pacific.

OPPOSITE: Squids open their eyes at night and squint during daylight hours. This Australian cuttlefish has cuddled its ten arms together in order to streamline its body. × 1.
ABOVE: The eight-armed octopus has no shell. The numerous suckers are used to grasp other mollusks and crabs. × 0.5.

The tusk shells

Of the three minor classes of mollusks, the Scaphopoda contains those mollusks probably simplest in shell structure and general anatomy. The shell, which is open at each end, resembles a miniature elephant tusk. All the thousand-or-so species are marine, and all live partially buried in sand or gravel in water depths ranging from a few feet to the deepest parts of the oceans. In size, they vary from minute *Cadulus* tusks, resembling grains of rice, to the five-inch-long, yellow Japanese tusks.

Despite the fact that there are hundreds of kinds of tusk shells scattered throughout various parts of the world, they show no great variations in structure other than the general differences shown between the only two known families—the typical *Dentalium*, resembling elephant tusks, and the *Cadulus*, which look like swollen cucumbers with a hole at each end.

Perhaps the most attractive of the *Dentalium* tusks is the four-inch-long Elephant's Tusk of the southwest Pacific. The shell is an attractive emerald green, fading to pea green at each end, and sculptured along its length by eight sharp ridges. In cross-section, the shell has an octagonal shape. Other tusks may be extremely long and slender, resembling delicate pink darning needles. The various species are distinguished by the number and shape of the longitudinal ribs, by the coloration and by the curious slots appearing along the edge of the smaller, posterior end.

Relatively inactive creatures, the scaphopods have a very low rate of metabolism and a very simple anatomy. There are no eyes, no gills and no heart. The mantle that lines the tubular shell serves as an adequate surface through which respiratory exchanges occur. The blood of the animal is contained in simple sacs extending from the mantle into the various tissues. The movement of the blood is accomplished chiefly through the contractions and expansions of the pistonlike foot, since there are no pericardium, arteries or veins.

The feeding mechanism is complicated and unique among mollusks. Food consists of microscopic, shelled foraminifera, a primitive form of single-celled sea creatures living in sand. The mouth of the tusk shell is surrounded by hundreds of long, fleshy filaments at the end of each of which is a sticky, ciliated pad. These curious capturing arms are called captacula; to feed, several of them gang up on a desirable foram and drag it through the sand to the mouth. There a set of radular teeth, not unlike that found in snails, cracks open the foram and passes it into the intestine.

The foot is probably the most vital organ of the scaphopod, since it aids in feeding, serves as a means of locomotion and, by contracting and expanding, keeps water passing in and out of the posterior half of the mantle cavity so that the blood is circulated. "Breathing," or the sudden exchange of old for new water through the small orifice that sticks up above the sand, occurs on the average of every five or ten minutes.

Tusk shells were used extensively by the western tribes of North American Indians. Long before the coming of white man, the tusks were cut into cross-sections and strung into necklaces. As late as the nineteenth century, the Indians of the Northwest fished tusk shells and strung them into money belts.

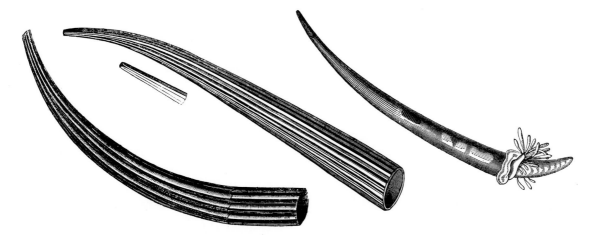

TOP: The four-inch Elephant's Tusk, *Dentalium elephantinum* Linné, is common in the Philippines. LOWER DRAWINGS: Tusks have many shapes and types of ribbing. The foot protrudes from the larger end.

The chitons

"Armadillos of the sea" is an appropriate nickname for the strange snaillike mollusks making up the Amphineura class. Also called chitons, coat-of-mail shells and cat's cradles, these creatures are recognizable by the presence of eight oblong shelly plates. These plates, welded together along their edges by a girdle, a band of leathery material, form an effective protective armor against strong waves and predators.

Strictly marine, the majority of the 600 living chiton species inhabit rocky seashore environments where their low dome-shaped shells are well suited to withstanding the violent surges of oceanic waves. All of them cling tenaciously to hard substrates. If one is removed from its rock, it will attempt to roll up into a ball to protect its fleshy undersurface.

Unlike univalves, the chitons do not have coiled shells. They are also much more bilaterally symmetrical, which is a biological way of saying that each side of a chiton is like the other. Chitons have a simple head that lacks eyes and tentacles. Behind is a large, flat, powerful foot, flanked on either side by a long series of leaflike gill platelets. The anus is at the very posterior end, whereas in most snails it is twisted around to face the front end. Although the shell of the chiton is formed into eight distinct valves, this mollusk is not segmented like the worms and crustaceans. Embryologically, the chiton has but one shell that in later development becomes broken into eight parts.

The leathery band, or girdle, encircling the shelly valves is part of the mantle, and in the chitons this organ is quite distinctive for each species. It may be smooth or bear bristles, spikes or scales, which overlap and resemble dried split peas. The mantle of the foot-long Giant Pacific Chiton of our western shores completely covers and hides the shelly valves. True cephalic eyes are absent in chitons, but a few families have developed independent eyes in the top surfaces of the shelly valves. To the naked human eye they appear to be minute black spots, but under high magnification each proves to have a cornea, iris, lens, retina and optic nerve.

Chitons are active at night, leaving their resting places under the ledges of rocks to venture out on browsing forays. Most species are herbivorous, and their strong radular teeth are constantly rasping off bits of algal growths. A few chitons, surprisingly enough, are predatory. The Veiled Pacific Chiton, a two-inch-long inhabitant of California, has modified the front end of its mantle into a hoodlike flap which it can raise and quickly snap down to capture small living shrimps and other tiny crustaceans, or amphipods. Tiny fleshy tentacles assist in guiding the captured food into the chiton's mouth.

Chitons employ a variety of methods of producing young. There is, however, no copulation. The males liberate sperm freely into the water, so that fertilization must occur in the freely floating eggs given off by the female or within the mantle cavity of the female. Some chitons lay jellylike strings of eggs, and a few brood their young along the gutters on either side of the foot. At least two species are ovoviviparous, giving birth to live young.

Chitons are used as fish bait in many parts of the world, and in the West Indies the foot is sometimes eaten raw, with appropriate condiments, or pounded tender and put in fish chowders. The valves of chitons are used extensively in the shellcraft industry and whole, polished as ornamental brooches.

TOP LEFT: From below, a chiton resembles a limpet snail. The central muscular foot and the head are clearly seen. RIGHT: From above, the eight shelly plates are seen bordered by the pebbly side of the girdle. × 1. LOWER LEFT: The radular teeth of a chiton are numerous and complicated. × 50.

The gastroverms

Although fossil representatives of the primitive class Monoplacophora had been described as long ago as had snails, their relationships to other mollusks were not realized until a living representative was dredged up from great depths off the coast of western Mexico by the Danish research vessel *Galathea* and reported upon in 1957. Within ten years, another five gastroverm species had been caught and recognized by oceanographers dredging in waters deeper than 3,000 fathoms.

The unusual feature of these strange limpetlike shells—dubbed in 1960 gastroverms for want of a better popular name—is that they are segmented like the worms and some of the other more primitive sea creatures. In each of the compartments, or segments, making up the body of the animal, the internal vital organs are duplicated. Thus, the segmented gastroverm has a number of pairs of kidneys, ovaries, testes, gills and other organs. All other mollusks, including the eight-shelled chitons, have but one pair of each of these various organs.

The shells of the gastroverms are not at all impressive. They are simple, depressed, limpet-shaped valves, less than an inch in size and quite thin and fragile. Like the snails, the early part has a coiled chamber and the outer surface of the adult is covered with a protective horny periostracum, or sheath. On the inner surface, the shell reveals a significant series of paired muscle scars, suggesting segmentation, one of the several features that relate this group to the segmented worms.

The soft parts somewhat resemble those of the chitons. The head lacks true tentacles and eyes. Behind the mouth is a curious cluster of frondlike appendages that serve to push food into the pharynx. The foot is round in outline and somewhat like that of a limpet, although it is not as broad nor does it have the musculature to suck onto hard surfaces. On either side, running along the mantle-cavity gutters, are five or six pairs of distinct gills. Internally, these are matched by pairs of kidneys, each with a separate exit, just as in the worms. Evidently the sexes are separate, although there does not appear to be any morphological difference between the shells of males and those of females. The eggs and sperm are probably expelled freely into the surrounding water.

The radular ribbon of the gastroverms resembles that of the chitons rather than that of most gastropods. From the nature of the individual teeth, it may be postulated that gastroverms ingest mud or bottom detritus. In actuality, the radular mechanism of the gastroverms is upside down as compared to that of other mollusks.

It is a general law of marine biology that the more primitive creatures are now generally confined to very deep waters. "Newcomers," with their more advanced, aggressive ways and apparatus, originate in shallow waters and exterminate the less efficient "old-timers." The few survivors among the primitive mollusks, such as the *Pleurotomaria* slit shells, the *Neopilina* gastroverms and the pearly nautiluses, all live in deep water, away from the more active competitors of the shallow seas.

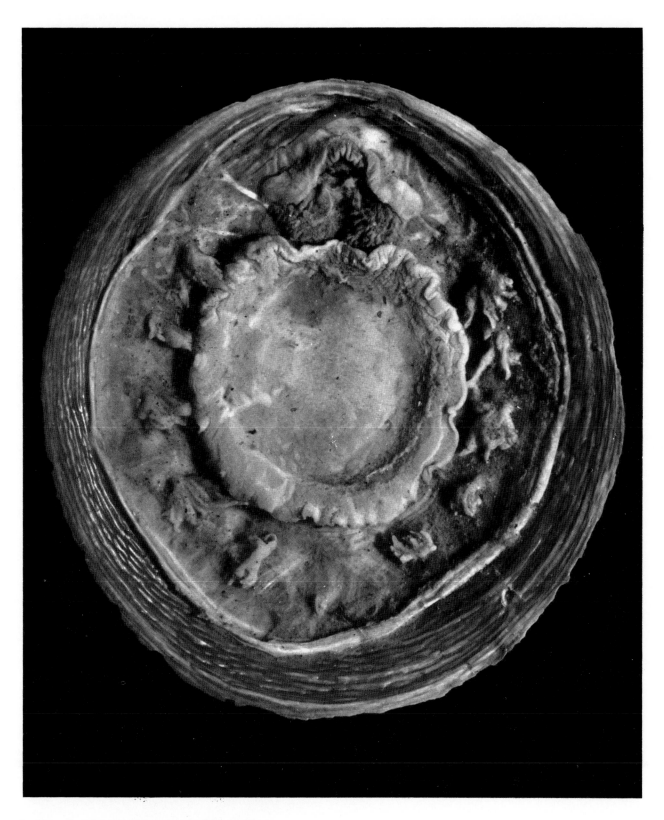

In this underside view of the recently discovered
Neopilina, the curious paired clumps of gills are shown on either
side of the somewhat retracted foot. Above is the head,
showing two fleshy palps, or mouth flaps. × 10.

How shells live 2

How shells mate

It is believed, on the basis of biological studies made on today's mollusks, that all primitive univalves and bivalves had separate sexes, that there were no accessory sexual organs and that the ova and sperm were directly and freely discharged into the seawater. This simple and rather chancy way of fertilization has been retained in many modern bivalves, the tusk shells and a few marine gastropods, such as the limpets and some top shells.

Spewing sperm and eggs loosely into the ocean is fraught with danger. They may be eaten by sea creatures or destroyed by adverse temperatures and currents or be unable to find each other. To offset these disadvantages, the mollusks produce enormous numbers of egg cells and sperm cells, or gametes, all in as short a period as possible and all at the same time. *Patella* limpets will breed only when the wind and waves have been extremely strong for several days. Northern oysters will shed eggs only when the water temperature goes above 60°F. Bivalves that cling to mangrove trees in estuaries will breed only on the first very high tide after a full moon. This assures the young of being spread about over as wide an area as is possible.

The sperm of all oysters contain a strong hormone that causes the muscle of the female to relax and at the same time increases the pumping rate of water. This allows the entry of more sperm. Some hermaphroditic wood-boring clams, *Xylophaga,* have a special sac for storing live sperm. Later, when the eggs have become mature, the sperm are released to fertilize them. This ensures a lone female adrift at sea in a log a supply of male gametes.

Sex change in an individual is not uncommon in some species. Some bivalves begin life as males and after a year change to functioning females. The

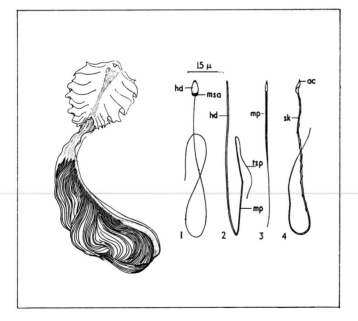

PRECEDING PAGES: This pair of nudibranchs,
Chromodoris quadricolor (Rüppell and Leuckart),
from western Australia, has just mated, and
soon gelatinous coils of eggs will be produced. × 10.

edible oyster alternates its sex—male one year, female the next. The common slipper shell, *Crepidula*, lives in clusters with one shell clinging on top of its neighbor. The four or five larger individuals at the bottom of the pile are all females. The younger and smaller ones at the top are males. Very often the middle ones are in the process of changing sex from male to female. Sexuality is controlled by a hormone that is constantly being produced by the female and exuded into the water. As long as the level of this hormone is high enough, it will prevent males from turning into females. Should the females die or cease to function because of old age, the hormone disappears and the snails at the top of the pile begin to lose their testes, the penis shrinks away and ovaries begin to develop. In a week, the males have become females.

Hermaphroditism is limited to certain groups of mollusks. The duck clam family, Anatinacea; most air-breathing land snails and the sea hares and nudibranch sea slugs are hermaphrodites.

The cephalopods have separate sexes; in fact, some octopuses go through a period of courtship. During this time, certain color changes are displayed by the male, and he may at the same time arouse the female by stroking her. The sperm, which occur in packets, are transferred into the female's oviduct by the tip of one of the male's arms.

OPPOSITE LEFT: Various shapes and sizes of sperm from marine snails. RIGHT: Underside view of a female slipper shell, *Crepidula*, being impregnated by a male riding on the back of her shell. At the left can be seen the extended penis. × 2. ABOVE: A male Australian Monoplex Triton extends his foot. Coming from the mantle cavity is the fingerlike penis. × 1.

Egg capsules and brooding

Ensuring protection for their eggs is one of the principal problems for the mollusks. Even the marine forms that shed their eggs directly into the sea supply a basic protective membrane around the ovum. A few bivalves lay their eggs in gelatinous capsules, while others deposit them with a sticky mucus to ensure their remaining safely on the bottom. A more advanced egg capsule, somewhat resembling a flying saucer, is produced by the Common European Periwinkle. Less than one-fourth the area of the head of a pin, the clear, pill-shaped capsules, each containing an egg, float through the water for a few weeks before hatching.

Although mollusks generally do not take care of their eggs or young, a few do. The female cowries, for instance, sit on top of their egg clusters to protect them from enemies. To keep off silt and parasites and help the flow of oxygenated water, the female octopus strokes the festoons of eggs she has deposited in her rocky lair.

Brooding is done in various manners among both univalves and bivalves. Many clams hatch their eggs within the mantle chamber and allow the veligers to grow into young clams within the protective gill

curtains. Some boring clams permit their young to remain within the burrow. Then they later begin their own independent tunnels in the wood.

The *Clanculus* snail and some sundials permit the young to crawl inside the umbilicus of the adult shell, and sometimes a mucus sheath is laid over the numerous infant snails that have lodged themselves in the spiral furrows of the mother's outer shell. Many slipper shells attach their leathery capsules to the substrate and then clamp down on them so that the mantle cavity serves as a protective hood. The *Trivia* cowries hollow out holes in ascidians—lowly marine chordates—and deposit their eggs deep below the surface of their hosts.

There are many dozens of kinds of capsules laid by marine univalves. In some cases, the eggs hatch and immediately escape as free-swimming veligers. However, in many kinds the veligers remain inside the capsule until they have metamorphosed into miniature snails. The young may eat their way out, or as in the case of some whelks, they eat their young brothers and sisters until only one large individual is left.

The *Colus* whelks, some volutes and the *Phalium* helmet shells lay towers of interlocking capsules. The *Busycon* whelk of the eastern United States lays wafer-shaped, leathery capsules attached by a cord in a snakelike row. Each capsule may contain from 50 to 120 miniature snails. The *Natica* moon snails that live on sandy bottoms lay a stiff, gelatinous collar with the inside containing microscopic eggs and the outside densely packed with sand grains.

A number of snails give birth to live young. The eggs are retained and hatch inside either the swollen oviduct or a special brood chamber located on the back of the head. Smaller young and deformed eggs serve as food for the survivors. Among the live bearers is a *Turritella* snail, which has been found in fossiliferous rocks many millions of years old, showing the tiny young snails closely packed inside the mother's shell.

LEFT: Neptunea whelks of northern Europe lay clumps of horny egg capsules from which the crawling young escape. OPPOSITE, TOP: Jelly capsules of the columbellid snail, *Anachis avara* (Say), on *Zostera* grass. × 30. LOWER RIGHT: Horny capsules of the drill, *Urosalpinx cinerea* (Say). × 20. LOWER LEFT: Capsules of the Tulip Shell, *Fasciolaria*. × 10.

How shells are built

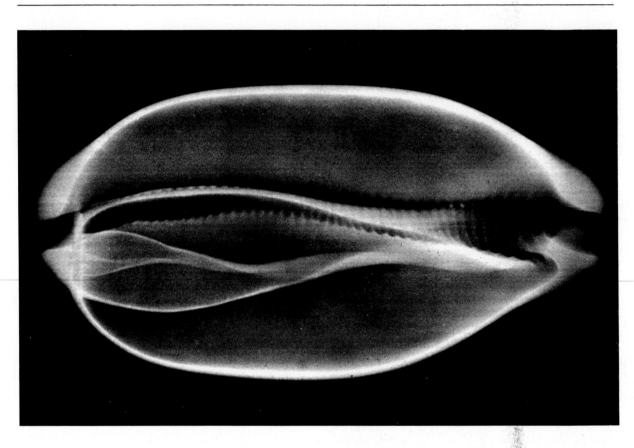

The hard shells of mollusks are made of a limy mineral, calcium carbonate. The degree of hardness and the microscopic structure of the shell material vary, depending upon the type of crystallization. The six-sided crystals may be prismlike, becoming calcite, or they may be very flat and thin, becoming aragonite. The latter is a heavier form of lime that gives a nacreous, or mother-of-pearl, effect.

The blood of the mollusk is rich in a liquid form of calcium. Most outer parts of the soft visceral organs—in particular, the fleshy cape known as the mantle—concentrate the calcium in areas where it precipitates into additional crystals. Most of the shell growth takes place at either the edge or the mouth of the shell, although a great deal of thickening continues farther back inside the shell. Solid crystals form either next to old crystals or on a matrix of conchiolin. The latter is a soft, brownish

material composed of proteins and polysaccharides that serves as a microscopic latticework for new crystals. This same material is also used in the formation of the outer coating, or periostracum, that covers the entire shell.

The mantle is the main architect of the shell, producing the various ribs, cords and spines. Production of new shell material is controlled and influenced by a number of factors, including sexual hormones, intrinsic rhythmical patterns, diet, acidity of the water and temperature. The size of the crystals is dependent upon the rate at which they are formed, and this, in turn, is determined by the temperature of the surrounding water.

In some mollusks, the inner layers of the shell, next to the viscera, may be reabsorbed to make room for growing gonads and to be reused to build a larger lip on the shell. A cross-section of a large, adult cone will show how the old whorls, once thick-walled, are now paper-thin. The calcium carbonate has been changed back into liquid form and carried by wandering amoebocyte cells to the mantle at the anterior end of the snail. There the mantle has secreted the calcium back into the edge of the growing shell. In the event of a major injury to a shell, this mode of calcium transport is used to mend cracks, to fill holes bored by sponges and snails and to repair a broken apex or damaged outer lip. Old spines that are beyond the reach of the mantle cannot be repaired.

Certain areas of the foot of gastropods may be endowed with glands that produce either soft conchiolin or hard shelly material. Such a region is located on the dorsal side near the back end of the foot. Here the operculum, or trapdoor, is secreted. The last part to be withdrawn into the mouth of

the shell, it serves as a protective barrier. The diameter and thickness of the operculum are increased on the underside where it is attached to the foot. The sides of the foot in the olive shells contribute to the glossy outer layers of the shell, whereas the posterior end of the foot of the Angular Volute from Brazil produces a long, shelly spike at the apex of the shell. The glossy and thickened backs of cowries, however, are the product of an enveloping extension of the mantle.

The largest prisms of calcite produced among the mollusks are found in the bivalve pen shells. The large crystals are readily seen with the aid of a hand lens or magnifying glass. The conchiolin separating the prisms contains a high percentage of water, thus giving the matrix and the entire shell an almost flexible quality. When recently collected pen shells are allowed to dry out, they become brittle.

OPPOSITE: X-ray photograph reveals the interior of a cowrie. × 3. LEFT: Microphotograph of the surface of a *Turbo* snail shows the stacks of lime crystals. × 1,500. ABOVE: A radial fracture of a minute piece of clam shell shows the structure of a thin layer of mother-of-pearl. × 2,500.

Shell colors and patterns

The many colors of shells and of the soft parts that produce them are due to the presence of organic pigments manufactured from the food of the mollusk and distributed throughout the body by the blood system. Glandular cells concentrate the pigments and mix them in with the fluid calcite just before the outer shell layers harden. Various colors are obtained by combinations of the four main types of pigments—yellow carotenoids, black melanins, green porphyrins, blue and red indigoids.

The basic colors and their patterns are genetically inherited for each species, although in many kinds of mollusks there is a natural variation, just as there is in hair color among human beings. Color phases, such as white, black or yellow, may occur in a genetic ratio among certain populations. Nonethe-

less, the environment and the diet are able to influence coloration within certain limits. Young abalone snails produce red shells when fed on red seaweeds. The rock dogwinkles, *Nucella,* normally a light gray or white, become yellow if given a diet exclusively of barnacles. Purple and brown markings will appear in the shell if the dogwinkles feed on blue mussels. A marked change in color in either a clam or snail, as it grows, may be due to a sudden change in diet.

Some colors, particularly the blue-green iridescent sheens of the interior of abalones and the outer shells of *Calliostoma* top shells, are the result not of pigments but of the odd refraction of light being bounced off the various layers of calcite shell. The wavelength of light is altered as it passes through and is reflected from the prisms. This is the same

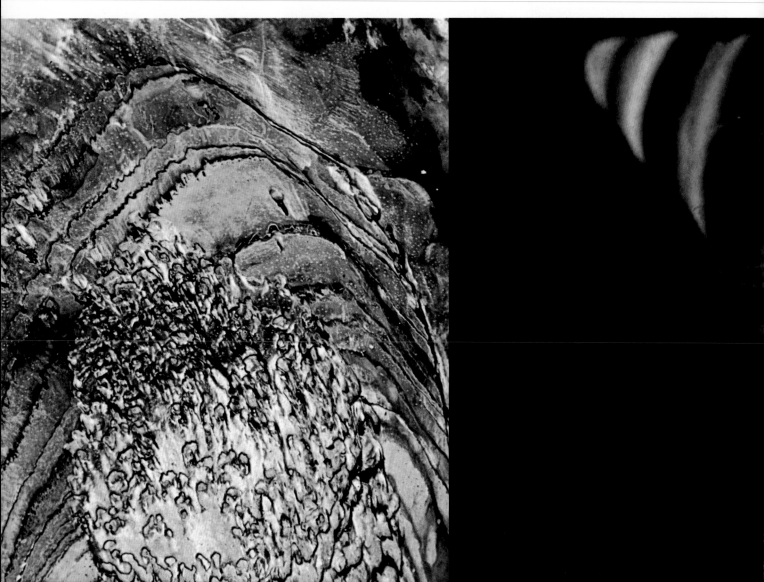

process by which butterfly wings appear to the human eye to be colored.

Most of the major clumps of color cells are located along the front edge of the mantle at the point where new shell material is being added. This would be at the rim of the mouth of a snail shell and along the free edges of the valves of a clam. A straight color line, or ray, is produced by a color center that remains at the same location on the edge of the growing mantle and that continues to produce pigment. If the production of pigments alternatingly ceases and starts up again, a series of dots or dashes will be created. If the color center migrates to one side, it will leave a slanting trail of color in the shell. Circles, triangles and odd figures are produced by other variations in the behavior of the color glands.

Some of the most brilliant colors in mollusks occur, not in the shell, but in the soft parts, such as the foot, the head and the mantle. The foot of some volutes rivals the shell in brilliance of color and detail of pattern. Many shell-less snails, such as the nudibranch sea slugs, sport brilliant reds, purples, yellows and blues in their fleshy exteriors. Although such coloration is undoubtedly valuable as camouflage, the factor of light intensity serves as a greater protection. For example, a darkly colored animal that inhabits a dark environment is better protected than a lightly colored creature, and vice versa. Many very colorful shells having beautiful and varied patterns are, in nature, covered with a thick brown outer periostracum. This completely hides the true color of the shell, demonstrating the uselessness of pigmentation for camouflage purposes in the case of cones, frog shells and certain tulip shells. The white, glossy shells of the Poached Egg Cowrie, *Ovula*, are usually completely covered by a black mantle, and the coloration of the enveloping mantle of some other cowries is not like that of the shell.

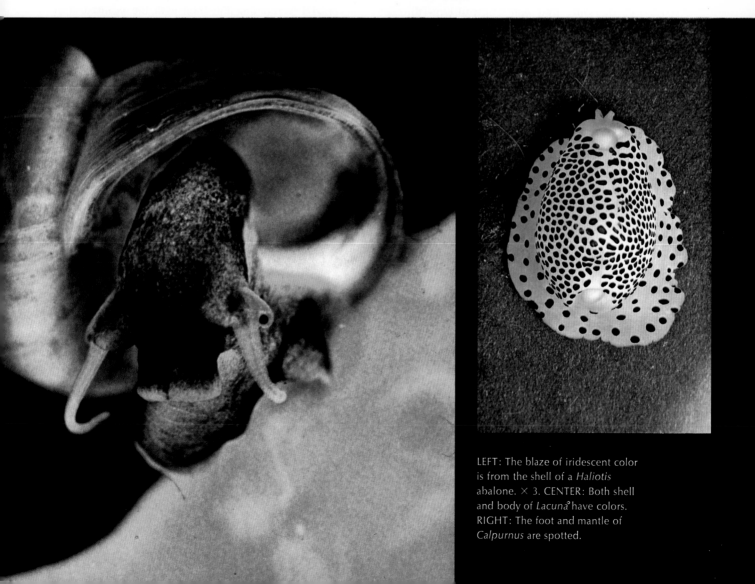

LEFT: The blaze of iridescent color is from the shell of a *Haliotis* abalone. × 3. CENTER: Both shell and body of *Lacuna* have colors. RIGHT: The foot and mantle of *Calpurnus* are spotted.

Strange shapes of univalves

Nature has created an almost infinite variety of life in the sea, and mollusks have produced shells of many shapes. Colors, color patterns, sculpturing and general form have been molded by millions of years of environmental changes and genetic mutations into literally tens of thousands of combinations.

If a snail lives in sand at the bottom of the ocean, it has a choice of having a large, spherical shell or a long, slender one. The ball-shaped shells produced by the *Natica* moon snails and the harp shells are associated with animals having a large, broad, shovellike foot with which to plow through the sand or to creep quickly over the surface. The *Terebra* augers and other slender shells offer less resistance to the sand and therefore have a relatively small foot.

Throughout their evolutionary history, the moon snails show a gradual diminution of the shell and a proportionately large increase in the size of the soft parts, particularly in the foot. Lewis's Moon of western North America and the Common Northern Moon of New England both have large, sturdy, almost ball-shaped shells. But other moons take on a more flattened spire and a proportionately larger aperture, such as shown in the Atlantic Moon (*Polinices duplicatus*) and Recluz's Moon of California. Still more flattened is the *Sinum* Western Baby's Ear and its Atlantic counterpart, *Sinum perspectivum*. They have an extremely flattened shell with an enormous aperture and a foot that envelops and hides the entire shell. Last and most extreme in this evolutionary progression is the Fingernail Moon, an inch-long, fragile shell with a minimum of spire in evidence and with its small shell completely buried inside the sluglike animal.

The most primitive form of a univalve's shell is cap- or shield-shaped. It is a flattened, open cone that keeps expanding along the edge of the wide mouth. Many diversely related gastropods have

such a simple shell—the limpets, the *Capulus* Hoof Snail, the Cup-and-Saucer *Crucibulum* and the strange opisthobranch Umbrella Shell, *Umbraculum*. Because a cone expanding in one direction tends to make the animal too long in proportion to the abilities of its foot and head, snails have taken to coiling. The early whorls of the limpets and similarly shaped shells are coiled about themselves. The vast majority of the univalves are coiled.

Usually, coiling is in a clockwise direction, no matter on which side of the equator the animal lives. Such a dextrally coiled shell may be recognized by holding the shell with the pointed apex up and the mouth of the shell facing you. If the mouth is on the right, the shell has been coiling dextrally and is sometimes referred to as being "right-handed." If the mouth is to the left, the shell has been coiling counterclockwise, or sinistrally, and is "left-handed." Some kinds of whelks, such as the Lightning Whelk of Florida, are normally left-handed. But in most right-handed species, a shell that coils around in the opposite direction is a rarity. There have been freak sinistral shells found in *Marginella*, cones, tulip shells and *Strombus* conchs.

Some snails do not obey the rules of regular coiling, particularly those that live in clumps of sponges or entwined among themselves as a colony. The *Vermicularia* worm shells, more popularly dubbed "Old Maid's Curls," begin life coiling regularly for a few whorls only; then they spiral off in any direction. The resulting shell looks more like a worm shell than a snail shell.

Although many univalves do not change the basic shape or outline of their shells during life, there are many that make a radical change when they reach maturity. The young cowrie, for instance, is a simple, coiled, rather fragile, elongate shell, resembling more an adult olive in shape than a cowrie. As the cowrie approaches sexual maturity,

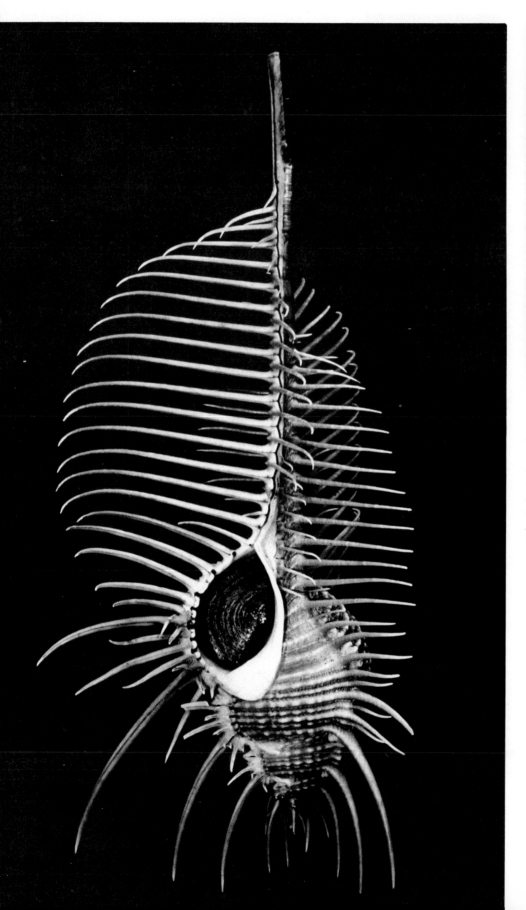

LEFT: This is a flawless specimen of a Venus Comb Murex, *Murex pecten* Lightfoot, from the Philippines. Soft protuberances of the mantle created the regular spines. × 1.5.
ABOVE: Two specimens of the sponge-dwelling *Vermicularia spirata* (Philippi) demonstrate uncontrolled coiling. × 1.

the shell does not grow larger to any great extent. Instead, the outer lip grows inwardly, thus narrowing the aperture to a mere slot. The mantle of the snail begins to thicken the outer lip and forms strong shell ridges, or teeth. An additional row of teeth is formed on the other side of the apertural slot. Meanwhile, the large, colorful mantle flaps that envelop the entire back of the shell begin to lay down the adult color pattern. Eventually the cowrie shell is quite thick and strong, and no further growth takes place. Should any sand grains or tiny shrimp become lodged between the mantle and the shell, they will be entombed with additional layers of calcite.

Perhaps the most radical change takes place in the Strombidae, or conch, family. The young resemble simple, inverted cones in shape and have a sharp, thin outer lip. When maturity approaches, the outer lip thickens and begins to flare outwardly, somewhat like the end of a trumpet. In some species, the upper part of the lip is produced into a long winglike extension, as seen in the West Indian Rooster-Tail Conch. At the other, or lower, end of the outer lip, a shallow U-shaped notch develops. This is to permit the conch to protrude its long snakelike eyestalk out into the water without its being pinched by the heavy shell lip. A further ramification of the outer lip is developed in a related group, the *Lambis* spider conchs. Each of its eight known species, which are inhabitants of the Indo-Pacific region, grow six to eight long spines, in addition to a sickle-shaped extension of the anterior siphonal canal.

Univalves vary in size from the adults of the vitrinellid family, which do not exceed one-tenth of an inch in length, to the huge *Pleuroploca* Horse Conch of Florida and the *Syrinx* Australian Baler, both of which obtain a length of two feet.

OPPOSITE PAGE, LEFT: Butterfly Moons, *Naticarius alapapilionis* (Röding), from the Pacific. × 1.5. RIGHT: The Shuttlecock, *Volva volva* (Linné), from Australia. × 1. ABOVE: A rare sinistral and a common dextral specimen of the Armed Vase, *Tudicula armigera* A. Adams. × 2. LEFT: Uncommon Noble Wentletrap, *Sthenorytis pernobilis* (Fischer and Bernardi), from the Caribbean. × 1.

Strange shapes of bivalves

It is difficult to imagine that such a staid and sluggish group as the bivalves could show much evolutionary imagination in producing novel shapes. Clams, mussels and oysters seem only minor modifications of the simple bivalve type. Yet around the world are found some very startling departures.

Although edible oysters vary in shape depending upon whether they grow in quiet or swift tidal waters, they do not show the marked departure in form exhibited by the Frond Oyster, which lives attached to the stems of sea plumes. This clinging oyster develops long curved fingers that enwrap themselves around the stem of the plume. In contrast to this, the Flat Tree Oyster of the West Indian mangroves, a member of the Isognomonidae family, attaches itself to mangroves by means of its hairy byssus, and its shell takes on the shape of a small fan. The two valves are so flat that the animal inside is no thicker than a sheet of cardboard. This permits several dozen oysters to clump together on the very small attachment area afforded by the mangrove roots.

Most novel of the shells of bivalves is that of the giant *Tridacna* clam of the southwest Pacific. A pair of its valves may reach a weight of 500 pounds and a length of just over four feet. Its free edge bears four or five huge triangular projections. In contrast to this is the *Pythina* clam, a tiny, translucent, smooth clam the size of a grain of rice that lives attached to the underside of shrimp and crayfish.

Bivalves that bore into mud, wood, rocks and other shells have all tended toward taking on an elongated, cylindrical shape. A half-dozen families have independently modified themselves in this fashion. The mussel family has developed the cigar-shaped date mussel, which somewhat resembles the seed of a date. One of them, *Lithophaga aristata,* has added a curious posterior extension resembling a pair of crossed fingers or scissors. The ark family, normally consisting of heavy, ribbed, boxlike shells, has an elongate, smoothish species that bores into rocks. The most radical departure among the borers is the teredo shipworm that develops a long, shell-lined tunnel in wood, resembling a white worm tube. At the anterior end a pair of rounded, half-globe valves is rotated back and forth to excavate new sections of the tunnel.

The problem of mud boring has been solved in a variety of ways. Clam diggers of New England and Europe are familiar with the *Ensis* razor clams, which reach a length of six inches and are not much thicker than a man's finger. This glossy, smooth bivalve produces deep, vertical burrows that permit the animal to zip down more than two feet in a split second. Contrasted to this is the immobile Watering Pot Clam of the Indo-Pacific. Shaped like a round nozzle of a watering pot, it even has, at its lower end, a convex cap punctured with many small holes. Tiny extensions of the foot protrude through these minute orifices. At the other end, which protrudes to the surface of the mud, is a wide opening that accommodates the intake and exhalent siphons. One would not suspect that this curious shelly tube was a bivalve unless one were to examine the lower end where a minute nucleus of two clam valves can be seen.

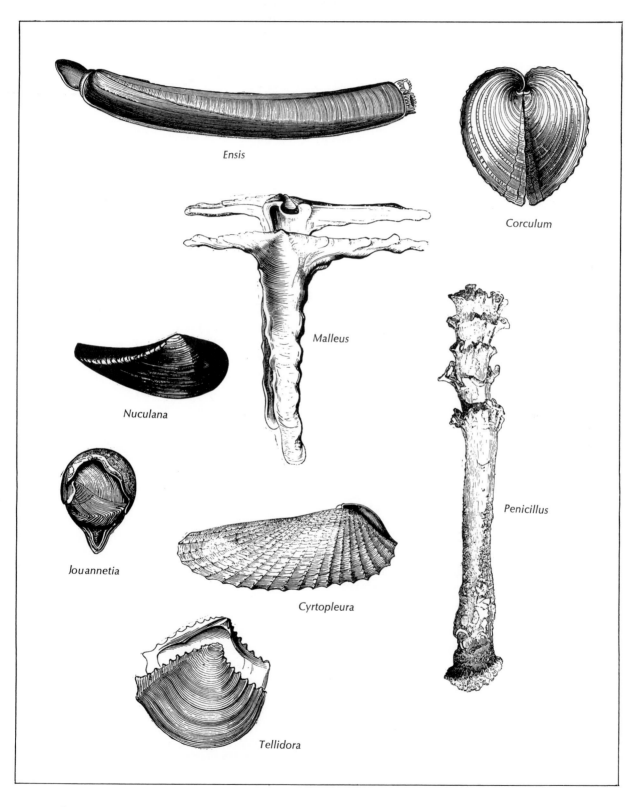

Ensis

Corculum

Malleus

Nuculana

Iouannetia

Cyrtopleura

Penicillus

Tellidora

Nineteenth-century drawings of curious shapes found in
common marine bivalves, from the elongate *Ensis* and
the heart-shaped *Corculum* to the Hammerhead Oyster,
Malleus, and the strange Watering Pot Clam, *Penicillus.*

How univalves feed

The univalves have developed a most remarkable diversity in feeding habits, from those of carnivores to herbivores, from snails that suck the juices from plant cells to those that tap the blood of sea anemones. There are cone shells that harpoon and swallow fish, and there are nudibranch snails that swallow other univalves whole as well as some that collect, filter and slurp up microscopic plankton. Some snails will feed only on the polyps of sea fans; others would starve if they could not find a particular species of hydroids. Yet some gluttons, such as the whelks, will ingest dead fish, crustaceans and putrifying mollusk meat, as well as lap up decaying vegtable matter.

The alimentary system of the typical univalve consists first of a mouth, which is usually flanked by a pair of small, horny jaws. Behind this, in the pharynx, is a tonguelike ribbon of many hooked, hard teeth that rasp off bits of food and pass them back into the esophagus. Salivary glands contribute fluids that assist in breaking down the food. Once entered in the stomach, the food may be further reduced by gizzard stones or by enzymes coming from a pencillike rod known as a crystalline style. A digestive gland, or "liver," contributes substances that complete digestion. The intestine of the snail winds forward into the mantle cavity, and, at the anus, feces are expelled.

Grazers on algae are numerous among the primitive univalves, such as the abalones, keyhole limpets, turbans and true limpets. Among the more highly evolved snails, the browsers include most members of the *Strombus* conch family, which feed mainly on red algae, and the rock-dwelling periwinkles that rasp off minute bits of the brown *Fucus* seaweed.

Plankton feeders exist among the snails that spend most of their lives fixed in one place, such as the *Crepidula* slipper shells that cling to one spot and the *Vermetus* worm shells that are cemented permanently to the substratum. The mantle cavity of the slipper shell is very large and amply endowed with gills that trap and collect particles of planktonic food, such as algal cells and minute eggs of other sea creatures. The food is entrapped in mucus and compacted into a trench where it is pushed forward toward the head. The snail reaches around with its proboscis and grasps, not bites, off a chunk of the compressed mucoid food. The vermetid snails that are anchored and living in still waters are also plankton feeders, but they are forced to "lasso" their food by slowly extending long pedal tendrils, sometimes a yard in length, out in the water. The sticky tendrils and the mucus strings waving at their ends entrap particles of food. Later, the snail pulls in the tendrils and then ingests the mucus strands.

Most marine univalves, such as the moon snails, whelks and *Murex* rock shells, are carnivorous. Some bore holes in living bivalves or other snails with their radular teeth and then extend the proboscis deep into the soft insides. Some enwrap the bivalve victim in their foot and pry the valves apart, using the edge of the outer lip. A large number of snails are ectoparasites, living on the exterior of their hosts. Many wentletraps regularly live and feed on sea anemones. The tiny *Stylifer* snail lives embedded in a wartlike cyst formed in the arms of starfish and the spines of sea urchins. The proboscis taps the juices of the host, and an open hole at the top end of this chamber permits the entry of water and the exit of wastes. A few highly specialized parasitic snails that have lost their shells live inside the intestine of the holothurian sea pudding, where they draw blood directly from the wall of the gut.

TOP RIGHT: The Cylindrical Sundial Snail, *Heliacus*, feeds exclusively on the soft coral, *Palythoa*. × 2. BELOW: *Cypraecassis testiculus* (Linné) removes the spines of a sea urchin before it eats the insides. × 1. MIDDLE RIGHT: *Acmaea leucopleura* (Gmelin) lives on the underside of the West Indian Top Shell, *Cittarium*. × 4.

BELOW: A Channeled Whelk, *Busycon,* approaches an oyster, pries it open, eats out the contents and leaves behind an empty shell.

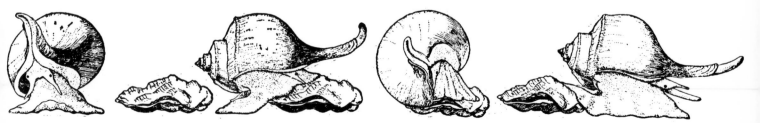

How other mollusks feed

The feeding habits of the bivalves differ markedly from those of other mollusks because of the loss in this class of the head and all head sense organs, the mouth parts and the radular teeth. The earliest bivalves, of which the nuculid nut clams are living survivors, collected food off the bottom by means of a pair of fleshy palps, or flaps, that pushed dead organisms into the mouth. Sometimes long proboscid extensions were developed in certain genera.

In another specialized group of bivalves, the septibranchs, small crustaceans and dead pieces of other invertebrates are drawn into the mantle cavity by a sudden inflow of water, produced by a pumping action of muscular septa, or walls of branchial tissues. Among these meat-eating bivalves are the deep-sea *Cuspidaria,* small clams with a long shelly snout at one end.

However, it was almost inevitable that the vast majority of clams would turn to the use of their gills as food collectors. Water being brought into the mantle chamber for purposes of respiration was inevitably contaminated with free-floating particles. Here was a ready source of planktonic food. The bivalves soon evolved an efficient mode of food gathering by increasing the area of the gills, by stepping up the production of sticky mucus and by multiplying the number of cilia, or tiny hairs, to transport the mucus and food toward the palps and mouth. The system was augmented by the development of long siphonal tubes that could be maneuvered over the muddy surface like a vacuum cleaner. The amount of water that an oyster pumps through its gills over the course of a year is estimated to be several thousand gallons.

The search for food and for protection has taken the bivalves into many types of habitats—the mussels and oysters to rocky coasts, the venus clams and cockles to sand bottoms, the shipworm to wood and the erycinid clams to the underside of sea urchins, scaly worms and shrimps. Like a certain genus of snails, the parasitic *Entovalva* clam uses the holothurian sea pudding as a host, living in its gut.

Most chitons are vegetarians, feeding on filamentous and encrusting algae. They feed at night by roaming over the shore rocks in search of new grazing areas. With the coming of morning light, the wandering chitons return to their original resting sites, usually hollowed-out pockets in the rocks. A few chitons are carnivorous, the most rapacious of which is the Veiled Chiton of California. It has a large head-flap that it holds up off the substrate in wait for victims. Should a small amphipod crustacean, shrimp or polychaete worm happen to wander within reach, it will bring the flap down suddenly, in the manner of a fly swatter, and entrap the hapless victim, which it will then devour with its radular teeth.

The most aggressive of molluscan feeders are the cephalopods. A squid, renowned for its speed, will flash through the water after a fleeing fish, grapple it within its suckered tentacles and quickly bite out a huge triangular chunk of flesh from the nape of the fish's neck. A school of hungry squid may decimate a thousand mackerel within a few minutes. The octopus concentrates on crustaceans, clams and snails. Like its squid cousin, its jaws are armed with a strong, parrotlike pair of chitinous beaks. These are backed up by a strong radular ribbon that can bore holes in shells, as well as tear up flesh. The salivary glands of some octopuses produce a potent venom that has, in some instances, caused injury and even death to human beings who have been bitten.

OPPOSITE PAGE, TOP: At the front end of a tusk shell tiny threads capture food and deposit it on top of the mollusk's foot. The foot tilts up so that the food can roll down to the mouth. A half-buried clam, *Nuculana,* uses palps to get food. BOTTOM: *Odostomia* sucking the blood of an *Ilyanassa* snail. × 5.

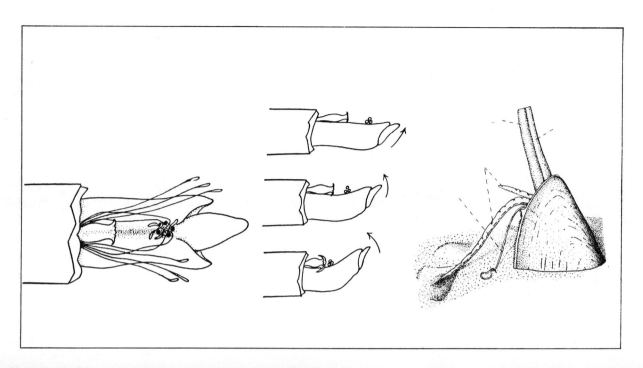

Where shells live 3

Mollusks of the rocky shores

The sea touches the land in a dozen ways, from quiet muddy bays to ruffled coral reefs, from mangrove-edged estuaries or reeded marshes to tropical sandy beaches. But for rigorous, dynamic challenge, the rocky shore offers the most inhospitable environment of all for the fragile creatures of the ocean. On a warm, quiet summer day the sea may heave gently against the barren rock-bound coast and suggest a peaceful haven for its marine inhabitants. But during a week of bitter winter winds the same sea may produce monstrous twenty-foot waves that mercilessly pound every square inch of every secluded crevice and scour every tide pool.

Despite the extreme vicissitudes of the rocky shore, this rugged meeting place of land and sea is surprisingly rich in mollusks. The occurrence of each species is usually restricted to a particular horizontal band, due to a number of environmental factors, such as the degree of wave impact, the slope of the shore, the nature of the rock substrate and the presence or absence of seaweeds and other animals. Characteristically, the mollusks of the shore are able to withstand many hours, and in some cases many weeks, out of water. The bivalves, such as the clinging mussels, are usually found in the low-water zone, where the tide is sure to reach them once a day. Periwinkles, on the other hand, are often found well above the high-tide line. The most landward species of the true marine snails is the tropical prickly-winkle, *Tecta-*

rius, whose members may be found fifty or more feet above the high-tide mark. The West Indian *Tectarius* may remain closed up and cemented to the rocks with its apertural mucus for as long as two months while it waits for storm sprays or rains to bring relief.

Most rock-dwelling snails make daily migrations, either at night to search for food or at any time simply to follow the wet intertidal zone. Some periwinkles remain all year near the high-tide region until the egg-laying weeks in summer. Then they will take up a place at the low-water line so that the eggs will float safely to sea. Limpets, nerites and chitons "make the rounds" at night, seeking out new algal pastures, and then return to their original resting spots. The zonal distribution of many herbivores is determined by their preference for certain kinds of seaweeds. The Northern Yellow Periwinkle, *Littorina obtusata*, for example, always selects *Fucus* weeds over others.

Of the carnivorous mollusks, only members of the murex family have successfully invaded the vertical rock shores, and most of these have been in the genera *Thais*, *Nucella* and *Purpura*. To feed, these snails bore holes in mussels, barnacles and chitons. In addition, they all produce a mucous fluid that turns purple in the sunlight and has a fetid, cabbagelike odor. This fluid is believed to have an anesthetizing effect on other mollusks.

Certainly one of the most abundant of univalves of the West Indian coral rock shoreline is the very inconspicuous and frequently overlooked *Spiroglyphus* snail. Less than a third of an inch in diameter, this small, coiled, brown, wormlike univalve is cemented in vast numbers to intertidal rocks and other shells. To the unsuspecting eye, they appear to be mere brown algal spots on the rocks. Other more conspicuous snails inhabiting this type of rock coast include species of nerites: the famous bleeding tooth, the Common West Indian Chiton, the prickly-winkles, the Deltoid Rock Shell, the West Indian *Purpura* and the Magpie Top Shell, *Cittarium*.

PRECEDING PAGES: Punctate False Cowrie, *Primovula punctata* (Duclos), from the Indo-Pacific, living on soft coral. × 20. OPPOSITE: Intertidal boulders abound with *Patella* limpets, *Littorina* periwinkles and *Nucella* dogwinkles.
ABOVE: The limpets, *Acmaea jamaicensis* (Gmelin), erode limestone shores. × 4.

Mollusks of the coral reefs

The largest and most impressive structure built on this earth was not the Great Wall of China nor the pyramids of Egypt but the 1200-mile-long Great Barrier Reef off the coast of eastern Australia. It is all the more a wonder when we realize that it was built entirely by lowly creatures, the coral polyps, each no larger than the tiny bell of a lily of the valley. The polyp animals are closely related to the sea anemones but differ in that they live in associated colonies and have an ability to secrete a hard, limy cup about themselves. The polyps multiply by budding into new individuals, each of which adds its new small amount of rock-hard coral base.

Proportionately few mollusks are directly associated with living corals, possibly because both of the groups are basically in competition for the calcium carbonate present in the seawater. To protect themselves, the living coral polyps probably give off a substance that is repugnant, for living snails are seldom seen crawling on living corals. Among the exceptions are the lavender-mouthed *Quoyula* snails, which live on the branches of finger coral. Yet *Quoyula* does not wander about on the coral. Instead, it sits fast on a depression it has created, and it feeds, in all likelihood, by drawing in food-laden water across its gills, much as do the sedentary bivalves.

The brain and sponge corals of the South Pacific are the nesting places of the curious, flat *Pedum* scallop. This bivalve is so thin and so deeply embedded in the massive coral that only its mantle edge shows within the long, narrow slot that serves as its burrow. The *Pedum* is completely surrounded by living coral, and in order to prevent itself from becoming entombed, it must keep growing faster than the corals.

More cases of commensalism occur among the soft, rubberlike corals than among the stony corals. Entire colonies of the large delicate *Rapa* snail, for example, live buried deep within the spongy flesh of the soft yellow coral growing in great sloppy piles in the shallow waters of Pacific reefs. The shelly siphons of these turnip-shaped snails project to the surface so that water may be drawn into the gills. Also associated with this type of coral and other, darker, soft corals is the beautiful Poached Egg Cowrie. Its shell is a glistening snow white, but the mantle covering the shell is pitch black except for tiny white-and-yellow dots. In the West Indies, the Cylinder Sundial, *Heliacus*, lives buried in clusters of the brown coral *Polythoa*.

The horny corals, or gorgonians, serve as hosts for many mollusks. On the sea plumes in the West Indies, the winged oysters are the mollusk most commonly encountered. They attach themselves fast with their strong, brown byssuses. The upper parts of sea fans serve as hosts for the *Cyphoma* and *Simnia* snails, while the rootlike bases serve as honeycombed compartments for the small coral snails, *Coralliophila*.

It is the great coral graveyards adjacent to the living reefs, however, that harbor a rich and varied population of mollusks. The worn, gray blocks of coral, torn loose by storms, serve as shelter for dozens of species of cowries, cones, miters and *Lima* clams. Old brain corals are riddled with *Lithophaga* date mussels, and the encrusting mats of calcareous algae and sponges hide numerous species of univalves that, even as adults, rarely exceed a few millimeters in size. A cup of shelly sand from the vicinity of a coral reef may easily contain more than sixty species of microscopic mollusks.

ABOVE: Certain specialized snails live closely associated with living coral reefs.
LEFT: Shown in the top row are *Magilus, Leptoconchus, Tolema* and the purple-mouthed *Quoyula madreporarum* (Sowerby). In the bottom row are the yellow *Rapa rapa* (Linné) that lives in soft coral, *Latiaxis mawae* Griffith and Pidgeon and the violet-mouthed *Coralliophila violacea* (Kiener). All are from the Indo-Pacific region. × 1.

51

Mollusks of the sandy bays

A sandy bay in the Gulf of St. Lawrence, Canada, within a few hundred miles of the icy waters of Labrador, and a sandy bay in the blue tropical waters of the Sulu Sea in the southern Philippines may look alike superficially, but even the least informed of oceanographers would realize that the sea life of each of these bays would have little relationship to the other. The cold-water buccinid whelks and *Aporrhais* Pelican's Foot Snails living off the coast of the Gaspé are not found south of Cape Hatteras nor are the cowries and olives of the southwest Pacific found north of Japan.

Despite the obvious geographical and climatic differences evident in sandy bays around the world, there are certain fundamental environmental condi-

tions present that give their inhabitants something in common. One of these is shifting sands. To avoid being smothered by them, snails and most bivalves of these bays had to solve this problem. (The oysters and mussels have never conquered this type of habitat; they remain aloof on their rocky perches.) For example, the tellin clams developed very·long, sinuous siphons that not only could project up through several inches of sand but could also be used in the manner of vacuum cleaners to suck in food detritus. To further combat the dangers of shifting sands, the tellins and their cousins the macoma clams developed the habit of orienting themselves sideways, instead of vertically, in sand.

The lucinid clams evolved in a different direction.

Having never developed successful siphons to project up to the water, they invented a system for getting fresh ocean water to their subterranean locations. They developed a unique round foot that projects upward through the sand and makes a firm tunnel by compacting the sand grains with mucus. When the tubular tunnel is complete, the lucinid clam withdraws its foot and uses the sandy tube to draw down fresh supplies of seawater.

The primitive cigar-shaped *Solemya* clam creates a similar tunnel by using its entire glossy body. Instead of making a simple vertical tunnel, however, it creates a V-shaped one, thus providing two entrances for itself, much like the gophers and some crabs. This has two advantages. A stomatopod crab or slender fish cannot corner it at the end of its burrow because it has an escape exit. Furthermore, the *Solemya* is able to zip down its tunnel very rapidly, since the build-up of water pressure is relieved at the other exposed entrance.

The univalves are well adapted to sandy conditions, and there are few families of snails that do not have sand-dwelling representatives. All harps, olives, volutes, nassa mud snails and members of the naticid moon snails are limited to a sandy substrate. Cones and miters are occasional sand dwellers. Because of their bulldozerlike forefoot and their long, projecting, fleshy siphonal tube, the olives are best adapted for moving through the sand by plowing, which they can do at a rather rapid rate. On the other hand, the moon snails, volutes and harps have very broad feet that enable them to glide rather easily over soft sand. The *Strombus* conchs seem equally at home on a sand or a rocky bottom and may even make excellent progress through algae forests. The conchs can manage this because they have, at the end of the very elongate, muscular foot, a curious sickle-shaped operculum that serves as a sort of pole-vaulting mechanism.

OPPOSITE: At low tide tropical sandy bays offer excellent conditions for collecting mollusks. TOP RIGHT: Jamrach's Volute, *Amoria jamrachi* (Gray), from northern Australia. × 1. BOTTOM RIGHT: *Oliva sericea* (Röding), Australia. × 1.

Mollusks of the mangroves

Brackish-water estuaries and lagoons of the tropics are characterized by the presence of the bushlike mangrove tree. Usually growing on the lee side of atolls and islands or in sheltered lowland areas near large rivers, mangroves thrive where silt and mud accumulate. Although they are fairly highly developed plants, with large seed pods and heavy foliage, their trunks consist of numerous thin, arching limbs that stick down into the mud. A mangrove jungle is a dark, quiet, cool haven for many forms of life. The tides rise and fall quietly among their maze of slime-covered roots. Birds, fish, crabs and mollusks predominate the mangrove faunal scene, whether the cluttered, saline grove be in Ghana, Bermuda, Florida, Australia or Ceylon.

When it is examined more closely, the mangrove will be found to grow under a rather wide set of oceanic conditions. Along the edges of reefs where pure ocean waters sweep at high tide, there are mangroves. In the Pacific, the Yellow Money Cowrie is found at the base of their roots; and in the West Indies, the Zebra Cowrie lives there. Not far from shore, where the trees become more abundant and yet where there is still a coarse bottom of coral sand and rubble, one will find *Lucina* clams, *Melongena* snails and an occasional *Cymatium* frog shell. But perhaps a half-mile farther inland, where some freshwater river spills its currents into the swamp, the scene changes completely. Here the bottom is deep, black, slippery, oozy mud, unfit for human tread. Mangrove oysters, Ellobiidae pulmonate snails, tiny *Assiminea* and *Neritina* snails predominate.

Some of the strangest shells in the world are associated with mangroves. The world's smallest known gastropods, including the one-millimeter-long *Rissoa*, the two-millimeter-long *Scissurella* and the three-millimeter-long *Amphithalamus* snails, are abundant in the green algae clinging to the mangrove roots. Yet, not far away in the higher intertidal mud flats are the world's largest known cerithid snails—the heavy, five-inch-long *Telesco-*

pium snails of the Pacific. Although there are relatively few species in the mangroves, probably no more than a hundred on a worldwide basis, they are each characterized by their huge populations. The False Ceriths, *Batillaria minima*, of the Caribbean probably exist in terms of billions per square mile. The *Cerithidea* of the mangroves of the Philippines would defy counting, since each of the ten thousand miles of mangroves probably supports several billion living specimens.

Some venerid clams, such as *Gafrarium*, a few lucinid clams, such as *Anodontia*, and some *Anadara* ark clams are found only in the muddy sands close to mangroves. The tree periwinkles of both the Pacific and the Atlantic are ever-present on the underside of the limbs and leaves of mangroves. Two or three species of oysters, including the *Ostrea* and the *Isognomon* genera, are apt to be common on the downward hanging limbs.

Most curious, and only recently discovered, is the so-called bivalve gastropod. A tiny opisthobranch snail related to the estuarine sea hares, it has two clamlike shelly valves encasing its body. The genus *Berthelinia* has been recognized for many years, but because it was known only from dead shells, scientists had mistakenly assumed that it was a bivalve. Not until a Japanese biologist happened to capture this tiny mangrove dweller, which lives only on the green algae *Caulerpa*, did anyone realize that it was truly a snail.

In the deepest muck of river mangroves in the southwest Pacific, one finds the extraordinary *Kufus* clam—a three-foot shipworm that looks like a huge shelled worm. The heavy, tubular shell resembles a small sewer pipe. This clam is a member of the *Teredo* family. At the front end, which is deeply set in the mud, there are two shelly, clamlike valves for boring into new territory. At the posterior end are two small siphons that circulate seawater to and from the long tube. The natives of the Solomons and New Guinea eat this giant species in a soup that is not unlike clam chowder.

OPPOSITE, TOP: The pea-sized nerites, *Neritina communis* Quoy and Gaimard, are abundant inhabitants of tropical Pacific mangrove mud flats. × 5. BOTTOM: *Littorina* periwinkles are as comfortable out of water as they are when submerged in the sea. × 6.

Mollusks of the open ocean

There are about thirty families—perhaps 200 species—of mollusks that live their entire lives at sea without touching bottom or shore unless they are in the throes of death. Still another thousand species spend at least a short part of their larval stages adrift in the currents of the sea. The latter might best be called members of the plankton, which is merely the Greek way of saying that they are wanderers, or accidental voyagers, in the currents of the ocean. The more permanent members of the open ocean community, such as the argonauts, squids, *Janthina* purple snails and pteropods, could be called independent pelagic creatures.

Certainly in size if not in numbers of species, the cephalopods are the dominant mollusks of the wide expanses of the seven seas. Bizarre squids exist from pole to pole and from the surface to an awesome depth of five miles. Over short distances, some species can probably outswim any creature of the sea, although the giant *Architeuthis* squid off Newfoundland is believed to be a slow and cumbersome animal. The largest specimen recorded of this species measured fifty-five feet, while in New Zealand, another species reached an official sixty-three feet. Many deepwater squids that seldom come to the surface are brightly bedecked with luminescent organs that presumably help the opposite sexes to find each other. Some species have huge eyes set out on pedicles, somewhat resembling the arrangement found in hammerhead sharks.

The remnant of one deep-sea squid, *Spirula*, is not infrequently found in the jetsam high upon tropical beaches. Within the cylindrical body is a segmented, coiled white shell. When the animal dies and the flesh rots away, this shell, composed of several loose whorls and resembling a ram's horn, floats ashore. The living *Spirula* congregate in schools in a vertical position at depths of about 500 feet. At the top, or front end, of the squid is a round luminescent patch, rather like a stop-light,

that assists the *Spirula* in identifying one another.

The *Janthina* purple sea snail is one of the few truly pelagic prosobranch gastropods. This beautiful violet shell, shaped like an inverted top, is kept afloat by a raft of irregular, foamlike bubbles, produced by the snail itself. Some species attach their eggs to the underside of this raft, but the common janthina gives birth to free-swimming veligers. *Janthina* are hermaphroditic, with the male phase occurring first. Because the male lacks a penis, it deposits its sperm in a large, feathery, mobile carrier that wiggles its way through the water in search of another snail that is in its female stage. *Janthina* feed on the floating siphonophore *Velella*, dousing their victims with a purple dye before beginning to chew off the stinging tentacles. The four or five known species of purple sea snails are worldwide in distribution. They are quite common in the Sargasso Sea, and during the spring months, easterly winds sometimes blow schools of them ashore in Florida.

One of the best sources of food for whales and pelagic fish are the vast hordes of tiny, butterflylike snails that belong to the order Pteropoda, meaning "wing-footed ones." Most of them have glassy, transparent shells less than a third of an inch in length. In shape they vary from the cigar-shaped *Cuvierina* and the needle-shaped *Creseis* to the butterfly-shaped *Clio*. Some species are shell-less, but all have ciliated pads attached to their winglike pedal lobes. Passing algal cells, such as diatoms and dinoflagellates, become enmeshed in the mucus of the pads and are passed along a ciliated gutter to a point where the radular teeth are able to shovel them into the mouth. As pteropods die, their shells rain down on the bottom of the ocean. In some areas of the world this process has been so continuous and so effective that the floor of the ocean has become several feet deep in what the oceanographers call pteropod ooze.

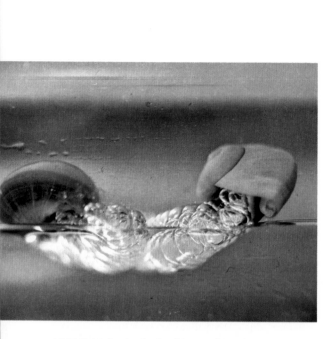

ABOVE: Violet Snails, *Janthina janthina* (Linné), spend all their lives at the surface of the ocean, buoyed by self-made bubble floats. × 1. BELOW: The *Cavolina* pteropod is a pelagic snail. × 5. RIGHT: Another free-floating oceanic snail, *Oxygyrus.* × 9.

Mollusks of the depths

About 70 percent of the surface of the earth is covered with ocean, and this is only on the top! A vast, watery world of darkness and great pressures lies below. Man is fairly familiar with the sunny shallow waters of the intertidal zones and the offshore reef waters. His knowledge of the continental shelves is also quite respectable, for he has long been fishing them and dredging them to depths of 600 feet, the limit of the edge of the average coastal shelf bordering large continents. But beyond this, the ocean floor slopes rapidly downward to depths of some 6,000 to 31,000 feet (one to six miles). The average depth of the oceans is 12,000 feet (about two miles). Although much of the vast bottom of the Atlantic and Pacific oceans is made up of undulating plains of red clay, earth deposits and oozes built up of the remains of minute plants and animals, there are great sections that are broken by enormous trenches, canyons and mountain ranges. Islands such as Bermuda, Hawaii and the Azores are merely the tops of ancient volcanic mountains. The tops of many smaller mountains, called guyots, are still hundreds of feet below the surface.

As one goes deeper, the diminution of light, and finally its absence at about five thousand feet, has a major influence on all creatures of the deep. At a depth of only several fathoms, all red rays from the sun have been filtered out by even the clearest of water. Violet light has been recorded as deep as 3,280 feet. Because of the varying altitude and strength of the sun, the roughness of the surface and the amount of suspended particles in the water, the depth at which algae will grow varies considerably. However, most grazing gastropods and herbivorous clams do not exist below 1,000 feet. The *Cuspidaria* clams, living at depths of 5,000 feet or more, contain bits of shrimp and fish, not algae, in their stomachs.

About 1,100 species of mollusks taken from abyssal depths—that is, from water over 5,000 feet in depth—have been recorded so far. Under these conditions, they are living in a constant temperature just above the freezing point and a pressure per square foot in the neighborhood of one million pounds. Ewing's Gastroverm was found living at 20,000 feet. But such pressures and low temperatures are of no great concern to a mollusk conceived and born at this depth. The pressure within its tissues and cells is the same as that on its outside. Were there any gases within its body and were the creature to be brought to the surface, then naturally it would explode.

Gastroverms and many other shelled mollusks of the depths lack eyes. However, the cephalopods that have luminescent organs and roam considerable distances at great depths have well-developed eyes.

There are three main sources of food for the abyssal inhabitants—neighboring creatures, dead plankton constantly raining down from the surface and vegetable and animal detritus sliding off the continental shelf in the form of mud. In the polar regions, diatomaceous ooze several feet thick has been formed at great depths as billions of algal diatoms have showered down from the surface. This permits some herbivorous species to live at fairly deep levels.

In color, mollusks of abyssal areas are generally a drab white, gray or brown, although red is not an unusual color. Below 100 feet, red would appear to be black, of course. Patterns of dots, stripes and bars are unknown in deepwater species. Among the gastropods found at great depths are the trochids, the naticid moon snails, the buccinids, the marginellids, the volutes and the turrids. The bivalves include the tellins, the *Pandora* clams, the cuspidariids and the *Verticordia* clams.

OPPOSITE PAGE: This delicate and highly organized bit of protoplasm, no larger than a grain of rice, is one of the eternal wanderers of the inky depths of the seas. Like its billions of brethren, this shelled pteropod, *Peracle,* knows no rest but must for the remainder of its life flap its foot appendages through its dark world. × 20.

Evolution of shells

Fossil shells

The realm of fossil shells is a world of timeless miracles, marked by meager remains from eons of time and a million little experiments of nature during the evolution of life upon our earth. By the time our planet had subsided from its fiery ball and cooled to the point of being able to support vast seas and turbulent atmospheric storms, the nucleus of life was stirring in primeval pools, where organic chemical combinations were leading to that magical spark. Mollusks were among the first of the primitive animal groups to come upon the scene during the Cambrian dawn of life, some 500 million years ago. By the Ordovician, a mere 100 million years later, all the six classes of mollusks had appeared, at least in some primitive stage of development.

Fossils are the remains of once-living organisms preserved in the ancient rocks of the earth's crust. The petrified impression of a snail's track or the burrow of a clam is also a fossil, although the molluscan creators of such formations are seldom accurately identifiable. The soft parts of mollusks are rarely preserved, although the outlines of the tentacles of squid have been found in very ancient rocks. Shells preserve well, though, and there are countless examples of shells having been buried in sand or mud and preserved intact over millions of years. The white, calcareous shells of the Pliocene beds of Florida are a typical example. Practically all the organic parts, including the outer periostracum and the pigments within the shell, are removed by time. Because of this loss of organic materials, the shells become porous. If conditions are right, other minerals, such as silica and lime,

will infiltrate the fossil, turning it to stone. Sometimes iron pyrites infiltrate, thus giving the fossil a more glamorous, shiny impression.

A clam or univalve may be buried and preserved in a layer of sedimentary rock. The interior of the shell becomes filled with a thick mud, which forms a cast. If during a later geological period, the original shell is dissolved, this internal impression, or cast, will be the only remaining evidence. Similarly, a shell may become encased in mud that later solidifies into a sedimentary rock. If acids in the mud leach a shell away, a hollow will be left in the shape of the original shell. If this hollow, or mold, fills with another mineral at a later date, the filled center becomes a cast.

Fossil shells abound in various crustal outcrops around the world, and some of them serve as ready indicators of the age of certain stratigraphic layers. The presence of fossil cephalopod ammonites immediately indicates that the rocks in which they are encased are between 70 and 390 million years old for this subclass existed only from the Devonian to the Upper Cretaceous periods. Some genera of ammonites existed for only relatively short periods so that the presence of these "index fossils" allows us to pinpoint the age of a fossiliferous rock with considerable accuracy.

The world has continuously changed the shape of its continents and seas, and today we can map out the limits of ancient oceans by studying the fossil mollusks present in such inland places as the states of Kansas and Nevada or the central part of India and the interior of Africa.

PRECEDING PAGES: Ammonite fossils, 150 million years old, *Asteroceras obtusum* (Sowerby), from the Lower Jurassic of Lyme Regis, Dorset, England. × 1. OPPOSITE, TOP: A row of living shells with their Pliocene progenitors below—a scallop, a volute, a cowrie and an ark. LOWER: A giant fossil scallop just dug from its matrix. × 1.

Ancient univalves

Although the univalves undoubtedly evolved just before the Cambrian period, some 700 million years ago, there are no definite records of them until the early part of that period. Fossil tracks attributed to gastropods were found in the Lower Cambrian of British Columbia and were optimistically given the molluscan name of *Archaeonassa*. The earliest forms considered to be true univalves were the somewhat cap-shaped *Coreospira* snails of the Lower Cambrian of North America. Some of these had already developed coiling, although in only one plane, like a wheel, not in a descending coil like that found in modern snails.

By the Late Cambrian and for the next 350 million years up to the Triassic—the beginning of the Mesozoic era—three great groups of snails dominated the scene—the bellerophonts, now extinct; the pleurotomariids, a few still living; and the

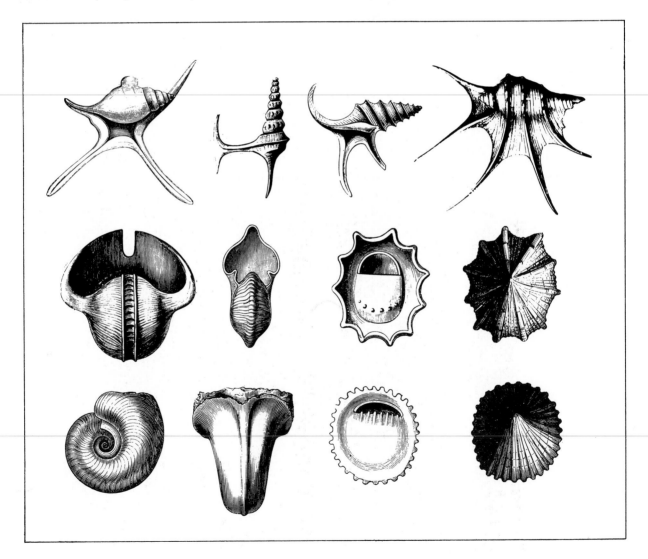

murchison snails, all extinct. The bellerophonts were magnificent coiled, cap-shaped shells with a slit, a notch or a series of holes along the center. They evidently had no operculum and probably had a pair of gills. Coiling was in one plane. The shell, reaching the size of a golf ball, was not pearly. The pleurotomariids were usually coiled so that the shell took on a typical conical, or top, shape. There were many genera, but most of them had pearly interiors and a deep anal slit in the lip.

The murchison snails were high-spired, with numerous whorls, and had an anal slit in the middle of the outer lip, indicating that the living creature had a pair of gills. This group died out in the Mesozoic, but it is believed that it may have given rise to several of our modern gastropod groups, such as the ceriths and turritellids.

A hundred million years later, by the Devonian, there were many well-established families that are not unfamiliar to the present-day scene. The nerites, with their shelly opercula, were flourishing, and by the Upper Cretaceous had given rise to the land helicinid snails. Turbans, *Patella* limpets, *Trochus* top shells and true *Nerita* were soon to follow.

The world was in a massive upheaval, with its climates and seas undergoing major changes. The great blossoming of the univalves did not begin until the end of the Mesozoic. With the coming of the Tertiary, most of today's genera sprang into existence. Certain families exploded during the Eocene and Miocene, particularly the warm-water groups, such as the cones, the *Terebra* augers, the turrids and the venerid clams. The Tertiary beds of southern Europe, southeast United States and southeast Asia are very rich in their molluscan faunas. The shells of the Miocene of the Paris Basin, the West Indies and Indonesia have much in common, for the ancient seas of these areas were interconnected. On several occasions during this period, the isthmus at Panama was open so that for many millions of years the mollusks of both sides of Central America were the same. Today, the resemblance among species is striking.

OPPOSITE PAGE: The Cretaceous *Anchura* snails of Europe developed bizarre flanges. Early gastropods included the slotted bellerophonts and limpet-shaped nerites.
RIGHT: During the Eocene in France the giant cerith, *Campanile giganteum* (Lamarck), reached a length of two feet.

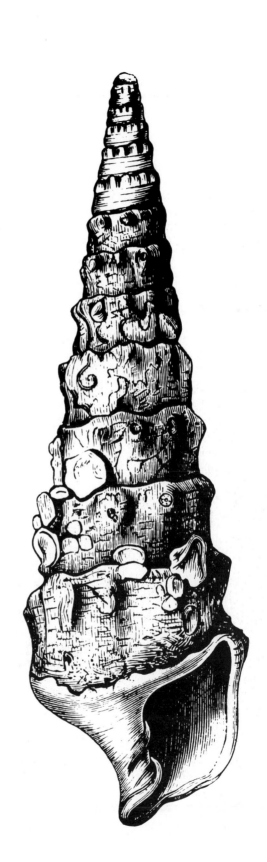

Evolution of the bivalves

The origin of the bivalves, probably occurring sometime during the early Cambrian when other molluscan classes were also becoming evident, is shrouded in mystery. Although they may have evolved from some curious mutant of the wormlike world, most students of this class prefer to believe that they came from primitive limpetlike mollusks resembling the gastroverms, such as *Neopilina*. The creation of two shelly valves, whether gradual or by a sudden mutation, exerted very serious limitations. It meant that having an active foot and a head possessing a mouth with teeth and tentacles with eyes was unnecessary. Protected by two hard valves, the bivalve mollusk could withdraw to safety and take a defensive, rather than offensive, attitude toward life.

Despite the seemingly sluggish and unimaginative nature of bivalves, this class is unique as an example of the evolution of life on this earth. They are common and well-preserved as fossils, starting at a very early geologic age and continuing abundantly through succeeding eras up to modern times where now they are at their peak of evolutionary development. Bivalves show, through the form and structure of their shells, the manner in which they have responded to their environment. They have also shown many cases of what is known in biology as adaptive radiation—that is, they developed many new and imaginative forms to enable them to fit into new habitats.

The cockle family, Cardiidae, a rather recent advent, is one of several classical examples of adaptive radiation. The family became widespread throughout the world in the early Tertiary period, some 65 million years ago. Several morphological lines developed in response to the type of habitat in which they found themselves. One of these lines consisted of cockles that developed stronger and stronger ribs until they culminated in the magnificent Ribbed Cockle, *Cardium costatum*, of West Africa, a veritable bauble of smooth, graceful white ribs. In contrast, the *Trachycardium* line, or prickly cockles, developed shells with increasing spinosity,

the most sophisticated of which being a shell that resembles a chestnut burr. Some cockles evolved in the direction of smoothness, others in brilliance of color and a few in drabness, as witnessed by the dull, brown *Cerastoderma* of subarctic waters.

The most curious of the evolutionary directions of the cockles was a compression or flattening of the shell, not from the sides, as one might expect, but rather from the front and back. This squashing of the cockle begins in the genus *Fragum* and culminates in the *Corculum* of the southwest Pacific. The *Corculum* Heart Cockle, squashed in an antero-posterior axis, turns out to be a very flat, heart-shaped clam. Its anatomy is so modified that it cannot function as a normal cockle. It is not adapted to wiggling into the sand, it has no extensive siphons for drawing in food—in fact, the *Corculum* clam can only sit placidly on the coral reef. To compensate for this unusual habitat, the shell has become very thin, thus allowing sunlight to penetrate through into the flesh of the clam. There, symbiotic algae grow in large numbers to provide internal food for the cockle, a feeding method very similar to that employed by the giant *Tridacna* clams.

Unique among the early bivalves were the rudistid oysters, which had large columnar shells resembling pipe organs with the upper valve serving as a lid on top of the lower valve. This group flourished in the warm Tethyan Sea in the Cretaceous era but for some mysterious reason died out. Perhaps some newly evolved disease or perhaps a parasitic enemy or possibly the consequences of overpopulation caused its extinction.

Boring bivalves appeared fairly early in the history of this class, as did the forms that attached themselves with their threadlike byssuses to sea plumes and other rodlike structures. Oysters did not appear until the Carboniferous era, at a time when the freshwater bivalves also began to appear. Among the Johnny-come-lately groups, the venerid clams, of cherrystone fame, and the giant *Tridacna* clams are outstanding.

Cockle shells of the family
Cardiidae display many shapes
and types of sculpturing.
LEFT: The true cockle,
Cardium costatum Linné,
comes from West Africa. × 1.
BELOW: Three genera of cockles
show various sculpturing,
Nemocardium, Laevicardium
and *Lophocardium*. × 1.

Fossil cephalopods

The most intelligent and morphologically advanced class of mollusks, the cephalopods, had their heyday some 400 million years ago during the Ordovician. So far, no less than 10,000 fossil species and 600 genera have been described, and there is no end in sight. Today, there are fewer than 500 living species and less than 150 genera. What caused their decline is not known. Today, the great nautiloid subclass that dominated the Paleozoic is represented by only four or five living species of *Nautilus* in the southwest Pacific.

The earliest nautiloids appeared in the Upper Cambrian and were entirely uncoiled. Later forms took on the familiar style of coiling seen in today's chambered nautilus. The largest of any known molluscan shell was an Ordovician nautiloid that had a diameter of fifteen feet. A German Cretaceous species that existed about 100 million years ago had a coiled shell just over eight feet in diameter; uncoiled, it would have been thirty-five feet in length.

Largest, and perhaps most curious, of the cephalopods were the numerous members of the ammonoid subclass. The interior of the shell had well over a hundred chambers. The adult shell was characterized by complicated external sutures that marked the presence of internal chamber septa. The sutures of some ammonites are so complicated that they have a dendritic, or mosslike, appearance. The classification of the ammonites is largely based upon these sutures and the internal septa. Many bizarre forms of coiling occurred, from great U-shaped monsters to forms that resembled *Turritella* snails. A few took on the superficial appearance of the nautiloids. Most ammonites lived at a depth of from 20 to 100 fathoms, although a few existed in water as shallow as 30 feet and as deep as 600 feet. Some forms seem to have dragged the shell along the bottom, while smaller species probably carried it upon their backs.

A third subclass of cephalopods, the Coleoidea, are well-represented in today's seas by the squid and the octopus. Only two living species produce a shell, and in one of these cases it is only an egg container made by the female argonaut. The small sepioid squid *Spirula* has an internal, loosely coiled shell of thirty to forty chambers. Each chamber, separating the concave septa, is perforated by a long, tubular siphuncle, which contains blood. The Coleoidea had greatly reduced shells, and today these have been reduced to either a spearlike blade of chitin or a soft limy bone, as is found in the Sepia Cuttlefish.

The oldest members of this subclass are the belemnites of the Carboniferous, some 345 million years ago. Their cigar-shaped shells are abundant in Cretaceous rocks, but the order soon completely disappeared. Fossil impressions of true squids are rarely found. The oldest known octopus was found in Cretaceous rocks of Syria, embedded there about 100 million years ago. The impression of its soft body and the ink sac, as well as a vestigial, saddle-shaped shell, were found still preserved.

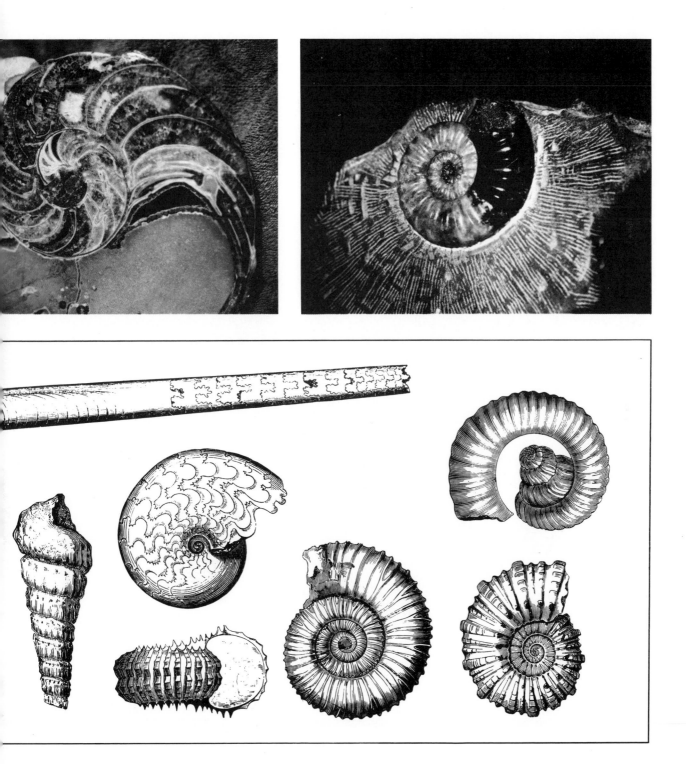

TOP LEFT: A Jurassic *Nautilus* from England has been sliced across in order to show the internal chambers. TOP RIGHT: Entirely extinct today, the subclass Ammonoidea contained the handsomely coiled *Asteroceras*. BOTTOM: A few of the numerous shapes of fossil ammonites.

Japan

Japan is a maritime nation with deep-seated associations and traditions regarding the sea. Her people have used shellfish, fish, algae and numerous other curious products of the sea to nurture her growing population. From this necessity has arisen a modern generation of Japanese biologists and oceanographers whose investigations and research results, including a well-classified molluscan fauna, are second to none in the world.

The sea kingdom of Japan is even more varied than that of many major continents. In the northern waters of Hokkaido, a host of huge buccinid and neptune whelks indicates that island's affinities with the Bering Sea and the bleak, inhospitable chain of

Aleutian Islands. Farther south, the temperate waters of Honshu Island and the shores of the Inland Sea abound with *Meretrix* clams and the dozens of muricid snail predators.

Southward lies the smaller, semitropical island of Kyushu, rather like Florida in climate—hot in summer and warm in winter. Here the tropical genera of shells, such as the cowries and the cones, put in an appearance. Toward Taiwan, even farther south, is the long chain of Okinawan Islands. The tropical waters of these islands support colorful olives, terebras, cones, cowries and scorpion conchs.

Offshore, on both sides of the Japanese archipelago, is a wondrous world of deep-sea mollusks,

most of which bear a typical Japanese stamp of appearance. The Emperor's Top, a beautiful top-shaped turban shell, is dredged from depths of 30 to 150 fathoms. Long-spined Star Shells, frilled *Latiaxis* snails, colorful scallops with brilliant hues of purple, orange, yellow and red, are commonly brought up in the net dredges of lobster and shrimp fishermen.

Pearls, both cultured and natural, are an important facet of Japanese sea culture, and the waters of the Inland Sea are abob with floating wooden rafts of pearl oysters, most of which have been impregnated with seed pearls. Associated with these floating conchological jungles is a host of other bivalves and predatory muricid snails.

Drs. T. Kuroda and Tadashige Habe, Japan's leading conchologists, estimate that the marine waters of their homeland support probably over 2,000 species. Many are less than a quarter of an inch in length, and more than half are to be found only in waters below a depth of 100 feet. Nevertheless, Japan ranks among the world's five leading areas for beautiful and varied kinds of mollusks.

Is there any shell that looks more Japanese than the famous Miraculous Thatcheria? This three-inch-long, graceful, cream-colored snail is a flowing swirl of frozen calcium designed in the best traditions of an Oriental pagoda. Which came first—the thought that this shell resembles a pagoda or the architectural development of a pagoda based upon nature's shelly example? The geometrically increasing whorls are arranged like the ramps of the Guggenheim Museum of Art in New York City—or did the architect take his inspiration from a simple principle of nature?

If the delicate filigree of Moroccan palaces or Thai temples seems intricate, let the shell collector attempt to assemble a complete collection of Japanese *Latiaxis* shells. These gorgeous, frost-imprinted shells of delicate pastel shades of rose, yellow and cream are truly studies in carefree symmetry. Curved spines, spiral rows of beaded threads and graceful contours are the common mode of these deep-sea shells, of which there are over thirty kinds.

The *Guilfordia* Star Shells, dredged from the inky waters of Honshu, are a surprising study of carefully planned spiral turns with sudden sunburst explosions of bold spines all along the periphery of

the shell. Why the spines? Perhaps they serve as protection from marauding fish, perhaps they are only an accidental expression of variation by Mother Nature.

The clumsy little frog shell, popularly known as the maple leaf, is a common shell of the shallow waters of Japan. This charming two-inch-long shell is a victim of commercial collectors who pass it into the markets of the world to be mounted and equipped with pins to serve as women's brooches.

PRECEDING PAGE: The common *Phyllidia* nudibranch of the Indo-Pacific sports a pattern of brilliant colors. × 12. OPPOSITE: The Triumphant Star Shell, *Guilfordia triumphans* (Philippi), is native to Japan. × 2. ABOVE: The Miraculous Thatcheria of Japan has the suggestion of a pagoda in its coiled architecture. × 1.

Australia

In actuality, the Great Australian Barrier Reef of Queensland has been grossly overrated as a source of seashells. Although this entire 1200-mile-long series of coral reefs and islands is replete with corals, fish, sea urchins and mangrove trees, it has no more in the way of marine shells than can be found just to the north in New Guinea and Indonesia. In fact, other parts of Australia, such as Victoria and western Australia, sport species that are more bizarre and sometimes in greater numbers.

The relatively accessible shallow banks of the Barrier Reef make shell collecting fairly easy at low tide. Mollusks, as a group, do not like to associate with living corals because of their stinging cells and the slime they exude. Of the thousand kinds of shells found in eastern Australia, probably no more than a dozen species live attached to corals or embedded in their calcium bases. However, dead corals, broken by waves and scattered in piles by tropical storms, offer a wonderful haven for many shell species.

Along the length of the Great Barrier Reef—from the truly tropical nature of the northern Torres Strait facing New Guinea to the cool-water habitats of the Capricorn Group far to the south near New South Wales—the mollusk fauna differs. A further lateral difference is apparent when one collects in the murky near-shore waters next to the continental shores of Australia. Certain kinds of conchs and volutes abound near Mackay, Townsville and Cairns. Offshore, several miles to the east, there is a long line of sparkling islands bathed by the clear blue waters of the South Pacific and the Coral Sea. Here, an entirely different and more cosmopolitan Pacific group of seashells is found.

Among the inshore species of Queensland, the *Ancilla* olives are the most attractive in design and color. The glossy exterior of the shell is the product of a soft body and a fleshy mantle that envelop the entire shell. So copious are the soft parts of the animal that the *Ancilla* bears no operculum but depends instead on its great production of sticky mucus to ward off predatory fish and crabs.

The Checkerboard Helmet, the *Phalium areola*, with its bold, squarish, red brown blotches is one of twenty fascinating members of the cassid family found in Australian waters; it is distributed from Queensland to southern Japan and as far west as the shores of Africa. The helmet shells live in sandy areas from the low-tide area to a depth of about thirty feet. Most of them feed upon sea urchins, sea biscuits or other members of the echinoderm phylum. The snout of the helmet is armed with a poisonous gland that exudes a fluid that paralyzes the sea urchin and causes it to drop off its spines.

The sundials are colorful, button-shaped shells having many whorls. The animals feed upon other sedentary sea creatures. To protect itself, the Pacific Sundial has a round chitinous trapdoor that completely seals the small aperture of the shell. This species is widely distributed throughout the Pacific, largely because the young of the species are tiny, free-swimming larvae that can float for many weeks and be carried for hundreds of miles by ocean currents.

How startling are the spiral, chocolate-colored threads enwrapping the Filaris Miter of the Barrier Reef! This and other miter species are plentiful in the shallow waters of Queensland. Since they are all nocturnal in habit, one must overturn old dead coral slabs or sweep away layers of sand to reveal these underwater jewels.

TOP LEFT: Australia has about sixty-seven kinds of volutes. This is *Amoria maculata* Swainson, from Queensland. × 1. TOP RIGHT: A spotted mantle hides the shell of *Ovula costellata*, Lamarck, from Zanzibar. × 1.5. LOWER LEFT: Red Cockle, *Nemocardium bechei* (Reeve), from Australia. × 1. LOWER RIGHT: A pair of Sieve Cowries, *Cypraea cribraria* Linné. × 2.

South Africa

The early explorers who depended upon sturdy canvas to sail them around the world had a healthy respect for two passages—one at the heel of South America, where only a fool would venture through the Straits of Magellan in the winter; the other around the Cape of Good Hope in South Africa, where high seas and strong winds tested the best of sailors.

South Africa has a rough, cool-water sea dashing vigorously against her shores most of the year. The shell fauna of South Africa is virtually unique; its hundreds of curious species have little in common with those of other continents. A few helmet shells, chitons and clams are startlingly like those of the cold waters of South Australia and Tasmania. This is somewhat expected, since the subantarctic seas are in continual circulation and contact around the southern third of the globe.

To the northeast of South Africa the shell fauna gives way abruptly to the strange muddy domain of West Africa from Angola to Dakar. To the west, up the coast to Natal, the collector is astonished to see more and more Indian Ocean cowries and cones the farther north he travels.

The typical South Africa shell assemblage consists of a dozen beautiful species of huge limpets, a wide color variation of the Roseated Cone and heavily corded *Purpura* rock shells. A walk along the shores of Jeffreys Bay in South Africa will quickly demonstrate the infinite variety of shells that exists just offshore. Winter storms blow millions of beautiful shells high up on the beach. Twenty to thirty miles offshore, the fishing banks are heavily populated by large volutes, including the large, green Gilchrist's Volute and a dozen other beautiful species of this aristocratic family of shells.

South Africa can certainly be called "limpet heaven." All along her rocky, wave-dashed shores, an astonishing array of many kinds of *Patella* and *Acmaea* can be found. So beautifully camouflaged are many of these algae-covered shells that the collector is apt to overlook them. And while one is searching for them, care must be taken not to be engulfed by one of those enormous waves that sometimes comes up out of the sea without warning. Limpets range in length from a fraction of an inch to more than four inches. Their colors may vary from the deep blues and grays of the shallow-water species to the rich golden reds and yellows of the offshore kinds. Some that live exclusively on the holdfast stems of great brown seaweeds are narrow, brown and with a base that enables the shell to cling around the tubelike algal stem. The vegetarian limpets feed mostly at night. The Long-ribbed Limpet, resembling a bursting star, is a moderately common species that is a favorite among shell collectors.

Cousins of the *Patella* snails are the keyhole limpets. These have a natural hole, resembling a keyhole, at the top of the shell. Through this orifice are shed the excrements and waste products, including water spent of its oxygen. In some keyhole limpets, such as the Fleshy Shield Limpet, the soft parts are enormous and almost entirely cover the shell.

Turbans and top shells, also vegetarians, abound in the shallow, rough waters of South Africa. The inch-sized Elegant Top Shell, adorned with red-and-white maculations and barred stripes, is common in tide pools. The Pheasant Shells, belonging to the genus *Tricolia*, are no larger than a pea, but their intricate spottings and colorful bands make them collectors' items. They have a small shelly operculum with which to seal off the mouth of the shell.

OPPOSITE, TOP: *Turbo sarmaticus* Linné of South Africa is commonly polished for the tourist trade. Normally the exterior is a drab gray. × 3. LOWER LEFT: Gilchrist's Volute from off Cape Town grows to four or five inches. LOWER RIGHT: The two-inch-long *Volutocorbis abyssicola* (Adams and Reeve) is an uncommon volute. × 1.

Thailand

 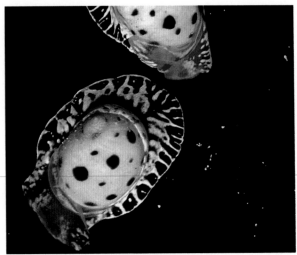

Thailand, once known more romantically as the Kingdom of Siam, hangs like a pendant from the throat of southeast Asia, deep into the seas of the Indo-Pacific. It divides the mysterious Indian Ocean from the equally enigmatic South China Sea. To the west its coralline shores are lapped by the Andaman Sea, a closed oceanographic domain with a hundred isolated, strange, endemic species of fish, sea stars and shells. To the east, the mangrove-bordered estuaries arch around the sullen, turbid Gulf of Siam.

The great contrast in faunas on each side of Thailand is accentuated by the continuing barrier to the south—Malaya and Singapore. In fact, the marine inhabitants of the Indian and Pacific oceans come together and struggle for superiority in the seas surrounding Sumatra, Malaya and Thailand. Engineers and economists, however, are planning blithely to dig a monstrous canal across the narrow girth of Thailand to afford cheaper passage for oil tankers and tourist cruise boats. With a rush, the life of the Gulf of Siam will mingle with that of the Andaman Sea, producing an ecological readjustment of amazing proportions and certainly unpredictable consequences.

Most delightful of the surviving natural spots on the west side of Thailand is the fifty-mile-long island of Phuket—a varied land of rocks, golden beaches, colorful coral reefs, teeming mangrove swamps and rich offshore waters. Helmet shells, figshells, olives, cowries and cones are moderately common in Phuket's semitropical waters. Rarely, one finds cast upon the white strand a broken chambered nautilus, a floating remnant that has ended its thousand-mile wandering from the Philippines where it was born and lived. Primitive roads around the island and a cobweb of side roads to sheltered bays offer an invitation to adventurous shell explorers to follow them.

Most seas are flushed with or replenished by some major current; for example, the Gulf Stream serves as a natural "sewer" for what otherwise would be a very stagnant Caribbean Sea. But the Andaman Sea, west of Thailand, has no such refresh-

ing stream and must, like the rest of the semi-isolated Indian Ocean, depend instead upon a seasonal backwash produced by the stormy monsoon winds. The upheaval is immense and disastrous to millions of acres of ocean-bottom life. Despite this violent seasonal change, several rare and unique species of shells survive in western Thailand. Lister's Conch and the Nivose Cowrie are two examples of this type of survival.

Among the other genera represented in Thailand's rich waters is *Umbonium,* a group of button-shaped, inch-long shells renowned for their multisplendored color patterns. So common are these shells on the shallow flats of the shores of southeast Asia and Japan that they are shoveled into great piles and used for making lime or bagged up and shipped to Japan where they are used in the manufacture of trinkets and souvenirs. The *Umbonium* is one of the few snails that has become an accomplished swimmer; it rapidly flips its long taillike foot to propel itself through the water.

The heavily forested mountains of Thailand shed rich nitrogenous wastes down the rivers and into the littoral areas just offshore. The build-up of rich sandy muds produces a host of detritus-feeding clams of many sorts. This gives ample opportunity for the development of gastropod predators, the most attractive of which is the Lined Moon Snail, a smooth, glossy shell designed with numerous, delicate axial flames of soft brown. Beneath that attractive shell lies an avaricious carnivore that pounces relentlessly upon clams at the rate of six or seven a day. The proboscis of the moon snail is doubly armed—with a circular sucker that emits a penetrating acid and with a set of radular teeth fixed to a ribbon that rasps back and forth over the shell of a clam until a neat hole has been drilled in it, giving access to the clam within, which provides the predatory moon snail with a tasty meal.

In addition to the unique kinds of Thai shells, there are many shell inhabitants of the coral reefs that are also widely distributed throughout the Indo-Pacific region. The Babylonia Turrid and the Spotted Miter are classic examples of widespread beauties.

OPPOSITE, LEFT: The Cardinal Miter, *Mitra cardinalis* Gmelin, is a common Indo-Pacific species. × 2. RIGHT: The China Moon, *Naticarius oncus* (Röding), of the Indo-Pacific. × 2. THIS PAGE: The common and widely distributed Tiger Cowrie, *Cypraea tigris* Linné, of the Pacific, has a retractable, frilled mantle. × 2.

Portugal

The Iberian country of Portugal, standing on the western flank of the Mediterranean, is a meeting place for mollusks from three general areas—the Mediterranean, the Bay of Biscay in France and the northwest African region of Morocco and its off-shore Madeira Islands. Primarily, however, the shells of Portugal belong to the eastern Atlantic marine province of Lusitania, a temperate water area characterized by the Saburon Bonnet (*Phalium*), the edible European oyster, a small noded Triton's Trumpet, several species of *Natica* moon snails and one cone species.

Portugal has about 800 marine species, while neighboring Spain and the Mediterranean have over 1,400 varieties. The lack of large, sheltered harbors and bays and the relatively cooler waters of Portugal probably account for its poorer fauna. The Mediterranean has a wide selection of shells, including the *Murex* shell that was once used as the source of the royal tyrian purple dye. Jacob's Scallop, the symbol of the medieval crusades, and the Prickly Cockle, *Cardium*, are common Spanish species also living in Portugal.

Some of the shells brought up in traps and nets by Portuguese fishermen are representatives of the African fauna. The attractive and uncommon Halia

Volute and the Neptune Volute are among the largest and most handsome. Despite the suitable temperature for some semitropical species, only one kind of cone shell, the drab, brown Mediterranean Cone, lives in southwestern Europe. Like its Indo-Pacific relatives, the Mediterranean Cone is armed with a tiny tooth resembling a microscopic hypodermic needle. Pacific species have stung and killed human beings, but the cone of European seas is evidently harmless.

The sandy shores of Portugal are well-stocked with venus and razor clams and small tellins. Their natural enemies, the boring *Natica* moon snails, are usually present nearby. The rocky shores, prevalent in Portugal, are well supplied with *Patella* limpets and periwinkles. Just offshore, where the bottom is a combination of rocks and seaweeds, several lovely *Calliostoma* top shells, the common European abalone and the strikingly colorful Magus Top Shell are all moderately common and are collected by snorkeling or scuba diving.

Limited to the Mediterranean and the North Atlantic is a family of charming little conchs known as the Pelican's Foot shells. During the last century, when shell collecting was the rage, every child's collection had at least one of these curious snail shells. The inch-long shell is characterized by a flaring outer lip with two or three prominent projections. Viewed from above, the shell vaguely resembles the foot of a pelican; hence its name. The shell is abundant wherever it lives, and for centuries it has been collected and sold as souvenirs and for shellcraft. A deepwater relative, the Serres Pelican's Foot, is much more delicate, with longer, more drawn-out projections. Some fossil European members of the Aporrhaididae had extremely long spines, rivaling those of today's Venus Comb Murex.

The Pelican's Foot is a sluggish creature and not an aggressive carnivore like so many northern univalves. It buries itself upside down in the sand and with its proboscis forms a conical channel down which detritus, mainly of vegetable origin, comes tumbling. By setting up a current by means of its gills, the Pelican's Foot may draw in several gallons of food-laden water every day. A similar type of behavior is found in the *Trichotropis* hairy snails of the North Atlantic.

Of great surprise to mollusk collectors is their

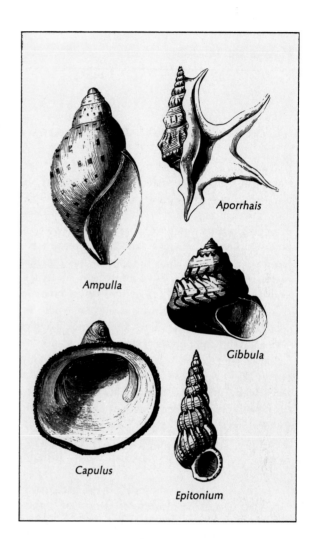

Aporrhais

Ampulla

Gibbula

Capulus

Epitonium

first encounter with an *Aplysia* sea hare, of which there are three species reported from Portugal. The lumbering, massive snail resembles a huge slug with two pairs of appendages, or "ears," at the front end. The vestigial shell is buried under the flesh of the back. Disturb or pick up a sea hare and it will exude a beautiful cloud of harmless purple ink. Sea hares are vegetarians that have been known to eat six times their own weight in green seaweed within twenty-four hours.

OPPOSITE: The mollusks of Portuguese bays are similar to those of southern France and Spain. ABOVE: Five typical kinds of shells found in Portuguese waters.

Hawaiian Islands

Hawaii is a submerged chain of mountains whose tops jut above the surface the length of a 1600-mile stretch, beginning with Midway Island and extending southeasterly to Lanai, Oahu, Hawaii and Maui. Thousands of years ago the sea level was a hundred feet lower than it is today and the temperature of the water was more akin to that of tropical Indonesia. At that time the shell fauna consisted of warm-water olives, cones, cowries and scorpion conchs, resembling those now living in Okinawa and the northern Philippines.

Today, the relatively cool waters of Hawaii support fewer species, and many of those that survived the chilling effects of the last glacial period have been modified into endemic Hawaiian subspecies. Others, such as the Tiger Cowrie, normally an abundant, shallow-water dweller, are large in size, rare and found living in Hawaiian waters at depths from 30 to 100 feet.

The black, volcanic shores of many parts of the Hawaiian Islands have produced a host of limpets, cowries and murex shells that are very dark in color, camouflaging them from the eyes of mollusk-eating birds and crabs. Although corals are present in substantial quantities, their production of calcium carbonate is at a much slower rate than in the warmer seas to the south. There are no extensive shallow flats of white shell-and-coral sand here.

Not far from Hawaii and, indeed, elsewhere throughout certain parts of the Pacific, there are ancient submerged islands, or guyots, whose tops have been planed smooth, possibly by wave action. Most of the several hundred guyots lie a half-mile below the surface, probably having sunk from their own weight as well as having been covered a few hundred feet by rising waters. The tops of these lost islands are littered with dead corals and harbor a moderately rich shell fauna, reachable only by deep-water dredging.

Although the mollusks of Hawaii are basically Indo-Pacific in origin, a few are evidently invaders from the cooler waters of the Japanese Bonin Islands. Among these is the common rock-clinging limpet *Patella,* a beautifully ribbed, shield-shaped snail adapted for resisting the pounding waves and surf. At night these snails crawl ever so slowly over the wet rocks, nodding their trunklike snouts back and forth as they graze on microscopic algae. The tiny radulae are strung on a very long, coiled ribbon. Because the hard rock surface is so abrasive, the radular ribbon is three times the length of the shell and is continually growing at the back end.

The *Patella* limpet was abundant at the time Captain Cook discovered Hawaii. The Polynesians eat the soft parts either raw or in stews. Today, human overpopulation has reduced the colonies to near extinction.

Although Hawaii can claim only about three dozen species of cowries, it can boast of some highly unusual and distinctive ones. Gaskoin's Cowrie, an inch-long, glossy jewel, is a soft yellowish fawn color with artistically arranged circular spots of ivory white. Along the edges a series of rich chestnut-colored spots divides the back from the ivory base of the shell. Along the left side of the back, a long, narrow white line marks the spot where the two fleshy mantle flaps come together. Other Hawaiian members of this group include Ostergaard's Cowrie, the Tessellate Cowrie and the curiously toothed Sulcidentate Cowrie.

Hawaii has a surprising selection of *Terebra* auger shells, although most of them are less than an inch in length. These many-whorled snails have extremely slender shells in order to permit them to dig down into the sand in search of their favorite food, marine worms. Miters abound under rocks and sand from a water depth of 20 to 200 feet. Among the many attractive species is the endemic Thaanum's Miter.

ABOVE: A hairy triton from Hawaii displays two unique characteristics of its family—giraffelike patterns on the foot and bifurcate strands of periostracum. × 2. LEFT: Mariel King and Cliff S. Weaver, two ardent collectors, dredge just off Diamond Head, Hawaii.

New England

The cold waters of New England from Maine to Connecticut contain about 600 marine species, of which only 150 are found in water shallow enough to allow the average collector to obtain them. The coastal waters are by no means uniform in temperature, clarity, depth or in the kinds of algae and shell life they contain.

Cape Cod, Massachusetts, which juts out into the ocean some eighty miles, is a natural barrier between the cold waters of the Gulf of Maine and the somewhat warmer areas from Buzzard's Bay south to New York. South of Cape Cod, the oyster, the Surf Clam, the Channeled Whelk and the venus clam are well known, but to the north in the Gulf of Maine they are absent or rarely encountered because of the unduly cold water. In some cases the restrictively low temperature will soon kill the larval or young forms.

Along the rocky shores of Maine, the intertidal rock pools are excellent places to collect a host of interesting and colorful forms of sea life. Bright red starfish, green sea urchins and many forms of brown, red and green marine seaweeds are readily found in the sparkling, clear waters of these pools. Pull aside the overhanging festoons of brown *Fucus* seaweeds and you will find the black periwinkle and the bright yellow Obtuse Periwinkle. Under ledges are the handsome *Nucella* dogwinkles, inch-long attractive white shells that lay small urn-shaped egg capsules. On the flat bottoms of the pools are small blue-and-brown mottled limpets, and by the edges are mats of the blue mussel.

On an especially low tide, great areas of ocean bottom may be exposed in the Bay of Fundy area. Normally deepwater species, such as the brown-corded New England Neptune and the Stimpson's *Colus* whelk, may be found among the granite gravel and seaweeds. Farther offshore, in twenty to eighty feet of water, there are large beds of the Deep-Sea Scallop, great circular grayish pink shells reaching almost the size of a dinner plate. The round adductor muscle is marketed for food.

Lobster and clambakes are a shore delight once enjoyed, before the days of pollution, by everyone

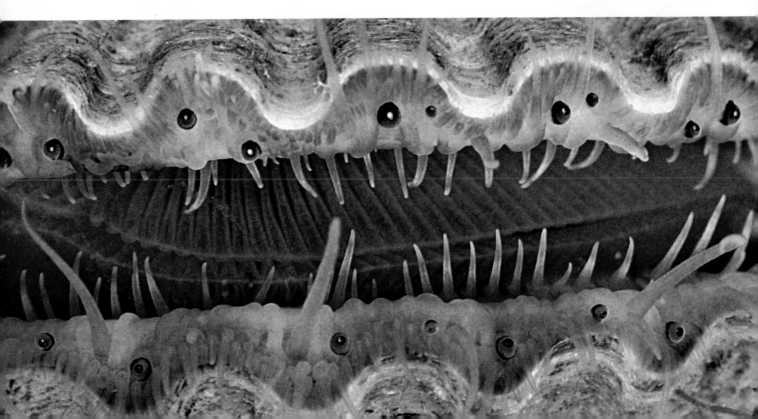

who went to the shore for the summer. The clam used in New England in seaweed-smothered fire pits is the "nanny-nose," or *Mya* Soft-shell Clam. The whitish gray shell is about three to five inches long with a wide gap at each end, one for the foot, the other for a long, fused siphon, or "snout," through which the clam draws and expels water. The clams live deep in the sandy mud, down about three or four times the length of the shell. At low tide clam diggers walk the shoreline flats looking for a small oblong hole about the diameter of a pencil. A stamp of the foot will produce a squirt of water from the hole if a clam, not a sea worm, is living below.

In southern New England, the six-inch-long Knobbed Whelk is a frequent occupant of shallow water and may sometimes be found eating a quahog, as the Hard-shelled Venus Clam is locally known. The whelk uproots the clam from the sand, enwraps it in its large muscular foot and then, by using the edge of its shell lip, laboriously pries the clam's valves apart. Once ajar, the clam falls victim to the jaws and radular teeth of the whelk. The Knobbed and Channeled whelks both lay a long ribbon of egg capsules, somewhat resembling an oversized rattlesnake tail. The ribbons are commonly washed ashore, puzzling newcomers to the sea. Each wafer-shaped capsule, usually about the size of a quarter, contains either hundreds of pin-sized eggs or dozens of hatched miniature whelks.

Other shells commonly found on the beaches of New England are the two tennis-ball-sized moon snails, the so-called Shark-eye with its brown button-shaped underside and the Common Northern Moon Snail. These snails bore holes through clam shells and feed upon the bivalve tenants. The snails lay curious egg cases. They are gelatinous ribbons coiled in the form of a shirt collar and covered with sand grains.

The delightful slipper shell is common in New England. Its shell is boat-shaped, and on its underside is a shelf that resembles a poop deck. These snails live one on top of the other and may pile up as many as six or seven in sequence.

OPPOSITE: The Common Bay Scallop, *Argopecten,* has baby-blue eyes. × 10. ABOVE: *Littorina obtusata* (Linné). × 2. RIGHT: Nudibranch, *Coryphella verrucosa* (Linné). × 3.

West Indies

The Caribbean Sea is the center for an ancient stock of shells that originally came from the Tethys Sea hundreds of millions of years ago. Since then the mollusk fauna has alternatingly spread to and shrunk from neighboring seas. At one time the Caribbean cut across Central America.

Today, the Caribbean fauna extends southward as far as central Brazil on the east coast of South America. Northward, the Gulf Stream is responsible for the presence of West Indian shells in Bermuda and on the shallow banks of the Carolinas. The West Indies proper are characterized by such snails as the Pink, the Rooster-tail, the Hawkwing and the Milk conchs and by colorful clams, such as the Sunrise and the Interrupted Tellin. Shelling is by no means as fruitful in the Caribbean as one would expect. In some coral-reef areas, it takes diligent

searching under rocks and in crevices to find cones and marginellas.

Shallow, muddy areas near large islands are usually conchologically richer than the bright, sandy coralline strands of small ocean-ringed islets. The tidal creeks, where oysters abound, sometimes support huge colonies of the Short-fronded Murex and the Giant West Indian *Melongena*. Areas of both muddy and clear coral water can be found along the Central American coast, in locations such as British Honduras, where offshore islands are moderately rich in shells.

The lower Caribbean from Venezuela to the Dutch Leeward Islands of Aruba, Bonaire and Curaçao is a semiisolated area containing species of cowries, spindles and olives found nowhere else in the West Indies. Unfortunately, the high winds of the winter season make shell collecting difficult. Collecting on rock shores on the lee side of islands, however, will always produce an abundance of nerites, purpuras, prickly-winkles and chitons.

Adjuncts of the West Indian fauna are found along the more southerly of the Florida Keys, where the warm Gulf Stream keeps local waters fit for tropical species. Northward into the Gulf of Mexico and up the west coast to Marco, Sanibel Island and Clearwater, the cooler waters are a haven for many beautiful and abundant species related to the West Indian forms.

The Calico Scallop is a small, colorful scallop occurring not only in the West Indies but also abundantly in the southeastern United States, where it is now being fished commercially for its small, edible muscle. Other scallops of the Caribbean include the large, nodose Lion's Paw, whose brick red, sometimes orange, hues make it a collector's item; Laurent's deepwater scallop, which has a smooth whitish lower valve and a slightly ribbed, rust brown upper valve and the Zigzag Scallop, which has a flat, fan-shaped upper valve and a deeply rounded, dishlike lower half.

Three large helmet shells are fairly common in the West Indies, of which the best known is the King Conch, *Cassis tuberosa,* and its dwarf brother the Flame Conch, which rarely exceeds the size of a grapefruit. The Queen Conch, carrying the scientific misnomer of *madagascariensis,* is the largest, reaching a length of thirteen inches. All are characterized by a large, glossy, enameled shield surrounding a toothed mouth. Helmets feed on sea urchins and are not hesitant about crawling up over one of these spiny creatures in order to break its spines and drill a hole in its fragile shell.

Among the rarer cassids are the deepwater Royal Bonnet, *Sconsia,* and the Dennison's Morum, found in thirty to eighty feet of water. The latter fetched fabulous prices at eighteenth-century auctions in Europe and is still considered a valuable shell.

OPPOSITE: The White Spotted Marginella of Florida and the West Indies has identical markings on both its soft parts and hard shell. Under the long siphon are the two eyes. × 5. ABOVE: The King Helmet, *Cassis tuberosa* (Linné), is one of three kinds of helmets common in the West Indies. They feed on echinoderms. × 1.

New Zealand

New Zealand conchologists take justifiable pride in the richness and uniqueness of the shell fauna of their picturesque islands. An almost complete census has been taken over the last century of the shallow-water kinds, and deepwater dredging operations are constantly bringing in new species.

Although the marine waters of New Zealand are perhaps best described as cool–temperate, there are unmistakable signs of semitropical invaders turning up at the northern end of the archipelago. Some of these, including a few cassid helmets, cowries and frog shells, show a very close resemblance to species from New South Wales, Australia.

For the most part, the central areas of New Zealand support a huge population of mollusks endemic to that area. The rich fossil records of New Zealand reinforce the belief that this fauna has been isolated and allowed to develop unique types for many millions of years. *Calliostoma* top shells and handsome whelks are today's common inhabitants.

Shells were a part of the life of the Polynesian Maori natives who inhabited the islands before the coming of the Europeans. Clams from the sandy, shallow flats were a favorite food staple, as was the abalone. The artistic wooden carvings of the Maori tribes were often inlaid with fragments of shells.

The farther south one travels in New Zealand, the colder the ocean water becomes. The most southerly portions border on the antarctic seas, and the snails and clams of those frigid waters show a close kinship to those of the subantarctic waters of Tasmania, Argentina and South Africa. Shells in these cold regions are thinner and less colorful than those of tropical waters. Clam species outnumber the kinds of snails, perhaps because the rich plankton food favors the filter-feeding clams.

Of the three species of *Haliotis* snails in New Zealand, the *Paua*, or iridescent abalone, is the largest and best known. In Europe this genus is known as the sea ormer or sea ear. The group is well represented in western American waters and, as in New Zealand, is appreciated for its delectable flesh and beautiful shell. To the novice, an empty abalone shell resembles one half of a bivalved clam, but a more careful inspection will show the unmistakable characteristics of a snail's coiling whorls at one end. The series of open holes in the shell are exhaust outlets for water coming from the gills of the animal. Abalones are vegetarians, and the females shed their eggs freely into the water where free-floating sperm fertilize them as they float by.

Cunningham's Top Shell is one of a dozen beautiful New Zealand species belonging to a worldwide family of Calliostomidae. The one- to two-inch-long shells are characterized by a pearly interior and a delicately beaded or speckled exterior. Colonies of these snails swarm amid the algae jungles found offshore at depths of 50 to 500 feet. The operculum of these snails is a very thin, amber-colored, circular wafer that can seal the aperture of the shell.

Normally, the spiny murex shells of the world are found in warm tropical waters, but an exception is the New Zealand Murex, a two-inch-long, whitish, spiny snail commonly found offshore. These rapacious carnivores feed upon deepwater oysters, mussels and clams.

New Zealand is not renowned for its spectacular *Patella* limpets, as is South Africa, but it does have one lovely psychedelically colored example, the little Fragile New Zealand Limpet. This beautiful little inch-long limpet is unfortunately cursed with the complicated name of *Atalacmea fragilis*.

LEFT: The cool waters of New Zealand abound in large whelks, such as the Dilated Siphon Whelk, *Penion dilatatus* Quoy and Gaimard. × 1. RIGHT: Typical of New Zealand is the spiny murex, *Poirieria zelandica* Quoy and Gaimard. × 2.

Philippines

For more than a thousand miles, the gigantic archipelago of the Philippines stretches across the richest tropical waters of the world. More than 4,500 islands, some large, most small, squat on a shallow marine platform bounded by the 34,000-foot-deep Philippine Trench on the east and the sultry South China Sea on the west. The Philippines have over 4,000 species of marine shells and almost that number in forest snails and river univalves.

Curiously, the marine fauna of the Philippines is not a uniform assemblage but rather a group of overlapping subfaunas. To the north, the island of Luzon has an open oceanic type of shell life that is almost indistinguishable from that of Okinawa to the north and the Marianas and Palau Islands far to the east. The Marble Cone, the Textile Cone, the Ricine Drupe, the Grossularia Drupe, the Lambis Scorpion Conch and many other western Pacific species are common to this area.

In the central Philippines, around Cebu, Leyte, Romblon and Negros, the Pacific species are mingled with many species that are uniquely Philippine. Here is the center of distribution of the chambered nautiluses, which occur in huge schools off the coast of western Leyte. Deep in the ocean, at a depth of around 200 feet, the chambered nautilus moves stealthily about in search of lobsters and crabs. This strange cephalopod, with its gas-filled chambers and more than ninety tentacles, is trapped in wicker baskets by the Filipinos. The flesh is eaten and the attractive, pearly shell sold to shellcraft dealers around the world.

The island of Palawan and the Sulu Archipelago, at the south end of the Philippines, are in the domain of the Moro tribes, and the fauna has much closer affinities with that of the Indonesian islands of Borneo and the Moluccas than with that of the Philippines. The region of Zamboanga and Cuyo support the fabulous Imperial Volute and the scarlet and orange Aulica Volute. Many other shells, such as the Noble Cone, are endemic to these seas.

Typical of the entire western Pacific is the large Triton's Trumpet, a magnificent marine snail sometimes reaching a length of twenty inches. In the Philippines this species seems to grow larger and more beautiful than in any other region. The Triton's Trumpet feeds on the blue sea star, known as *Linkia*, although on rare occasions it will attack the Crown-of-Thorns sea star that does so much damage to coral reefs. A large triton takes about six years to reach its maximum size. The female lays clumps of sausage-shaped egg capsules under protective rocks. A cousin of this triton, known as the Variegated Triton, lives in the Caribbean but is not as large or as graceful. Tritons have been used as trumpets by South Sea islanders and by Orientals for hundreds of generations.

Strangest of the conch family is the extraordinarily slender Tibia Shell, an eleven-inch-long architectural wonder with a long spire of many whorls and an equally long shelly snout at the anterior end. Settled safely under the soft ooze of Manila's bay, the tibia can draw fresh seawater down its long "periscope." These delicate shells are brought up in fishermen's nets during the summer months. Miraculously, many specimens fall to the deck of the ship amid sponges and sand rubble without breaking.

The tiny, pea-sized Pacific Emerald Nerite is found clinging to eelgrass that grows in the sandy meadows of the shallow Pacific waters. Under a microscope, the delicate paintings of white and black stripes are very pronounced. In deep offshore waters, the Oriental Turrid is a bejeweled wonder sometimes dredged from as great a depth as 1,000 feet by biological expeditions.

The miter family of univalves reaches its climax in the Philippines. Some experts believe that there are over 400 kinds in these waters alone. Shells of the genus *Mitra* can be recognized by the three to five toothlike folds within the mouth of the shell.

TOP LEFT: Shell collecting on your doorstep is possible in the Philippines. At high tide the water rises eight feet.
LOWER LEFT: *Homalocantha zamboi* Burch and Burch was named after the builder of the above house. × 1.
ABOVE: Limited to the southern Philippines is the eight-inch Imperial Volute, *Volutocorona imperialis* (Lightfoot).

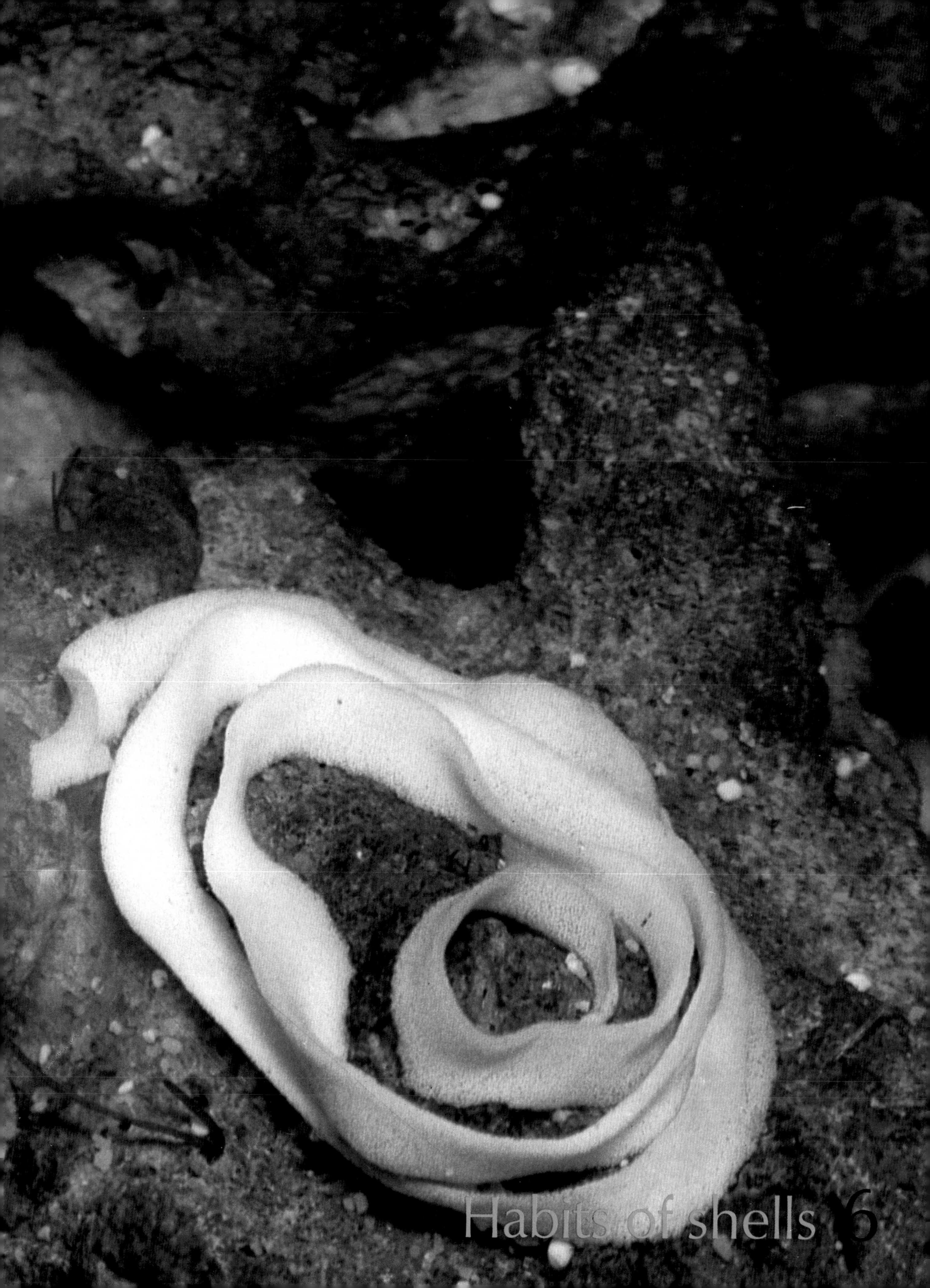

Habits of shells 6

Giant clams

The oft-told tale that giant man-eating clams have clamped down on the arm or leg of a diver and caused him to drown has never been authenticated. A four-foot-long giant clam, cleaned of its meat and with its huge shell valves agape, certainly looks capable of locking down on the arm of a man. But when one looks closely at a living *Tridacna* clam and studies its behavior, it becomes evident that the chances of a person's being caught, much less being eaten, by this placid bivalve are very remote.

A large giant clam, between three and four feet in length, is capable of opening its valves no more than six inches, and between the prongs of the shelly valves is the huge, fleshy, serpentine mantle edge that serves as a cushion for any object jabbed between the valves. The last thing a giant clam wants is an intruder between its valves, so it gives a warning by contracting its valves to a width of an inch or less. This warns the intruder, be it a crab,

fish or swimmer, that it is "stepping on someone's toes," so to speak. It takes several harder jabs deeper into the clam to make this giant bivalve almost close its shell. Smaller *Tridacna* clams, between four and six inches in length, are more dangerous, since they can completely shut their valves within a few seconds.

The largest known giant clam is four feet six inches in length. The heaviest pair of shell valves weighs 579.5 pounds. There are six species, all living in the Indo-Pacific region. The largest is *Tridacna gigas*, which lives in the shallow reef waters of the southwest Pacific. The smaller, but beautifully fluted, Squamose *Tridacna* Clam has a wide distribution extending from the Red Sea to Polynesia.

All species are alike in that they live upside down, with the hinge of the valves buried in sand or deep inside a soft coral block. The free, toothed edge is uppermost. When the clam is covered with water at high tide, it protrudes its huge, colorful, fleshy mantle over the edges of the two valves, so that they resemble two undulating worms.

The maligned "giant killer clam" is strictly a vegetarian, but unlike most bivalves that suck food-laden water into their mantle cavities, *Tridacna* farms its own algal food within these fleshy mantle lobes. A unique species of symbiotic algae, called *Zooxanthella*, lives in great quantities in the clam's phagocyte blood cells near the surface. There the single-celled seaweeds, bathed in sunlight most of the day, multiply and serve as a ready supply of food. In order to step up production, the clam has produced clear lenslike organs in its skin, which allow more sunlight to penetrate deeper. The vivid, multicolored designs in the mantles of giant clams are due in part to the presence of *Zooxanthella*.

The giant clams, although solitary squatters on the sea bottom, cannot claim to be lonely, for

many dozens of other sea creatures are associated with them. As many as thirty species of mollusks have been removed from the outside of a *Tridacna*'s shell. A veritable jungle of algae, bryozoans, sponges and tiny snails exists on the outer surface. Ten species of palaemonid shrimp have been found living deep within the mantle cavity of the clam, where they feed on food scraps brought in through the clam's siphonal hole. Occasionally, one can find a school of half-inch-long fish swimming just in front of the clam's intake siphon. The fish apparently enjoy the current it produces, and when they are in danger, they may use the mantle cavity for protection.

Giant clams have many uses for man, although today the shells are used mainly as decoration or bird baths. South Sea islanders and Malayans eat them raw or cooked, and in some areas there is some commerce in dried *Tridacna* flesh. The large adductor muscles are the tastiest parts of the clam, as is the case with our commercial scallops. For centuries the natives of coral atolls have used the shells as basins, mallets, hoes and scrapers. The Solomon islanders make from them large, centrally perforated disks about six to nine inches in diameter that serve as money in the purchase of brides.

Pearls of a white, nonnacreous nature are sometimes formed in the giant clams. A specimen from Malaita Island, Solomons, produced one that is the size of a golf ball. The largest known pearl, a badly misshapen one, weighs fourteen pounds.

PRECEDING PAGES: A nudibranch has just laid its coil of gelatinous eggs. This is one of numerous species of *Chromodoris* found in Australian waters.
OPPOSITE: Shell and soft parts of this Giant Clam weighed nearly 500 pounds. Note that the clam, despite rough treatment, has not completely closed its two valves.
ABOVE: The soft flesh of *Tridacna* clams contains commensal colonies of nutritious algae upon which the clam feeds.

Carrier shells

Among the various kinds of protection that are employed by creatures is the simple and obvious process of camouflage—developing a coloration or formation that blends in with the natural surroundings to enable the creature to escape notice. This, of course, is a relative matter because what serves as a case of camouflage to one enemy may not deter another potential predator. An orange scallop attached to an orange sponge may elude a human diver but not escape the hungry color-blind crab that hunts by smell and touch.

Most intriguing among the purported cases of molluscan camouflage are the several examples found in the family Xenophoridae. The Latin name *Xenophora* means "bearer of foreigners," a name bestowed by a Russian in 1807 on a strange trochid-shaped snail that attached stones, bits of coral and dead shells to its outer shell surface. Today, we know of a dozen species of these strange shell-collecting shells. Curiously, each species has its own degree to which it will collect foreign bodies. The Pallid Carrier Shell of Japan and the Common West Indian Carrier Shell are veritable pigs when it comes to collecting shells. From a fish's or human collector's viewpoint, these two species appear to be mere piles of dead shells. Longley's Carrier Shell from deep water off Cuba is not a very enthusiastic collector, for it adds only an occasional shell. Laziest is the Exustus Carrier that attaches no foreign objects but produces an edge resembling attached objects.

The pinnacle of evolution in this family is the Sunburst Carrier, *Stellaria solaris,* a deepwater species from the Philippines and Malaya. The entire peripheral edge is studded with long projections of shell material. This saves the snail the task of hunting for objects and gluing them to itself. The Sunburst Carrier was known to European collectors as early as 1705 but was for over 200 years considered a rarity. After World War II, deepwater fish trawlers in the Philippines began netting them in increasing numbers, so that today this treasure is represented in many leading collections.

Two mysteries about this family have prevailed for centuries. Only one has been solved—how do carrier shells hunt, hold and glue other shells and bits of coral to themselves? An amateur conchologist in Florida recently captured and kept alive a specimen in his salt water aquarium. One night, under a dim light, he caught his carrier at work. The snail selected the shell it wanted with its waving proboscis and then snuggled its "shoulder," or the part of the mouth of its own shell where the mantle is located, up against the foreign body. Holding still for several minutes, the snail added a few millimeters of new shelly material to its apertural edge. At the same time, it cemented the new object. It then lumbered off to another part of the aquarium and spent the rest of the night quietly consolidating its new acquisition.

No one knows exactly why carrier shells are collectors. In some cases it may be for camouflage purposes; but even carriers that live in the deep parts of the ocean where there is no light have excellent collections attached to themselves. Some malacologists speculate that the added bodies give additional strength to the shell or may even prevent the shell from sinking into the soft mud.

LEFT: Resembling a pile of dead clam shells, the carrier snail, *Xenophora conchyliophora* (Born), has attached foreign objects to its own shell. × 1.
BELOW: At the left is the Japanese Carrier, *X. pallidula* Reeve, a common Asian species. At the lower right is the curious Sunburst Carrier, *Stellaria solaris* (Linné), from the tropical Pacific depths. It produces its own ornamentation. × 1.

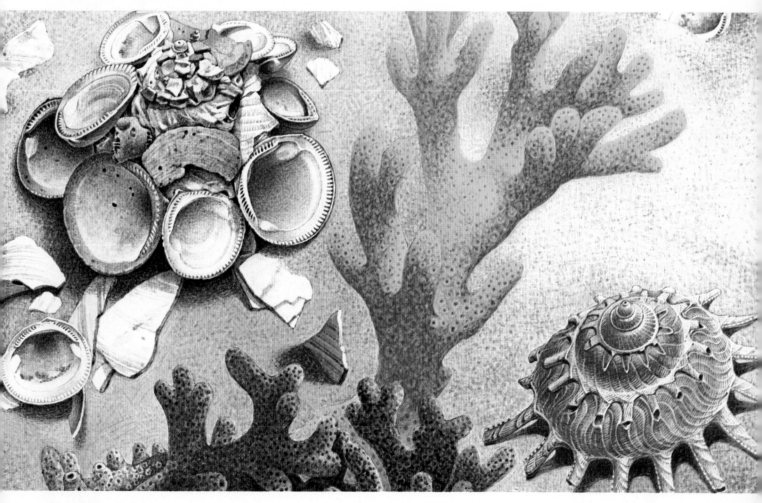

Sea-fan snails

ABOVE: In tropical reef settings of the West
Indies, it is not uncommon to find the snail, *Cyphoma
gibbosum* (Linné), clinging to sea fans.
The spotted mantles cover their orange shells. × 1.
OPPOSITE, TOP: The Common West Indian
Simnia lives only on sea whips. × 3. BELOW: The
Fingerprint Cyphoma of the Caribbean is identified
by its striped mantle. × 2.

There is probably no sea-fan snail on the West Indian reef scene more striking and conspicuous than the curiously named Flamingo Tongue. It is neither tongue-shaped nor flamingo-colored, except perhaps when it has been killed and cleaned of its beautiful soft parts. Known technically as *Cyphoma gibbosum*, this inch-long, cucumber-shaped, glossy orange shell has a mantle stretched over it that looks much more like the hide of a spotted giraffe than the color of a flamingo.

These snails live all their lives attached to the colonial animal structures of the sea-fan and sea-plume families. Young, free-swimming larvae of the genus *Cyphoma* land by happenstance on a sea plume, attach themselves to it firmly and then spend the remaining years of their lives slowly grazing over the polyp surface of their coelenterate host. There seldom are more than one or two pairs of *Cyphoma* snails on one sea plume, for overcrowding would destroy the host. Never does a *Cyphoma* feed upon sea-fan polyps faster than the sea fan can regenerate them.

Nature has endowed *Cyphoma* snails with the territorial characteristics of the tiger. Once a male has established itself on a sea plume, it will violently attack any newcomers of the same sex. Females—there may be two or three per male—lay their small capsulelike eggs firmly on the stems of the sea plumes. Hatching occurs within three or four weeks, whereupon several dozen free-swimming veliger snails are produced that sail out into the blue sea in search of a neighboring sea fan.

There are four kinds of *Cyphoma* snails, all limited to the Caribbean marine province. The shells of these various species are similar enough to be very difficult to distinguish from one another. However, the soft, fleshy mantle that extends over and completely covers the hard shell of each species is quite distinctive. The common Flamingo Tongue, ranging from Bermuda to Brazil, has orange and black spottings resembling those of a giraffe. The Fingerprint Cyphoma is marked with many crowded black lines, which together resemble an

inked fingerprint. McGinty's Cyphoma, on the other hand, has very subdued tan blotches. The fourth West Indian species is the Intermediate Cyphoma, whose shell has been known for over a hundred years, but whose mantle has not been properly described.

The relationship between the sea fan and the snails is a one-way form of symbiosis. The host supplies them with shelter, food and a convenient station in life. So far as we know the sea fans do not gain any benefits from this association, although further research may prove this untrue. If the *Cyphoma* snails are to be classified as predators, they certainly are very slow about the process and do not "eat their way out of house and home."

The lively scallop

Clumsy clams and sedentary oysters have not done much to improve the reputation of the bivalve class as being an active group. But there are probably no more sprightly mollusks than the scallops, a large group of bivalves known to the public more for their culinary assets than for their colorful shells or ability to swim.

Among adult mollusks, swimming is confined to relatively few groups—the swift squids, the butterflylike pteropods, the plodding sea hares, a few nudibranchs, still fewer shelled snails and perhaps three or four families of bivalves. The principle of progression used by all bivalves is the water jet stream—the sudden expulsion of water produced by the rapid closing of the shell valves.

Adult scallops sitting placidly on the ocean bottom will, upon threat from a predatory fish, crab or starfish, suddenly leap into action and zigzag away into the watery distance. One of the prime preconditions for such a reaction is a full set of highly developed eyes. All along the edges of the mantle of a scallop are a series of relatively large, colorful eyes that are highly sensitive to the slightest change in light. A passing cloud will stimulate a scallop to shut its valves; the shadow of a fish will often startle a scallop enough to make it snap its valves and beat a hasty retreat.

Curiously, the scallop has two ways of swimming. The most obvious one, already mentioned, is the so-called escape reaction. The scallop snaps its valves together, and the resulting exodus of water propels the animal backwards in the direction opposite to the opening of the valves. In other words, the hinge end of the scallop moves forward.

However, there is an alternative method of progression, and this is possible only because the scallop's soft parts consist of a curtainlike mantle edge. When the valves are suddenly closed, the scallop holds the mantle curtain firmly in place. The water cannot squirt out at the front end. It can only escape backwards past the hinge end. This results in the scallop's moving forward. In action, the scallop looks as if it were "biting" itself forward.

The ability to swim is so highly developed in the scallop that it can, by controlling the muscles of the mantle flaps, take any direction it wishes, left or right or up or down. In fact, large beds of the edible deep-sea scallops off the coast of New England make gradual migrations, evidently not only to avoid unfavorable conditions but also to find richer feeding grounds.

Of the several dozens of scallop species, only a few are good swimmers. These include the true *Pecten*, such as the Zigzag Scallop of the Caribbean. Other scallops seldom take to swimming except in emergencies. During their hours of anchorage, the sedentary species of scallops, such as the *Chlamys* group, attach themselves to rocks, seaweeds and other shells with a byssus. If abruptly disturbed, the scallop will release its byssal anchorage, swim off to a new haven and immediately begin to spin new anchor threads.

In its gradual evolution toward developing the ability to swim, the scallop family has modified its internal, as well as external, structure. Within, a very large adductor muscle has developed so that the valves may be snapped shut. Between the hinge edges of the valves is a triangular-shaped elastic cushion that serves to keep the valves apart when the muscles are relaxed. In the scallops this ligamental wedge is unusually large. Externally, the scallops have modified their shells for swimming by making them brittle and much lighter in weight. In many cases, this has necessitated the formation of radial ribs to give added strength.

TOP: Related to the scallops and also a lively swimmer is the lima file clam. Here, *Lima scabra* (Born) of the Caribbean displays its delicate tentacles. × 2. BOTTOM: Eyes and short tentacles bedeck the mantle edge of this Australian scallop, *Mimachlamys subgloriosa* Iredale. × 3.

Nest-building clams

Close cousins to the scallops, and fellow swimmers, are the lima, or file, clams. They are unique among the bivalves in possessing numerous very long, colorful tentacles. The shells of the lima clam (pronounced "lee-mah") resemble those of the scallops but are smaller, less fan-shaped and micro-sculptured with fine scales or beads. Whereas the scallops depend upon speed and agility to protect themselves, the lima clams depend upon their sticky, detachable tentacles and their ability to seclude themselves in self-built nests.

Lima clams usually swim backwards—that is, with the hinge in advance and the graceful tentacles flapping behind. Annoying small fish are deterred from nipping at the lima because the sticky tentacles break loose at the slightest provocation and entangle in the mouth of the would-be predator. Limas can also manipulate forward by using the tentacles in a "rowing" fashion. Some species are capable of burrowing into pebble bottoms, using their valves to shove aside the tiny stones. In well-aerated areas where the bottom is of clean shell gravel, lima clams may abound in large numbers.

Limas are prodigious producers of byssal threads.

Place a captured specimen in an aquarium overnight and in the morning there will be a long line of tufts of brown threads attached near the waterline. During the night the clam will have swum to the surface, spun an attachment thread with its small abortive foot, and then, feeling restive about its artificial environment, cast off and moved along seeking a new place to lodge. In an evening, the lima will have left a trail of dozens of abandoned byssal tufts.

In more natural surroundings the limas put their byssal manufacturing to good use in producing complicated nests in the crevices of rocks. Unable to escape their enemies as quickly as scallops, the limas have taken the tack of secluding themselves in these nests. Often they do this in colonial groups. When a rock is overturned, it is not uncommon to find five or six specimens entwined in a community basket of threads.

Smallest of the family is Bronn's Lima, a tiny white bivalve barely larger than a swollen grain of rice. Largest is the deep-sea species found off the Philippine Islands at a depth of over a thousand feet. The shells of these deep-sea clams quite often reach the size of large dessert platters.

Nest building is not confined to the family Limidae. Many members of the mussel family, namely the *Musculus* tribe, spin finely threaded mats that serve as protective nests. Some of the more highly evolved Bladder Clams, notably the *Entodesma* of the American Pacific coast, live their entire adult lives encased in a self-made byssal bag. This serves as a protection not only against rough waters but also against crab and fish predators. The nests also provide a home for several other forms of life, including algae, bryozoans, worms and parasitic *Odostomia* snails.

The most famous of the byssal producers among the bivalves is the two-foot-long *Pinna* clam of the Mediterranean. This fragile, fan-shaped clam is found almost completely buried in the mud bottom, anchored by means of a large clump of golden byssal threads. The ancients of the Mediterranean world gathered, cured, carded and spun these threads into a valuable cloth. Mussels, pearl oysters and a host of other sedentary bivalves are anchored by byssal threads, but these "beards" are of no economic value.

OPPOSITE: A magnified view of a lima clam shows the delicate, annular structure of the tentacles. They stick to collectors' fingers but are harmless. × 50. ABOVE: A lima clam is shown in the process of building a protective nest of byssal threads and bits of debris.

Boring clams

Most of the bivalves plow their way down into the soft substrate to protect themselves against predators and adverse currents. Since most groups of life have explored almost every evolutionary avenue toward survival, it is natural that many families of bivalves would have extended their burrowing habits into a more specialized form of boring. Hard clay, soft limestone, dead coral and wood were boring materials available to the bivalve experimenters.

The true boring bivalves, of which there are over a hundred species belonging to a dozen families, arrived at their tunneling existence through two main evolutionary routes. One way was found by the byssal-attached bivalves that kept snuggling against the hard substrate. Some wiggled down into protective cracks; others, with the help of the byssal anchor, twisted back and forth and hollowed out a groove or basin. Among this type of borer is the small species of *Tridacna* clam, *crocea*. It now lives almost completely buried inside hard coral blocks, maintaining its position by constantly moving its shell back and forth.

But to produce a neat, hollow tunnel in a hard rock requires more on the part of a shell than mere industrious scraping. The *Lithophaga* date mussels have solved this problem by producing an acidlike secretion that literally melts soft calcium carbonate rock. To protect its calcium shell from being destroyed by its own acid, the date mussel has covered itself with a thick, impenetrable coating of brown, chitinous periostracum. Date mussels are commonly found riddling the underside of small brain corals.

While some families of clams were learning how to nestle and wiggle into crevices or were taking short cuts by producing dissolving agents in their mantles, the great piddock family, Pholadidae, and its close cousin the Teredinidae shipworm were attacking the problem head on. The pholads have been Trojans in their efforts to bore into clay, shale and hard rocks. Acting much like a bore bit, the anterior ends of these clams, which are twisted against the rock, bore holes in the hardest of substrata by incessant abrasion. In fact, one kind of pholad glues tiny bits of minerals, such as garnets, to the edge of its shell to facilitate its boring activities. The power to bore is provided by a huge, suctionlike foot that protrudes through the anterior gape in the shell to hold fast to the tunnel end.

Perhaps the most adroit of the boring clams is the large, worldwide clan of shipworms, a misnamed family of clams resembling worms but modified into molluscan engineers dedicated to drilling holes through wooden ships, floating logs, old coconut shells and manila hemp lines. Ever since man launched his first dugout canoe or bamboo raft into the ocean, the molluscan shipworms have been destroying his nautical handicrafts. A healthy shipworm can penetrate a six-inch-thick plank in less than a year.

The business end of a teredo shipworm is at the anterior, where two serrated shell valves are constantly at work rasping back and forth scraping off minute shreds of wood. As the shipworm enlarges its tunnel and grows in length, it adds to the long, shelly encasing tube that fills the older parts of the tunnel. Contact with the vital oceanic waters, rich in oxygen and food, is maintained through two small posterior siphons that protrude from the surface of the wood.

It may be said that almost every wooden ship in history has succumbed eventually to the ravages of the shipworm. Only fire and submergence into sterile muds have prevented a molluscan end to all sailing ships. But this is also true of millions of tons of fallen trees that have floated out to sea. Were it not for the scavengerlike activities of the shipworm and other sea creatures, our oceans would be clogged with a monumental logjam.

LEFT: Many kinds of clams bore into coral blocks, creating tunnels by rotating their shells or producing a mild acid to dissolve the rock. BELOW: Within a few months a colony of *Teredo* and *Bankia* shipworms can destroy a wooden piling. Boring is done by the shell valves at the front end of the long, wormlike body of the clam.

Tibia shells and other snorkelers

One of the basic problems facing the shy marine snails that bury themselves deep in mud or sand is being able to keep in contact with the watery world above, necessary to obtain a supply of oxygenated and food-laden water. To accomplish this, many snails have produced either a fleshy or a shelly tube that can be used as a sort of snorkel. In technical terms this instrument of watery communication is known as the anterior siphonal canal. In plain language, it is a tube at the snail's front end that permits water to be drawn into the mantle cavity wherein lie the gills.

Most striking of the shelled snorkels is that produced by the long, graceful *Tibia* snail of the Indo-Pacific. Although a member of the heavy, lumbering Strombidae conch family, the ten-inch-long *Tibia* of the Philippines is one of the narrowest, most streamlined of seashells. Its twenty coiling whorls begin with a sharp, pointed apex and end in an extremely long, sharp siphonal canal. It is the hatpin of the shell world. But this long, hollow snorkel permits the *Tibia* to live safely several inches below the sandy bottom and yet to suck in fresh seawater.

Other families, notably the *Fusinus* spindle shells, have also developed long siphonal canals, although of a more sturdy build. In some instances, the siphons become grossly distorted or even doubled because of injury during growth.

Not all burrowing snails have a shelly siphon. In fact, the large majority of carnivorous sand-dwelling snails, such as the olives, the miters, the volutes and the cones, have only a fleshy siphon, which they poke up through the sand. These deeply buried snails can glide along rather quickly without coming above the surface of the bottom. Only a siphon protruding above, much like the periscope of a submarine, reveals the presence of the snail. The siphon performs the additional service of notifying carnivorous snails when a luscious prey is in the offing. This can be readily demonstrated if a piece of smelly crab or fish is dropped into an aquarium tank containing *Nassarius* snails. These little carnivorous univalves usually lie at rest beneath the surface with their siphons just peeking above the sand. Within ten seconds, the fishy odor will have spread throughout the tank, and with an almost electrifying response, the dozens of siphons will pop up and wave about to locate the enticing source of food. In another half minute, little mounds of sand will be erupting from the bottom and out will come *Nassarius* shells, almost galloping toward the fishy feast.

If any univalve deserves the name "periscope snail," it certainly is the strange *Terebellum* conch, a small, smooth, slender member of the family Strombidae. *Terebellum,* a native of the tropical Indo-Pacific, spends most of its hours buried in soft, white sand. Its bright blue eyes are mounted on the ends of a pair of very long stalks. Protruding a delicate fleshy stalk and an eyeball up through the gritty sand would not be very comfortable, even if at all possible. But by sending up its firmer, hollow siphon, *Terebellum* can readily follow with its periscope eyestalk. While crawling forward under the sand, *Terebellum* keeps one eye always at the surface. It literally "eyeballs" its way across the lagoon floor, always keeping its wary blue eye on the lookout for hungry fish. *Terebellum* is also capable of zipping forward through the water at a speed greater than that of a human swimmer. It propels itself by rapidly flicking its long, muscular foot in a springlike fashion.

OPPOSITE, TOP: Most sand-dwelling snails, such as this miter from Hawaii, have a long fleshy siphon with which to draw in fresh seawater. × 5. BELOW: The Spindle Tibia, *Tibia fusus* (Linné) of the southwest Pacific, has a shelly tube to protect its siphon, which may reach a length of five inches. × 1.

Venomous cones

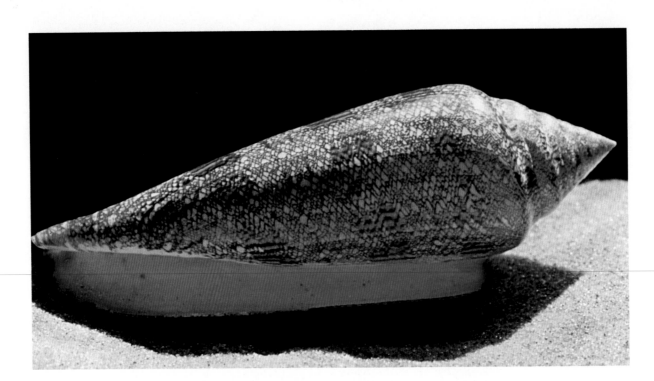

"When man bites dog, that's news!" a sage editor once reported. When a snail harpoons and eats a fish, that's malacological news. In 1955, Dr. Alan J. Kohn, working in a Hawaiian marine biological laboratory, discovered that the Striate Cone harpoons, paralyzes and swallows whole fish. As early as 1705, the Dutch naturalist Georgius Rumphius had recorded that cone shells were capable of inflicting a serious bite on human beings. Today, more than forty cases of human beings' having been stung by cones have been authenticated and recorded, ten of which have resulted in the death of the victim.

The Striate Cone, like most members of the genus, is nocturnal in habit, and when the sun's rays have left the reef, the snail ventures out from underneath a rock in search of a goby or blenny fish. The snail can sense, through the passage of water odors to its osphradium, or "smelling gills," the presence of this kind of fish. When within two inches of the fish, which generally sits placidly on the bottom minding its own business, the snail slowly protudes its long, red, wormlike proboscis. The swaying snout bends and stretches slowly toward the unsuspecting fish.

In a flash, a tiny, glassy harpoon is thrust into the side of the fish. A shot of yellow, viscous venom is immediately injected through this hypodermic tooth. The fish thrashes violently, stirring up a temporary cloud of sand, but within a dozen seconds the poison takes effect. The fish soon languishes helplessly on the bottom, and the snail slowly withdraws its proboscis. The snail pulls the harpoon, with the fish impaled at the end, to the lips of its snout. As the fish approaches the head of the cone, the snail's mouth opens like a tropical flower in the morning. Down the dying fish slides, swallowed slowly by the engulfing funnel. Frequently, the fish is half the length of the snail, and the dying victim is held within the protruding pharynx and digested before it is swallowed.

Not all cones are fishermen. In fact, the majority

feed on annelid worms and other mollusks. Although the mechanism is generally used for obtaining food, it is occasionally used as a defense against such predators as the snail-loving octopus. An octopus stung by a Textile Cone is likely to die within twenty-four hours. Cones have stung shell collectors, and death may ensue within four to ten hours after the injection of the venom. The initial symptoms are a sharp stinging and localized numbness which later spread to the lips and mouth. Blurred vision, excessive salivation and paralysis of the voluntary muscles may follow. In severe cases, coma may ensue, followed by death due to cardiac or respiratory failure. The venom is a neurotoxin, and the victim should be treated like a person suffering from snakebite. The best emergency treatment is an injection of 2 milliliters of Anthisan and 0.5 milliliters adrenalin. Lancing of the wound and removal of the venom by suction are recommended as soon after a sting as possible.

All known human deaths resulting from cone stings have been limited to the tropical Pacific. One unsubstantiated case of a mild sting from a Florida Alphabet Cone was reported in 1969. Because all cones have the venom duct, the necessary harpoon-like teeth and the muscular bulb to inject the poison, care should be taken in handling all live cones. In the worst cases, the species responsible for the sting has had a harpoon about one-eighth the length of the shell, whereas mild stings have resulted from species having a very small harpoon, about one-thirtieth the length of the shell. Deadliest of all the species are the Geography and the Textile, or Cloth-of-Gold, cones of the Pacific.

OPPOSITE: The famous Glory-of-the-Seas Cone, *Conus gloriamaris* Chemnitz, has harpoonlike teeth and a venom sac but to date has not killed anyone. × 1.
ABOVE: *Conus aurisiacus* Linné, a rare cone from the southwest Pacific, probably feeds on polychaete worms it finds in reef rocks. × 2.

The chambered nautilus

Oliver Wendell Holmes's stately poem about the chambered nautilus was a zoological catastrophe that mixed two widely different families in one beast and attributed to it habits that were greatly distorted. It was as if he had written a poem about a graceful antelope who had the back half of a leopard and the habit of flying over the arctic ice.

We can excuse Mr. Holmes, for in his day not many scientists, much less poets, appreciated the difference between a paper nautilus, or argonaut, and a chambered, or pearly, nautilus. The paper nautilus is a thin, white, cradlelike container made of stiff, parchmentlike shell material. It is the egg case made by the female *Argonauta,* an eight-armed close cousin to the octopus. It has no compartments and no iridescent shelly material.

The chambered nautilus has from sixty to ninety small arms, four internal gills and no ink sac, while all other living cephalopods, belonging to the octopus and squid groups, have only from eight to ten suckered arms, two internal gills and an ink sac. The *Nautilus* lives within its hard shell, which is made up of gas-filled chambers formed as the animal grows. The outside of the shell is creamy white with broad, rusty brown stripes. Within, the shell is a brilliant mother-of-pearl. Running back through the middle of each chamber and piercing the curved septa separating the compartments is a soft siphuncle that aids in adjusting water and gas pressures.

The animal lives in the last and largest chamber. When attacked by predacious fish, it cringes within its shell and covers the entrance with a tough, leathery hood. *Nautilus* feed on crustacea, and their crayfishlike, striped color pattern may be associated with the fact that they bob through the water at great depths among schools of lobsters. The natives of the Philippines and Melanesia bait large basketlike traps with smelly lobsters and catch nautiluses abundantly at depths ranging from about 200 to 400 feet. The *Nautilus* swims very slowly, using its small, fleshy funnel to jet propel itself forward. By changing the pressure, and hence the volume of the gas in the chambers, the nautilus can, to some extent, control the depth at which it swims.

There are three well-known species of *Nautilus,* all of which live in the southwest Pacific. They are the Common Pearly Nautilus, *Nautilus pompilius* Linné, which is widely distributed from the Philippines to the Fiji Islands and which has no indentation in the side of the shell; the New Caledonia Nautilus, which has a small, deep hole, or umbilicus, on each side of the shell; and the Large-holed Nautilus of New Guinea and the Solomons, which has a large, ramplike umbilicus. Three other reported species may be only varieties of the Common Pearly Nautilus.

The shells of the *Nautilus* have been used in the decorative arts for centuries, by both Europeans and South Sea islanders. The pearly layers of the shell lend themselves to delicate sculpturing and carving. In Samoa, the early whorls, with their glistening round septa, add to the beauty of the village maidens when worn as head ornaments.

The chambered nautilus is buoyed up by gases in its dozen or so internal chambers.
It has about ninety short tentacles with which it seizes its favorite food,
lobsters and crayfish. There are three common species in the Pacific;
this one, *Nautilus macromphalus* Sowerby, comes from New Caledonia. × 1

Nudibranchs—the naked shells

Without question, the most exquisitely colored and most delicately structured mollusks are the nudibranch gastropods—small, shell-less sea slugs commonly found in shallow waters and usually associated with sea anemones, bryozoans and sponges. "Sea Fairies" and "Rainbows of the Sea" are two of the names applied to this beautiful clan.

Nudibranchs occur in many bizarre shapes, and the casual observer finds it difficult to realize that they are, indeed, snails. Most of them are less than an inch in length, although the giant *Dendronotus* of the Pacific Northwest may reach a length of ten inches. Being without shells, they resemble the land slugs but differ in that they bear appendages on their upper surfaces. In front are two great antennae resembling Martian electronic reception units and behind may be a series of multicolored trees, balloons and feathery plumes. If any mollusks could claim psychedelic coloration, the nudibranchs would qualify.

There are over 800 species of nudibranchs found in both tropical and temperate seas. Their variation in form is so great that marine biologists are still attempting to unravel their history so that they may be properly classified. Commonest of the types are the dorids and the eolids. The dorids have a great plumelike circle of feathery gills set on the back at the posterior end. At the front end are two antennalike rhinophores used to sense chemical and temperature changes in the water. The rhinophores are made up of numerous saucer-shaped platelets. When attacked by fish, some dorids can retract the entire rhinophore into an open socket. Sponges serve as the food of dorids, whose stomachs sometimes become greatly distended by indigestible sponge spicules. Dorids that feed on bright yellow colonies of sponges take on a similar protective coloration—hence this nudibranch is some-

times called a sea lemon. Its long, ribbonlike gelatinous egg mass is also bright yellow.

The eolids are the most beautiful of the nudibranchs, and most of them sport fleshy appendages, called cerata, on the back. In some species the cerata are balloon-shaped, in others they are leaf-shaped or resemble branched twigs. Extensions of the animal's stomach protrude into some of these cerata, often giving them bizarre colorations. One group of eolids feeds on particular kinds of hydroids and sea anemones. These forms of food contain many microscopic stinging cells, or nematocysts, similar to those found in jellyfish. To counteract these, the eolid pours a copious amount of mucus over part of its victim and then bites off large chunks. The stinging nematocysts now can travel to the eolid's stomach without breaking and releasing their poison. Within half an hour the nematocysts are moved up into the cerata on the back of the snail. There they are stored just under the thin epidermis. When a predacious fish nibbles a ceras, it gets a face full of exploding, stinging cells.

Strangest of the feeding habits among the nudibranchs is that of the fish-egg-eating *Calma*. The nudibranch's mouth is shaped in the form of a half-globe hood that fits over the eggs of small gobies and blennies. The *Calma* sucks an egg against its mouth, carefully slits a hole in it with its saber-like radular teeth and then drains off the contents of the egg. *Calma* feeds only once a year, during the season when these fish are laying their eggs. The content of the fish's eggs, in their early stages, is so highly digestible and readily absorbed that the gut of *Calma* has become blind, there being no anus. The *Calma* gorges on egg juice for only a few days, but can store a surplus quantity in its stomach for many weeks.

OPPOSITE, TOP: Dorid nudibranchs, such as this *Chromodoris* from the tropical Pacific, have two towerlike sensors at the front end and a clump of feathery gills on the back near the posterior end. × 8. BELOW: Eolid nudibranchs, such as *Aeolidia papillosa* (Linné) from northern seas, have on the back fleshy extensions of the digestive system. × 6.

Collecting shells 7

Where to look

Most people, including the native fishermen of remote tropical shores, are poor shell hunters. The clam diggers of New England, the oystermen of the Chesapeake Bay and the pearl divers of Japan are all very familiar with their own specialties, but they seldom take note of other mollusks and very rarely collect them. A casual beach stroller or a novice conchologist may see the large and obvious shells cast up by the waves, but the dozens of minute species underfoot go unnoticed. Even a well-experienced malacologist suddenly placed in a new habitat will take five or ten minutes to "turn on his collecting eyes." It sometimes takes that much time to find the first mollusk in a rock tide pool, but in the next five minutes a dozen kinds and a hundred specimens will be seen. A mud flat, at first seemingly barren, will begin to reveal more and more snails, and the sand bars will begin to turn up more clams.

Camouflage is a built-in protection for many mollusks. Novice collectors expecting to see the bottom of the sea dotted with bright and colorful shells are bound to be disappointed. The purple-dotted cone is covered with a thick, brown periostracum; the long-spined orange *Spondylus* is hidden by a thick growth of algae, sponges and bryozoans and even the tiny *Nassarius* mud snail is heavily covered with a thick film of mud.

Shyness and a dislike for bright sunlight are two additional mollusk characteristics that make most of them difficult to find. A snail venturing over the sand in broad daylight is a likely target for predators; a clam or mussel nestled in a crevice on the underside of a rock ledge is less likely to be found by a marauding fish or crab.

To the novice, the beach is the obvious place to find shells. There are certainly few places as pleasant to stroll when the weather is fine and the clean sand is firm. However, few beaches harbor many mollusks. Dead shells, of course, may be cast up along the tide line, particularly after storms, but usually subsequent tides sweep the strand clean again. Some beaches, because of the rather sudden drop-off, rarely have any shells. The two great

exceptions in the world are Jeffreys Bay in South Africa and the west coast of Sanibel-Captive Island in western Florida. At the latter, the beach becomes strewn with millions of tons of fresh shells once every few years, usually after a chilly three-day blow from the northwest. Minor incursions occur once or twice a year, but for the most part the pickings are poor to bad in the off-seasons. In New Jersey, where the ocean beaches have few shells most of the year, the strand will become deeply littered with surf clams, *Spisula,* and moon snails during February when a combination of near-zero temperatures, heavy offshore winds and unusually low tides kill billions of mollusks.

In the tropics, sand beaches are apt to be more productive, for a number of clams and *Terebra* snails live in the moist slope below the midtide line. As the tide begins to rise and each wave is larger and sweeps farther up the slope, the large *Donax* clams begin to pop up above the surface for a few seconds to feed. At times, the beach may be dotted by small clams wiggling themselves back into the sand as each wave recedes. Higher up on the beach, well beyond the reach of the average wave, there may be a zone shaded by trees and overgrown with vines where moist humus and coconut husks harbor a vast kingdom of salt-loving pulmonate snails, including *Melampus, Pythia, Ellobium* and *Truncatella.* Collecting on this high land zone is best just after a rain.

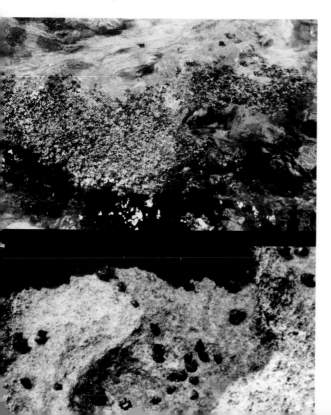

Beaches are not always sandy. Some are made of boulders and small stones. If the slope is not too steep and if the stones are fairly well anchored, a respectable community of mollusks may exist on the sides of the rocks and in the narrow mud or clay interstices. In cooler climates, festoons of brown *Fucus* weeds add additional protection for mussels, periwinkles and *Nucella* dogwinkles.

The sand and mud tidal flats are lower extensions of the beach and harbor vast colonies of mollusks, since that area is underwater for long periods, is richer in food and is less subject to the rigors of wave action. Some mollusks roam at low tide, others move about only when there are several inches of water above them. In areas such as this, night is the time that most mollusks come out of the sand and travel in search of food and mates.

Although in most parts of the world rocky shores harbor the same general types of mollusks, there are many variations and curious novelties limited to certain geographical regions, to certain types of rocks or to various tidal levels. In England, hard sandstone is bored into by the piddock clams, whereas in the West Indies the coral limestone rocks are penetrated by an entirely different family, the *Lithophaga* date mussels. In Peru, the offshore sedimentary rocks are bored by the elongate ark clam, *Litharca.*

The upper levels of rocky coasts seldom are washed by waves, but during storms sea spray may be carried inland for many yards. The periwinkles, *Littorina* and *Tectarius,* attempt to venture as far inland as possible, moving mainly at night and during rainy periods. Since they must return to the sea or to rocky pools of seawater to lay their eggs, the adults do not completely desert the ocean. A few species, notably the Zebra Nerite, *Puperita,* of the Caribbean, can survive in hot, supersaline pools isolated on the high rocks. Their ability to withstand changing temperatures, from 60° F. to 110° F., and salinities, from very salty to pure rainwater, attests to the adaptability of littoral snails.

Rock pools in the midtide zone are usually well-stocked with mollusks, both large and minute. In cool waters, the pools are lined with colorful algae, sponges and bryozoan growths. Colorful starfish and sea urchins may dot the bottom. Limpets, peri-

PRECEDING PAGES: The author and his wife, shell collecting in the Bahamas. THESE PAGES: Shells are found in many places, including wharves, shipwrecks, coral reefs, floating seaweed and rocky shores.

winkles and blue mussels are dominant, but hidden among the more delicate green algae or nestled in the sandy cracks there are apt to be dozens of species of minute snails, some adults being less than four millimeters in size. In the tropics, an even richer fauna inhabits the intertidal pools. Nerites, chitons, *Purpura* rock shells and occasionally a large tun or frog shell from deeper water are found in these deep, rockbound pools.

In the Caribbean, pelagic species of the open ocean wafted shoreward by winds are sometimes trapped in these pools, but lack of oxygenated, cool oceanic water usually results in their death. Among the inhabitants of the large floating mats of brown sargassum weed are the little brown snail *Litiopa* and the brown-and-white nudibranch *Scyllaea*. In surface waters nearby are usually found the violet snails, or purple sea snails, *Janthina*, that keep afloat by bubble rafts they create with their feet.

A whole world of mollusks is found living as commensals or symbionts with other marine organisms. The phylum of starfish, sea puddings and sea urchins, known as the Echinodermata, plays host to dozens of species of univalves and bivalves. There are snails, such as *Thyca*, that live like limpets enwrapped about the spines of sea urchins. Deep inside the urchins' pencillike spines live the tiny, white *Stylifer*. Shaped like an old-fashioned electric light bulb, the *Stylifer* creates for itself in the spine a hollow cyst that has a small opening for taking in fresh seawater. A parasitic clam attaches to the underside of urchins. Even the lumbering sea cucumber, *Holothuria*, has tiny white *Melanella* snails attached to its anal end, and deep within the intestine is sometimes found another shell-less family of parasitic snails.

Almost everywhere one looks, one is apt to find mollusks—clams boring in waterlogged planks, manila rope, ship bottoms and floating coconut husks. Snails live on the leaves and roots of mangroves. Upwards of seventy kinds of minute mollusks have been found living on a Red Abalone.

OPPOSITE: The sea beach is
not a productive place to collect
shells, except perhaps after a storm.
LEFT: Sedges of salt marshes
are the habitat of *Littorina*
periwinkles. ABOVE: Skin divers
compare their shell finds of the day.
Rubber jackets keep them warm.

How to watch mollusks

All too often the real enjoyment and profit of shell collecting is lost by the hasty and greedy impulse of grabbing up a living mollusk, throwing it into a dark bag and not looking at it again until it is time to drop it into boiling water or some deadly preservative. In today's world where man is rapidly bringing thousands of species to extinction, it seems little enough to ask of seashore visitors that they spend more time watching than collecting.

Overcollecting is occurring in more and more places around the world, although it is not this activity, but rather massive pollution from cities, manufacturing plants and ships, that is endangering coastal marine mollusks. Locally, some kinds of mollusks are becoming very scarce because of commercial collecting. In some states, even the constant revisiting of biology classes, week after week, has decimated certain small, once-productive spots. Shell watching and limited shell collecting is becoming more popular, if not a necessity, for the conchologist of the future.

It is surprising how much information may be obtained by simply observing undisturbed living mollusks for a few minutes. Trails in the sand tell a tale, and if you follow a furrow in the surface of a Florida tidal flat, you may find a hump in the sand caused by an olive shell, a venus clam or a small *Busycon* whelk. If whelk and clam happen to meet, you will see the snail envelop the bivalve in its black foot, press the edge of its shell between the clam's valves and slowly but surely pry open its victim. Equally fascinating, but seldom seen except by snorkelers or scuba swimmers, is the process of egg laying by a whelk. The capsules are formed in a pore in the sole of the foot and passed up by the oviduct, where several eggs are injected into each wafer-shaped case. When filled, the capsules, strung together like the segments of a rattlesnake's tail, are pushed up out of the sand.

Many profitable and interesting hours can be spent observing living mollusks in a homemade aquarium. In fact, the strange habits and life cycles of such mollusks as the fish-eating cone and the sea-anemone-sucking wentletraps were first discovered and documented in saltwater aquariums. The tank need not be elaborate and space-consuming. A clear gallon jar, with a large, round opening, will keep most small mollusks overnight. The tricks are not to overcrowd and not to put natural enemies together.

The best aquariums are ordinary square plastic boxes, no larger than cigar boxes, available in kitchenware departments. Keep only four or five of the smaller mollusks, such as periwinkles and nerites, in one miniaquarium.

Mechanical aeration can be set up by attaching a tube to an inexpensive aquarium pump and branching it out to several miniaquariums. Where the lid of the box overlaps the bottom section, file a round hole to accommodate the air tube. For very tiny mollusks, aeration is not necessary, but a lid should be kept on to prevent evaporation of the water. Be sure that the porous stones and algae-covered rocks remain moist. Young snails that have crawled up the dry sides should be brushed down at least once a day. When replenishing evaporated seawater, add only fresh water or the salinity will rise too much.

The following genera have been kept in small unaerated miniaquariums for from one to five years: *Cerithium, Batillaria, Planaxis, Littorina, Neritina, Nerita* and *Marginella*. When feeding carnivores, say once a week, in aerated tanks, remove pieces of uneaten shrimp, clams and mussels.

Many important habits and morphological details of small mollusks may be observed in small watch glasses of new seawater. Although a hand lens of seven-power magnification will reveal a great deal, for comfort and better vision, a binocular dissecting microscope is recommended.

TOP LEFT: Scuba diving has opened new areas for collecting and observing mollusks, but this method can be dangerous without prior professional training. UPPER RIGHT: On an exposed sand flat a snail leaves a telltale trail. BOTTOM LEFT: Cyphoma snails spend their adult days on sea fans where they feed and lay eggs.

How to catch shells

Although bending over and picking up a specimen is half the story of shell collecting, there are many other factors that contribute to the success of this enjoyable pastime. Whether you plan to stroll the beach, wade across shallow-water flats, snorkel in reef waters or scuba dive in the depths, some thought should be given to the tides, the weather and the vagaries of the unpredictable sea. If you have been cooped up all winter, do not underestimate the strength of the sun. Many a vacation has been ruined by severe sunburn. To prevent this, use lotions or wear a long-sleeved shirt and long pants, no matter how silly you think you may look. Plan in advance the best times to collect— times when the tides are unusually low. You can purchase a guide to the predicted tides of your area from the Superintendent of Documents, U.S. Government Printing Office, Washington, D.C. 20402. Seashore papers and fishing guides also carry such tide tables. In some areas, a tide a few inches lower than usual can expose several extra miles of flats and reefs.

If you plan to do extensive snorkeling or scuba diving daily, it pays to wear at least a lightweight upper wet suit, even in the most tropical of waters. Be sure to dab some alcohol in your ears after diving in order to prevent a tropical fungus from developing. Watch the weather and listen to the advice of local fishermen. They know when unexpected squalls are likely to arise and when currents are particularly dangerous. If you do not use flippers when swimming, be sure to wear soft canvas shoes or sneakers. Going barefooted guarantees a cut foot and an infection.

Many seaboard states have passed laws which are primarily intended to conserve edible mollusks, such as oysters, scallops and clams. It would be wise to inquire about the local laws before you collect commercially important species. In some states you must have a license to collect venus clams (Maryland, Maine, Massachusetts, New Jersey, New Hampshire); in others (British Columbia and California) you must have a license to collect abalones as well as clams.

ABOVE, LEFT: Various types of shell-collecting gear, including an underwater camera.
RIGHT: A triangular dredge brings up marine treasures. OPPOSITE, LEFT: Box
screens with various-sized meshes are used to sort shells from sand. CENTER: A proud
snorkeler has captured a helmet. RIGHT: A knife in a safe holster comes in handy.

The simplest gear to use for intertidal collecting is either a cloth bag or, preferably, a small plastic bucket, a knife and a pair of forceps, the latter to get into narrow crevices for small mollusks. If you intend to keep some of your catch alive at home, bring a jug to fill with seawater. If you are not in the mood for swimming, a glass-bottomed bucket will give you an absolutely clear view of the bottom while you are wading in water less than three feet in depth.

Except when waves are breaking, though, the easiest method is to use a face mask and snorkel, even in water less than two feet in depth. Both in snorkeling and scuba diving, a heavy plastic bag, eight inches in diameter and about two feet long, is much better than a "goodie bag" or a cloth salt bag. Nudibranchs, limas and delicate shells fare well in this type of water-filled container.

The Jensen belt is used by those swimmers working in areas where small shells are likely to be found. It is a canvas belt two inches wide that is fitted with open pockets of elastic canvas into which

polyethylene screw-top bottles slip. As the shells are collected, they are placed in these bottles. Without water, the bottles serve as a life preserver for poor swimmers; if the collector wishes to dive to the bottom, however, he must fill the bottles with water.

Waders or those walking across exposed reefs will find most of their mollusks by overturning stones and rocks. Be sure to roll the rocks back or the young mollusks and eggs will be destroyed by sunlight. Many good specimens may be obtained by bringing old coral blocks to the surface and smashing them open. It is urged that you do not carelessly destroy live coral stands. Although storms will ultimately pare them back, the continuous breakage by collectors can make an area quite desolate in a few months.

Night collecting is usually more profitable than are daylight operations. A waterproof six-battery flashlight will provide sufficient light—if you are diving, a lead weight will have to be attached to it. Needless to say, night collecting should not be done alone if you plan to stray any distance from shore, al-

though sharks do not seem to bother divers or waders any oftener at night than in the day. In some tropical areas care should be taken not to touch or bump into stone fish, feather or lion fish and long-spined purple sea urchins.

There are many special ways to collect shells, most of which have been designed to take advantage of either the mollusk's unique habitat or its peculiar habits. Baiting and trapping, for instance, are used to obtain carnivorous species. In the Philippines olive shells and *Conus bullatus* are captured with tiny fish hooks that have been baited with bits of conch meat and left overnight. These hooks are attached to lengths of fishing line, ranging from two to five feet in length, which have been tied every inch along a six-foot iron pole. If you are in the lower West Indies and find one live Music Volute, you may flush the others out of the sand within an hour by anchoring the carcass of a fresh Pink Conch in the sand. Crushed crab, shrimp or lobster, put in a bag to protect it from small fish, serves as an ideal overnight attractor for meat lovers, such as *Harpa*, *Fasciolaria* and olives. Visit the bait at night; or in the morning, stir up the nearby sand for hidden molluscan visitors. Traps are moderately successful, particularly at depths below 200 feet where diving is not efficient. Traps should be made of nonmetallic material.

Most productive of all specialized collecting procedures is dredging or trawling. Small metal screen dredges with strong metal strips at the open end should have a capacity of no more than half a bushel and no opening larger than seven by fifteen inches, mainly because of the labor involved in pulling in and emptying a dredge larger than that.

Large dredges may be used if you have engine-run winches aboard your boat. The metal screening should have quarter-inch or three-eighths-inch square holes. The four chain leaders should come together about two feet in front of the dredge. It is usually necessary to tie a five-pound weight at this point in order to keep the dredge's front end on the bottom. Always play out three or four times as much line as you have depth. Dredging in ten feet of water would require thirty or forty feet of line. Dredge very slowly, at a speed of not more than two or three knots. By holding your hand on the line, which should be three-eighths-inch nylon rope or

five-eighths-inch manila rope, you can tell whether the dredge is swimming over the bottom (it will flutter) or is properly digging into the sand.

The contents should be dumped onto a long, wooden sorting board, the big shells put in a bucket of seawater and a couple of gallons of shelly sand put in a cloth bag for future drying and sorting at home. Under a hand lens or microscope a sand sample may reveal over a hundred different species, depending upon where you are dredging. Coral sands and rubble are the most productive. Some shell dealers sell bushels of such rich sand.

An operation similar to dredging is the use of box screens in shallow water. Bottom sand and mud are shoveled onto the screen and cleared of silt by bouncing the screen up and down in the water.

Many interesting and seldom-collected mollusks live in beds of algae or the red algal coverings of mangrove roots. Put several handfuls of algae into a bucket and fill it with fresh water. Shake the pieces of algae as you remove them one by one. The minute mollusks will drop to the bottom of the bucket. What appears to be sandy grit and sludge will turn out to be swarming with little snails and clams when examined in a separate dish with

124

a hand lens. If fresh water is not readily available in the field, you can stuff a bag with algae and give it the bucket treatment when you return to your lodgings. Among the algae-dwellers are *Caecum, Assiminea, Rissoa* and the clam *Musculus*.

Fish stomachs are an excellent source of deep-water mollusks not usually obtained in any other way. Naturally, only freshly caught fish should be investigated, for the digestive juices of the fish quickly dissolve the calcareous shells. The rare Fulton's Cowrie of South Africa has been found only in the stomach of the musselcracker fish. Paper argonauts, sometimes with the shell intact, are found in the stomachs of sailfish off Florida. The following fish also feed on bottom-dwelling mollusks: cod, halibut, king croaker, sea robin, puffer, sculpin and flounder.

Other productive places to collect shells are navigational buoys and floating logs and boards. A homemade plankton net, made from a coat hanger over which a nylon stocking has been stretched, towed very slowly at night will bring to light living pteropods and larval gastropods.

OPPOSITE: Live mollusks may be put into a floating mesh container until ready for the home aquarium or to be photographed. Many malacologists release their mollusks after observing and studying them. ABOVE: Close and patient inspection of a tide-pool floor reveals an amazing number of otherwise overlooked mollusks.

How to clean and preserve shells

The attractiveness of a collection or display of shells, whether it serves the hobbyist, scientist or museum visitor, depends largely upon how well the mollusks have been cleaned and preserved. When a live mollusk dies, which it does soon after it has been out of the ocean for a few hours, it smells very unpleasant. Many a lovely specimen has been tossed into the trash or back into the sea because the collector did not realize that the inside meat had to be removed or because too many specimens were collected to be properly cleaned.

There are six easy ways to clean shelled mollusks —freezing, boiling, preserving, salting, rotting out or bleaching out. Freezing is the most modern method, adopted within the last twenty years, because there are few homes, hotels and motels that do not have facilities for freezing packets of food. Fill a plastic bag with your mollusks and place the bag, tied shut, in the lower part of the refrigerator for a couple of hours. Then place it in the freezer for two or three days. When you are thawing the contents, put the bag back in the lower part for half a day and then in a cold water soak. This process is done gradually to prevent fine cracks from developing in the enamel of large, glossy shells. When completely thawed, usually over a period of twenty-four hours, most meats of univalves will come out completely by pulling on them in an unwinding, corkscrew fashion, using a fork or bent safety pin. Save the operculum with each shell.

Boiling live mollusks in fresh or salt water is usually successful and can be done in a relatively short time. Because a rapid change in temperature will craze the surface of shiny shells, be sure to start with warm, not hot, water. Boil bivalves for one or two minutes, univalves for six to ten minutes. Let the pot stand for an hour or add one-third more cold water to bring the temperature down gradually. The shells of those few univalves that don't pull out completely can be soaked in a preservative or buried for a week to rot out.

The best preservative for mollusks is 70 percent grain or ethyl alcohol. This is the "drinkable stuff" and is 140 proof. It is sometimes available from museums if you need a small amount for preserving some special mollusk for research purposes. Rubbing alcohol, isopropyl alcohol and other poisonous forms should be used in a 50-percent strength. This type of alcohol hardens the mollusk's flesh and makes dissections difficult, but mollusks soaked in it for a week will not rot. In most cases, "alcoholed" snails will pull clean, and tiny gastropods, if soaked for ten days and dried in the sun or in a low oven for a couple of hours, will need no further cleaning. A 5- or 6-percent formalin mixture (formaldehyde comes in bottles at 40-percent strength; mix one part of that to eight of water) is a good preservative for fish and shell-less mollusks, but it may be used on shelled mollusks only if it has been buffered with two tablespoons of baking soda per quart of formalin—otherwise the acids of this preservative will etch away the shell within a few weeks.

In an emergency, live univalves may be packed in table salt in cardboard or wooden boxes. Sometimes a supersaturated solution of salt serves as a preliminary brine bath, but after a journey of a few weeks in pure salt, the mollusks will have to be soaked and cleaned by hand. If time is of no concern, live shells may be buried in soft sand in the shade. Generally, rotting and sometimes ants or blowflies will readily clean out the meat, but because of odors this method should be done away from the home. Commercial shellers dump live or smelly shells in a 50-percent solution of chlorine bleach. This will dissolve away the flesh and the outer organic growths.

The exteriors of shells can be cleaned by giving them an overnight soak in full-strength bleach. If the shell is dried, picking at the surface or giving it a sharp, quick rap with an old dentist tool will chip off the white encrustations. Brushing with warm water and detergent will suffice in most cases. The use of muriatic acid is not recommended. Baby oil, used sparingly, will give some shells a brighter color.

Cleaning shells is not always fun, but it is a necessary chore after collecting live specimens. Deep freezing overnight or boiling for a few minutes softens the mollusk's muscles and permits the soft parts to be removed. Alcohol is the best preservative of soft mollusk parts.

The beginner's shell collection

The thought of organizing the first few shells that one acquires generally does not occur to the novice collector. In the first place, the new collector is usually not yet bent on obtaining many more shells. But as the specimens begin to accumulate—a box or two here, a jar of local beach shells on the bureau and one or two large shells on the mantelpiece—the thought occurs that things could get out of hand. Second, the beginner is usually not aware that shells can be identified, classified and organized into many different ways of display and storage.

There are two kinds of beginners' collections—one for the youngster and one for the adult. Since the younger children, however, will welcome guidance from the older collector, the basic instructions suit both age groups. The difference in the collections will depend upon the amount of time, money, artistic ability and thought put into them. The collection should be divided into a more or less permanent display section, preferably under glass, and a mobile boxed section, also covered with glass or clear plastic. An understanding mother might pack away at least one shelf of seldom-used dishes in the glass-fronted china cabinet for her child's bigger shells. An adult with a little money may obtain a secondhand cabinet or glass-fronted set of bookcases. The shells should be neatly labeled with the common name and the country of origin. By folding the label so that it will stand up like a place-setting card, it will be visible.

Smaller shells are more difficult to handle, but an inexpensive way to house them is to use an oblong cardboard candy box about one inch deep. Line the box with an inch-thick layer of white or colored cotton and place on it the shells, with small paper labels under each kind. Stretch a piece of clear plastic wrap over the box and fasten it with Scotch tape on the underside. It is best to obtain a number of boxes of the same size or at least multiples of each other, so that two smaller ones equal the next

larger size, and so forth. This makes a much neater arrangement and makes them easier to store away in a closet, trunk or cabinet when not on display. Very small boxes, such as match boxes or powder boxes from the druggist, are also useful, but again, it helps to have units of uniform size. Lidded plastic boxes, measuring about two inches by two inches, are ideal. If you cut out and add small squares of half-inch-thick green foam cushioning to the bottoms, the shells will be prevented from rattling around. The label if placed under the rubber foam can be read by turning the box over.

The collection may be divided into various categories. Some people prefer to arrange shells by

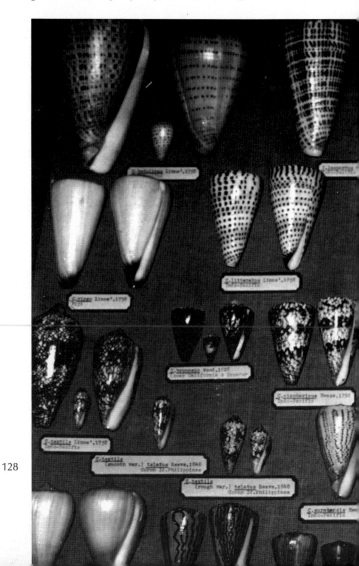

OPPOSITE: A beginner's collection may be arranged as a display, usually in a large glass-covered frame. Labels should give identifications and locality data.

families; others keep a geographical division, with shells from one beach or country together; others put all shells of one color or shape in the same box. A box may be devoted to a particular subject, such as dyes and sources of color obtained from murex shells, and accompanied by a neatly typed story. More elaborate habitat groups, such as one sees in museums, may be attempted by painting appropriate background and adding rocks, corals, dried sponges, sea fans or dried seaweeds.

Display boards are popular for schoolrooms planning to introduce sea life to the young students. The background may be white, tan, blue or green, just as long as it furnishes enough contrast for the shells and accompanying labels to show up. There are many themes possible, including "What Is a Mollusk?" "Shells of Our Shores," "How Shells Breed and Grow" and "How Shells Help Mankind."

If you are collecting shells in one immediate area near a summer beach house, specimens may be preliminarily sorted and placed in empty papier-mâché egg cartons. Note the locality on the outside of the box and store the specimens away for future wintertime study. Empty shoe boxes are useful for storing large shells and duplicates that you can use to exchange with other collectors. When possible, record the name of the town or beach where each shell was found.

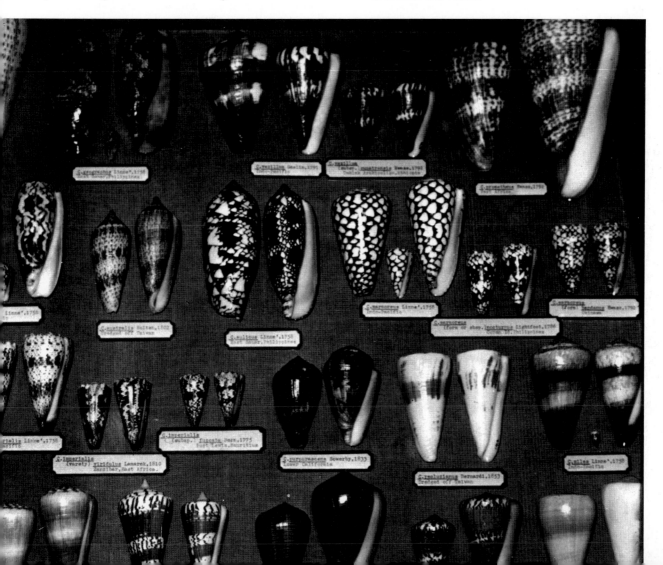

The advanced private collection

When a person finds himself enjoying the study and collecting of shells more with each passing season and when he realizes that his growing collection and his observations can serve the advancement of science, he has become an advanced collector. Now he must channel his efforts into making his future collecting meaningful and put his collection in such shape as to make it useful, not only to himself, but to scientists and amateur conchologists who wish to obtain more information. Geographical and ecological data now become more important. Shells with insufficient locality date, such as *India* or *Florida,* are sold or given away to make room for growth series with more detailed information such as: "Collected on mud flats, 1 mile southwest of Marco, Florida; John Doe, collector; September 28, 1972." If the collector was biologically minded, he might have added "found feeding on dead shrimp."

Advanced collections are arranged, for convenience' sake, in a standard systematic order outlined in most malacological texts and handbooks. The gastropods begin with the primitive families, such as the *Pleurotomaria* slit shells and *Haliotis* abalones, and are arranged in regular, evolutionary sequence, up through the periwinkles, conchs and cowries to the advanced cones, turrids and *Bulla* bubble shells. The bivalves begin with the *Nucula* and *Arca* taxodont clams and end up with the shipworms and the *Cuspidaria* dipper clams. The system is universal and makes consulting and adding to the collection easier and, at the same time, instructive.

The housing of a study collection should be as dustproof, as lightproof and as inexpensive as possible. Keeping the specimens in individual wooden drawers, 2½ by 3 feet, with plywood bottoms and sides of pine, 2 inches by ⅜ inch, is the simplest. An oblong cabinet with a hinged door and wooden runners 2½ inches apart should hold the drawers, say twelve to a cabinet. If large shells are added to the collection, slide the drawer on the runner below to allow clearance. Shells of one species from one locality, collected at a certain date, are put in separate low, white, cardboard trays, say ¾ inch deep. The outside dimensions should be multiples of the smallest tray. This unit may measure 1 by 3 inches, the next largest 2 by 3, then 3 by 3, then 3 by 4, then 3 by 6, and the largest 6 by 6, or even 6 by 9. In this way, a sampling of various sizes will line up in the drawer with neat regularity. The outside of the drawer should be fitted with two brass tacks spaced 5 inches apart, onto which slips an end-slotted card bearing the genus and species content of the drawer. A white label, 1 by 3 inches and fitting into the smallest cardboard tray, should bear the name of the owner of the collection and have room for entering the name of the shell, the locality in which it was found, the name of the collector and/or donor, the date and the catalog number.

A catalog is maintained solely for the purpose of keeping the collecting data and the shell together. If the catalog entry, the label in the tray and the specimens from that one lot, or sample, all bear the same number, mixtures and spills can be unscrambled by matching up the numbers. Specimens that are too small on which to write a number in india ink may be placed in a round shell vial with a numbered slip and then plugged firmly with a wad of cotton. The catalog should be a sturdy, bound, 300-page ledger, with the numbers kept consecutive in the first column. With two pages spread open, the left-hand page can have a column each for the catalog number, the name of the shell (not always necessary) and the locality. The right-hand page can have four columns—one each for recording the name of the collector, the date of collecting, from whom received and remarks (habitat notes, the extent of its rarity, etc.).

The handmaiden of a good collection is a working library of books on identification and classification. Because names are apt to change and classifications become more accurate with new information, it is best to choose the most recently published

LEFT: The conchologist's home study room may combine the charm of informal displays and the utility of formal arrangements in pull-out drawers. BELOW: Some advanced collectors house their collections in beautifully made wooden cabinets.

ones and those that have been written by experienced, professional malacologists. A bibliography of the most useful books is at the end of this book. Reprints or separates of interesting articles and research results are available from secondhand book dealers and sometimes directly from the research authors, who are usually eager to share their knowledge. Reprints should be arranged in your library by author and date, but a cross-reference subject card file can be made up for your own convenience.

The professional museum collection

The great public museums that include mollusks as one of their specialties are the inheritors of many generations of shell collectors and are the guardians of the specimens that have served thousands of scientists in the preparation of their research and discoveries for many hundreds of years. Throughout the world today, there are about fifty major museum collections of mollusks. It is estimated that, all told, they house 50 million samples of mollusks. The number of specimens would well exceed half a billion. It is from this great reservoir of dependable, documented samplings of the world's mollusks that malacologists can function as biologists, conservationists, evolutionists and specialists in identification and classification. The field of malacology usually knows no national boundaries nor the possessiveness of private collectors. It is a comradeship of interests and endeavors that finds its focus in the fifty taxonomic centers of the world. It is a realm of intense study that needs and welcomes the labors of myriads of interested amateur collectors. In fact, it may be justly claimed that over half of the world's scientific museum collections were assembled by hobbyists and serious amateurs.

The basic purpose of a professional museum collection is to increase the amount of knowledge about mollusks. Second comes the equally important function of the diffusion of knowledge about mollusks. This can be accomplished through exhibits, lectures, films, popular books and scientific monographs and reports. To meet these broad goals it is necessary to have in charge a professional malacologist who is trained in modern biological procedures, familiar with all aspects of malacology, expert in curating procedures, accomplished in public relations, knowledgeable in business administration and sympathetic toward the struggling and potentially helpful amateurs.

Museum collections serve as a sort of "bureau of standards," or guide to the proper identification of mollusks. In many related fields this service is often a great necessity. The control of fatal freshwater diseases depends upon the elimination or control of certain species of snails. Oyster research workers need to be able to identify damaging drill snails. Oceanographers, fish experts, engineers, general biologists, archaeologists and biochemists are constantly coming to museum malacologists for identifications.

Many large collections assembled during the eighteenth century were acquired by European states and served as nuclei for national museums. Among the oldest mollusk centers still active in Europe are the British Museum of Natural History, the Musée d'Histoire Naturelle in Paris, the Zoologische Museum in Amsterdam and the Zoologische Institut in Copenhagen, Denmark. Other very large professional collections are in Frankfurt, East Berlin, Brussels, Cardiff (Wales), Geneva, Vienna and Madrid. The largest in the world is housed in the U.S. National Museum, Smithsonian Institution, Washington, D.C. It contains about 700,000 samples. Other large museum collections are in Cambridge, Massachusetts; Philadelphia; New York; Ann Arbor, Michigan; Honolulu; San Francisco; Los Angeles; San Diego and, more recently, Greenville, Delaware. There are also large collections in Australia, New Zealand, South Africa, India and Japan.

Material is obtained by museums either from scientific expeditions or as gifts from volunteer amateur collectors. Seldom are funds available for purchases, except for historically important collections that need preserving. When time and personnel are available, exchanges are carried out between museums. Large, carefully documented mollusk collections assembled by hobbyists and amateur collectors, unless bequeathed to well-funded museums, are apt to be destroyed by time and neglect.

Professional museum collections of mollusks serve as a sort of bureau of standards where research workers may identify and study millions of specimens. The Delaware Museum of Natural History has more than 500 steel cases and 13,000 square feet devoted to its scientific collection of shells.

Collector's Items 8

Rare shells of yesterday

The terms *rare shells* and *collector's items* are not necessarily synonymous, for there are many species that have been described from one known specimen and never collected again, yet have no commercial value. Some of the rarest shells in the world are less than five millimeters in size, lacking in color and of ordinary shape. Many of these shells are rare only because no one has happened to sample their optimum habitat. It might well be said that there is no such thing as a rare marine shell, since any species living today must have a large enough population, certainly of several thousands of individuals, to sustain the species.

If a shell is large, handsome, beautiful, known only from a few specimens and sought after by avid, wealthy collectors, it may qualify as a collector's item or be classed as a so-called rare shell. Lister's Conch, *Strombus listeri,* was originally known from a single specimen brought back to England from the Indian Ocean as early as 1620. It was first illustrated in Martin Lister's *Historia Conchyliorum* in 1685, but it was not given an official scientific name until 1852. A second specimen of this regal conch was purchased from Ceylon by Madame de Burgh in 1869. Being one of the two well-known female conchologists in Great Britain at that time, the other being the indefatigable Jane Saul of Limehouse, she prevailed upon the period's leading conchologist, George B. Sowerby II, to name it *Strombus mirabilis*. Four more specimens turned up from Burma during the 1880s, but it was not to be rediscovered until almost eighty years later, first by me on the International Oceanographic Expedition ship *Anton Bruun* in 1963, a year later by a Japanese trawler and, in Arabia, by Richard W. Foster on Cruise Nine of the *Anton Bruun*. By now, over 50 specimens were known in scientific circles. As late as 1970, despite the fact that enterprising fishermen in Thailand and Burma had trawled up over 500 specimens a year earlier, uninformed amateurs were still paying as much as $1,000 a specimen.

The reputations of rare shells die hard, sometimes almost a generation after the species has proved to be common. Most touted of the rarities was the Glory-of-the-Seas Cone, a magnificent, graceful, finely patterned shell first described in 1777 and known from only a couple of dozen specimens for the next hundred years. False tales and high auction prices built this malacological paragon into a holy grail. In 1856, it was erroneously published that the great Danish cone collector Chris Hwass had in 1792 purchased one at an auction and immediately crushed it underfoot to make the one he already possessed all the more valuable. A second false tale was published in connection with the discovery of two specimens in Bohol, Philippines, by Hugh Cuming in 1837. A few years later it was reported that an immense earthquake had swallowed up the living grounds of this now-extinct shell. This added to the desirability and sale price of the Glory-of-the-Seas. By 1957, twenty-four specimens were known; by 1964, twice that number had been discovered in New Guinea. The jackpot was found by two Australian scuba divers, Gibbins and Bailey, in 1970, when they collected over one hundred fifty specimens on the north shore of Guadalcanal Island, Solomons.

Among the other handsome species that brought fantastically high prices in the early days, but which are now known to be rather common, are Florida's Junonia, *Scaphella junonia;* Martin's Tibia, *Tibia martinii;* the Miraculous Thatcher Shell of Japan, *Thatcheria mirabilis;* Beau's Murex, *Murex beaui;* the Clavate Murex, *Murex elongatus;* the Snowy

Cowrie, *Cypraea nivosa;* and the Precious Wentle-trap, *Epitonium scalare.* Many of these sold for several hundred dollars apiece at one time but today may be obtained for less than five or ten dollars.

The Precious Wentletrap was a rare and favorite collector's item from 1700 to about 1890. Some-time during this period it was reported that clever Chinese had manufactured perfect replicas out of rice paste and sold them for several hundred dollars apiece. The story may not be true, for no one, even after ardent search, has rediscovered one of these unique counterfeits, which probably would today be worth ten times the value of a real specimen.

Unlike stamps and coins, rare shells do not in-crease in value. If anything, they are likely to drop in value as more specimens are found. Only species rapidly becoming extinct might have an increasing value, but such cases exist among the land and freshwater shells, not among the marine species.

PRECEDING PAGES: Part of a scallop shell collection assembled by a private collector, Mr. Hal Lewis of Philadelphia. × 1. ABOVE, LEFT: First specimen ever found of the rare Dennison's Morum, *Morum dennisoni* (Reeve), from the West Indies. × 1.5. CENTER: The once-rare Junonia, *Scaphella junonia* (Lamarck), from Florida. RIGHT: Lister's Conch, *Strombus listeri* Gray, from Burma, has been rediscovered in large quantities. × 0.5.

Rare shells of today

Despite the fact that many species considered to be very rare are now known to be fairly common, if not abundant, there have been quite a number that have defied the best collecting efforts of modern dredgers and scuba divers. Naturally, many deep-sea species remain scarce in private and public museum collections, but this is because funds have not been available to finance deep-sea dredging expeditions.

Probably the most enduring of the collector's items, and one which has for years been intensively hunted in its well-known habitats, is the Golden, or Orange, Cowrie, *Cypraea aurantium*. This gorgeous, bright orange, glossy, four-inch-long cowrie, with white ends and creamy base, has appealed to South Sea Island natives and Europeans alike for many hundreds of years. The Fijians used it as a chieftain's badge, drilling a hole in it and stringing a neck cord through it. It was used in earlier days as a major article of barter and was passed eastward to the Polynesian tribes before the coming of white man. The distribution of the Golden Cowrie extends throughout the Southwest Pacific arc from the Ryukyu Islands through the Philippines and Micronesia to the Fijian Islands.

There are probably less than a thousand specimens in collectors' hands, despite the intense demand that has prevailed for them for over two hundred years. At present there are three areas where they seem to be most frequently found—northwest Mindanao Island in the Philippines where at least thirty have been obtained recently; the northern coast of San Cristobal Island in the British Solomons and the southwest end of Viti Levu Island in Fiji. Three or four specimens have turned up in widely scattered areas in such places as Truk, Guam, New Guinea and other Solomon Islands. They live in recessed, submarine caves on the front of reefs facing the open ocean at a depth of about twenty-five to forty feet, usually in places where red sponges are dominant. Undoubtedly many more will gradually come on the market, although the present-day value of these cowries, about $200, or more, will undoubtedly prevail for years to come.

There are a number of rare shells that live in such inaccessible shallow-water places that they are not likely to become common. Some of these are so far obtainable only from the stomachs of mollusk-eating fish. These ex *pisces* specimens are turning up in increasing numbers in areas where enterprising collectors are catching and opening shell-loving fish, particularly in South Africa, the Philippines and Brazil. From 1966 to 1970, approximately $20,000 worth of ex *pisces* shells were sold around the world. Among such species still considered fairly rare are *Cypraea barclayi*, *Cypraea fultoni*, *Cypraea broderipi*—all cowries from South Africa; *Morum matthewsi* and *Cypraea surinamensis* from Brazil and *Cypraea leucodon* and *porteri* from the Philippines.

Among the rare cones that do not seem to be very easily obtained, as yet, are the Glory-of-India, *Conus milneedwardsi*; the Glory-of-Bengal, *Conus bengalensis*; *Conus thomae* from Indonesia and perhaps the rarest of all ex *pisces* shells, the Du Savel Cone, *Conus dusaveli*, known from only one specimen coming from a fish caught off Mauritius in 1871 in 180 feet of water.

The outstanding rare collector's items are usually limited to the better-known and more popular groups. The six leading families are the cones (Conidae), the cowries (Cypraeidae), the volutes (Volutidae), the murexes (Muricidae), the slit shells (Pleurotomariidae) and the scallops (Pectinidae). If a rare and desirable shell belongs to some other family, it generally will have some very unusual characteristics, a large size and a purported rarity, at least in private collections. *Morum dennisoni, Trigonostoma pellucida,* and from the Seychelles, *Vasum crosseanum* are examples of species underrated by collectors governed by cupidity. Many other rare and beautiful species await recognition and exploitation. Fortunately, their marine environments are usually sufficiently inaccessible and extensive enough to endure the greedy onslaught of man.

OPPOSITE, TOP: Glory-of-India, *Conus milneedwardsi* Jousseaume, from off India. × 1. TOP RIGHT: *Cymbiola cymbiola* (Gmelin), volute known from only a few specimens; probably a native of Indonesia. × 1. MIDDLE RIGHT: Famous Prince Cowrie, *Cypraea valentia* Perry, from southwest Pacific. This is the type specimen. BOTTOM: Heart Lyria, *Lyria (Cordilyria) cordis* Bayer, 1971, is a stunning Caribbean volute known only from two specimens. × 2.

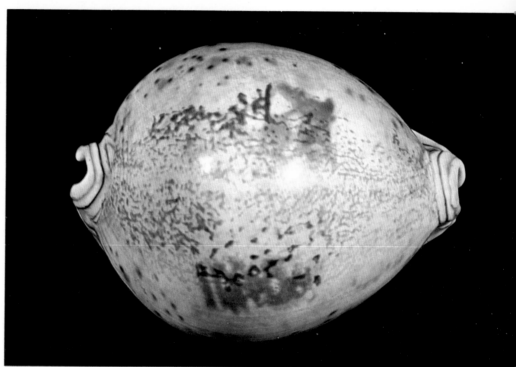

African volutes

The huge continent of Africa is surrounded by four main and distinct faunal regions. Each has its own peculiar types of sea life, including unique communities of mollusks. To the north lies the Mediterranean, but no volutes survive in that sea despite the fact that dozens of varieties have been found in the fossil beds of France and Italy. The exception is found just at the very western end, in the vicinity of Portugal and Spain. There the once-rare Halia Volute lives in waters from 25 to 150 fathoms deep. This delicate, ball-shaped, glossy gem, seldom over three inches in length, is a rosy tan and adorned with spiral rows of small red-brown dots.

Strangest of the volute faunas is that of the mud-bottomed shores of Africa, from Spanish Morocco south to Angola. There, from the intertidal sand flats to a depth of about 200 feet, are eight species of large, thin-shelled *Cymbium* volutes, unique in harboring their young in the oviduct until they are ready to crawl out as independent, miniature volutes. The Elephant Snout Volute, a shallow-water species of the Gulf of Guinea, has a sunken, snout-like area that replaces the spire. The thin outer periostracum is usually covered with a brown-sugar-like glaze. It reaches a length of thirteen inches and has a large brown body and foot. Equally handsome is Neptune's Volute, *Cymbium pepo,* from the west bulge of Africa. The golden orange, very wide-mouthed shell is large, heavy and quite globose. When living, the shell's exterior is covered with a heavy brown periostracum.

The cool waters of South Africa harbor many interesting, and in some cases quite rare, volutes. New species, or at least curious ecologic forms, continue to come up in the nets of commercial trawlers. In 1848, H.M.S. *Samarang* brought up on her mud-caked anchor in the harbor at Cape Town a strange volute with a curious latticework sculpturing. It was a "living fossil" previously represented only by fossils from Alabama and Texas. *Voluto-corbis abyssicola,* as it is now known, remained a rarity until the famous expedition ship H.M.S. *Challenger,* in 1881, and, much later, numerous commercial trawlers, brought up many more specimens. A very similar species, Helen Boswell's Volute, was described as recently as 1969. Another previously uncommon, magnificent, greenish volute, *Neptune-opsis gilchristi,* was found off the Cape of Good Hope in 1898. It is unusual in having a large, whelk-like horny operculum. The graceful, spindle-shaped shell may reach a length of eight inches.

East Africa, basically part of the vast Indo-Pacific faunal province, has several rare and unique volutes. Rarest of these is the Festive Lyria, known to French collectors as early as 1810. This handsome knobbed volute, blotched with orange and black, has been found from Arabia to Mozambique, but probably no more than four or five have been brought to light during the present century. The lyre-shaped lyria, a five-inch-long, elongate, ribbed beauty, was considered very rare during the nineteenth century when it was first found. It was not until after World War II that its homeland was discovered, and in the last ten years over a hundred specimens have been brought up in fishermen's nets off Mombasa, East Africa. The most exquisite of the lyrias is Delessert's, a rosy, two-inch-long, sharply ribbed species from Madagascar. Discovered in 1842, it has since appeared on the European market quite frequently. The operculum is large and claw-shaped.

ABOVE: The Festive volute, *Festilyria festiva* (Lamarck),
was first described in 1811, but fewer than a dozen
specimens are known. One sold for over $2,000 a few years
ago. This specimen, collected in the 1800s, is now in
the British Museum (Natural History). $\times$ 1.5.

Pacific volutes

Among the so-called aristocratic families of shells, the volutes have been favorite collector's items ever since conchology gained prominence in the early eras of world explorations. Architecturally, they include some of the most stunning shells, and from the point of view of color, there are few to rival the purple cobwebbing of Bednall's Volute or the glossy brilliance of an Australian *Amoria*. Some of them reach a length of twenty inches, a fact that has always guaranteed them a place of prominent display. Among the 200 known species, thirty are still known from only one or two specimens and over a third of them are still rated as uncommon. To acquire a complete collection of volutes is probably impossible for any private collector or, indeed, any museum.

Volutes are carnivorous, feeding on small invertebrate animals and other mollusks. A few live in shallow water, but the majority inhabit the zone from ten to one hundred feet. There are at least twenty species that live below a depth of a half mile and one that has been dredged from two miles down. The sexes are separate, and in most cases the females lay large leathery capsules that contain several eggs. The family is largely a tropical one, although quite a few species exist in cold abyssal seas, as well as in the temperate regions of New Zealand, Argentina and southern Alaska.

The Indo-Pacific and neighboring seas are rich in volutes, possessing almost three-quarters of the known species. Australia can boast of the most colorful and diversified representatives. Leading of these is the genus *Amoria*. These very glossy, elongate shells are from three to five inches long and very brightly colored. Commonest among them is the two-inch-long Zebra Amoria that is found along a 2,000-mile stretch of Australia's eastern coast, usually from the low-tide line to a depth of a few fathoms. Its outer shell is creamy ivory with numerous axial streaks of dark chocolate brown. This beautiful animal has a zebra-striped foot and tentacles camouflaged with zigzag stripes of yellow brown. Other amorias include the charming little Channelled Amoria, which is spotted with bold blocks of orange and delicately streaked with fine reddish axial lines. Damon's Amoria, four inches long, from Western

Australia is a study in feathery purple-brown cob-webbings.

Perhaps outstanding among the northwest Australian members of this family is the strangely patterned Bednall's Volute. Its curious, squarish color pattern, somewhat resembling that of chicken wire, is capped with a bulbous apex of salmon brown. Discovered about a hundred years ago, it was known only from five or six specimens until Japanese pearl luggers invaded the Australian offshore waters in the late 1950s. Hundreds of specimens were taken back to Japan, some gaining a place of honor in leading shell collections of that country but many being sold to Americans and Australians at high prices. It is still not a very common shell in collections.

Mammoths of the volute world are the seven melo volutes, known only from the waters from southeast Asia to Australia. The shells are monstrous in size, some reaching a length of twenty inches. The aperture of the shell is very large, and the shell material itself is thin but strong. Some species, such as the Ethiopian and Georgina volutes are marked above with a circular crown of curved spikes. The egg capsules of the melos are built in towerlike clusters about eight inches in height.

Commonest of the volutes of the Southwest Pacific is the Bat Volute, a sturdy three-inch-long, spined shell with a rather dull olive brown to reddish color. It is quite variable in color and in the degree of development of spines. In New Guinea, it is commonly collected at night in knee-deep water, but its range extends from the Philippines to Australia. About one in every ten thousand specimens is coiled sinistrally, a genetic aberration turning up even more rarely in *Melo* and *Scaphella* volutes. Among the rare Pacific volutes are *Cymbiola cymbiola* and the Golden-mouthed Volute, *Cymbiola chrysostoma*, both probably hiding in large numbers in some unexplored bay in Indonesia. Kaup's Volute, described in 1863, is known from only one dark, mysterious specimen now buried in the Berlin Museum in East Germany. The original locality of this rust brown, spotted, two-inch-long volute is entirely unknown.

The volutes shown here are from Australia. All × 1. OPPOSITE, TOP LEFT: Bednall's Volute, *Volutoconus bednalli* (Brazier). BOTTOM LEFT: Lightning Volute, *Ericusa fulgetrum* (Sowerby). RIGHT: *Cymbiolacca thatcheri* (McCoy). THIS PAGE, TOP LEFT: *Cymbiolacca wisemani* (Brazier). LOWER LEFT: *Amoria grayi* Ludbrook. RIGHT: *Cymbiola nivosa* (Lamarck) laying eggs.

American volutes

The Americas have a rather poor but nonetheless diversified assemblage of volutes. Two species became known at rather early periods in Europe, one of them the Music Volute, depicted in seventeenth-century books and paintings; the other, the famous Junonia, reached Paris soon after the French Revolution. The Music Volute, so-called because its patterns resemble the bars and notes of written musical scores, was common in the lower Caribbean and was brought back in fairly substantial numbers from the "Sugar Islands," mainly Barbados. It was one of the first shells named by Linnaeus in 1758, and because of its variability, it received no less than twenty-four additional names in the next hundred years.

The Music Volute is the characteristic type of the genus *Voluta*. Only two other living species are known, and all have a long, clawlike, horny operculum. The Hebrew Volute from northeastern Brazil is similar but lacks the musical characters and grows to a much larger size, sometimes reaching over five inches in length. The third kind, the Greenish Musical Volute, found in the western part of the Gulf of Mexico in waters from ten to eighty fathoms deep, has five knobbed whorls, a dull greenish blue cast and a slightly reticulated surface. Formerly, it was considered quite rare.

A typically American group is the genus *Scaphella*, represented by the once-rare, purplish-brown spotted *Junonia* of southeast United States. Three other species live in deep waters off south Florida and Cuba, most notable today being the Dubia Volute, which has received fifteen other names because of its variability in spotting and spiral sculpturing. The *Scaphella* clan flourished during the early Tertiary period, and fossil representatives, still showing their square color spots, are not uncommon in the Pliocene beds of Florida. A similar genus, *Volutifusus,* has three rare deep-sea Cuban representatives, of which Torre's Volute with its beautiful salmon-pink enamel finish, overlaid with a few reddish spots, is a masterpiece of nature.

Turning southward to the cooler waters of Brazil, Uruguay and Argentina, we find several unique species, including the chunky, colorless Brazil Volute that lays numerous single egg capsules resembling tennis balls. After a storm the beach may be littered with them. Largest of the American volutes is *Adelomelon beckii,* named in 1836 in honor of the early conchologist Beck. It reaches a length of eighteen inches, and because it is carnivorous, it is sometimes captured on baited hook and line. The most beautiful of the cold-water species of southern Brazil and Argentina is the stunning, glossy Angulate Volute, *Zidona dufresnei.* Its very long, pointed spire, entirely covered by a bronzed brown glaze, is on occasions so elongated by this additional glaze that it may be drawn out into a two-inch-long pencillike spike.

The Pacific side of the Americas is poor in volutes except for a few scarce deepwater species dredged off the coast of Central America and Ecuador. The one existing specimen of the Benthalis Volute of Dall, found in 1896, was dredged from the impressive depth of 10,000 feet. Better known is a related species, Stearns's Volute, which is occasionally brought up by commercial trawlers from forty fathoms along the western sections of Alaska and the Bering Sea under the floating ice packs. The shell has a very crude gray exterior and a dull brown aperture—a lack of coloration typical of arctic mollusks in general.

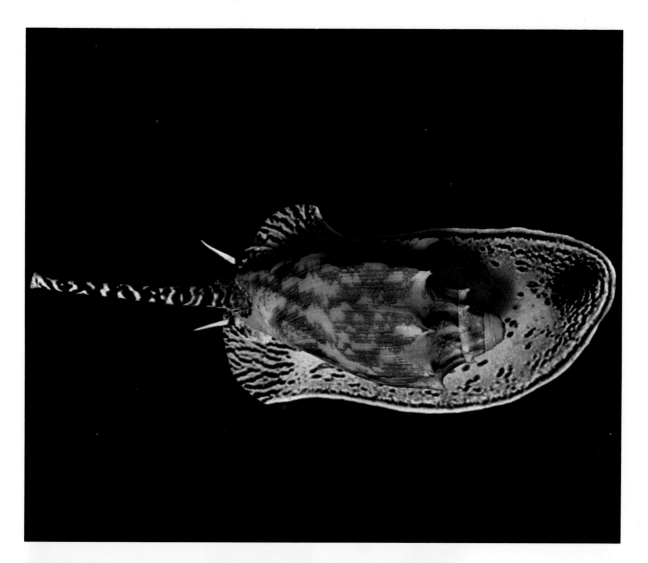

TOP: Common Bat Volute, *Cymbiola vespertilio* (Linné), from the southwest Pacific, does not have an operculum. BOTTOM: Uncommon Greenish Musical Volute, *Voluta virescens* Lightfoot, from deep water in the Caribbean. Unlike most volutes, this species has a small, horny operculum.

Cones

It is probable that more amateur conchologists have attempted to amass a complete collection of cones than of any other family of mollusks. This is undoubtedly because of the cone's great beauty of color and design, the relative abundance of most kinds and the constant presence of several rare species that always seems to lure the collector to seek more specimens. There may be as many as 400 good species of *Conus*, despite the fact that there are about a thousand extra synonymic names cluttering the literature.

Part of the reason for the large number of species in existence is the specialized mode of feeding that has evolved in this family. The radular teeth, shaped like harpoons, are kept in a quiver behind the pharynx and used to spear fish, worms and other mollusks. In tropical Pacific reef areas, there may be as many as 200 species coexisting in a relatively small and similar habitat. Each species feeds on a particular kind of worm or mollusk. Whenever only one species of cone occurs in a given area, it has been found to use a wide selection of foods.

The Indo-Pacific area extending from East Africa to Polynesia has the lion's share of cone species,

146

probably supporting 60 percent of the known living kinds. Most are shallow-water inhabitants living on either intertidal rock or sand flats or dwelling on sandy bottoms down to 200 feet, but a dozen species have been recorded at great depths. The majority of species feed on tiny reef worms, and most of these species have a very wide distribution, usually extending some 6,000 miles across the Indo-Pacific expanse. The common Hebrew Cone, the ever-present Miliaris Cone, the abundant Flavidus Cone, are examples of ubiquitous species. Even some of the strikingly beautiful cones, such as the black-and-white checkered Marble Cone, the Cloth-of-Gold *Conus textile* and the handsome but deadly Geography Cone are widely distributed.

In contrast, there are a number of attractive and distinct cones that have very restricted distributions. Some of these were once considered rare. The Noble Cone and *Conus thalassiarchus* were beauties that commanded high prices at nineteenth-century auctions, but about 1956 Fernando Dayrit, the conchologist of the Philippines, began turning them up by the hundreds. Their particular area had been found. *Conus nobilis* had been hiding in the Sulu Sea and *Conus thalassiarchus* was found abundantly only on Palawan Island. A rare form or subspecies of the Noble Cone, called *Conus victor,* was recently unearthed in goodly numbers in central Indonesia. Even the treasured Rhododendron Cone, an exquisite lavender shell with a yellow aperture, bound to extract the highest of ransoms from conchologists, has proved to be available in the Cook and Phoenix islands.

Some cones defy discovery. Leading the list are Du Savel's Cone from Mauritius; *Conus cervus,* probably from the Indian Ocean, and *Conus thomae* from Indonesia. However, numerous specimens of the Glory-of-India, *Conus milneedwardsi,*

OPPOSITE, LEFT: Geography Cone, *Conus geographus* Linné, has stung and killed several people. × 1. RIGHT: Rare Victor Cone, *Conus nobilis victor* Broderip, is from Indonesia. × 2. THIS PAGE: Nineteenth-century paintings of the Caribbean Cedonulli Cone. X 2.

in Mozambique and the Glory-of-Bengal in the Andaman Sea have recently been discovered. Even *Conus excelsus* has given away its habitat—it has been recently dredged in the northwest corner of the Bay of Bengal. The deglorification of the Glory-of-the-Seas, once the paragon of early European collectors, has gradually come about with the discovery of more than 150 specimens in the British Solomon Islands.

The tropical Americas have a rather rich assortment of cones—not nearly as many as has the Indo-Pacific but certainly a high proportion of species as compared to that of most American families. The coast of western Central America, from the Gulf of California to northern Peru, is blessed with several dozen exquisite species. Few of them reached Europe before 1840, and they escaped the frantic auctioning of the century before. The West Indian species, on the other hand, were well known only a hundred years after Christopher Columbus's adventures. The Mouse Cone, the Crown Cone and the Alphabet Cone were all named and illustrated before 1793.

The two earliest glamour cones of the West Indies were described by Linnaeus in 1758. One was the Glory-of-the-Atlantic, *Conus granulatus*, a brilliant scarlet, two-inch-long cone that once brought the highest price of any shell in a Rotterdam auction of 1853. For some reason—perhaps because of its unimposing name of *granulatus* or because too many specimens reached Europe too soon—it never reached the exalted status of the other famous Caribbean cone *Conus cedonulli*. This was the cone known as early as 1734 as the "Second to None" and the "Matchless Cone." Albert Seba, the Amsterdam apothecary, was sufficiently impressed with a specimen to write: "While I had this beautiful specimen in my hand and could examine it closely, I was shaken by its remarkable beauty and by the pattern of all its various colors and ornamentation which it possesses." The two earliest known specimens ended up in royal hands; one went, in 1731, to the king of Portugal, the other to King Christian VI of Denmark. Pierre Lyonet, an early eighteenth-century Parisian collector, possessed two specimens and refused to

LEFT: The uncommon *Conus barthelemyi* Bernardi, from the Indian Ocean. × 1. RIGHT: Two small *Conus litteratus* Linné and one large *Conus leopardus* (Röding). OPPOSITE, LEFT: *Conus omaria* Hwass. × 1.5. RIGHT: The rare *Conus thomae* Gmelin. × 1.

part with either, although the duchess of Portland offered today's equivalent of $1,000 for one of them. Between 1854 and 1865, the species brought about $100. Because of technical nomenclature, the name *cedonulli* was abandoned for *dominicanus* in the twentieth century, and with scuba divers obtaining numerous specimens in Curaçao, the value of the shell has been reduced to that of a pair of shoes. Nevertheless, a perfect specimen is still a breathtaking sight.

Delessert's Cone, described in 1843, was long known from only one specimen, erroneously credited to the Red Sea fauna. As more specimens turned up from its true Floridian home, it was given a second, unnecessary, name, *Conus sozoni*. To the south, along the Brazilian coast, several undoubtedly good new species have been turning up since 1967.

The Panamanian fauna on the Pacific side of central America is rich in cones. Earliest to reach Europe, probably through the auspices of the Spanish conquistadores, was the beautiful Prince Cone that Linnaeus described in 1758. When cleaned of its thick outer periostracum, the shell is a deep, nonglossy salmon pink overlaid by numerous black-brown, axial, wavy brush lines. For delicacy of pattern, nothing exceeds the Lucid Cone with its latticed filigree of markings on a lavender background. A few of the Panamanian cones are obviously recent escapees from Polynesian waters, as evidenced by Dall's Cone, a member of the *Conus textile* group, and by the presence of the Hebrew Cone in Costa Rica.

The Mediterranean has few cones. In fact, only one species lives there, but because of its numerous variations in color and shape, the frustrated, cone-conscious European conchologists gave it more than 190 names over a period of two centuries! The species, however, can lay claim to being one of the only two living cones ever found coiling about sinistrally. The other is *Conus floridanus*.

The largest cone in the world is the Promethean Cone of West Africa. It reaches a length of over nine inches. Heaviest is the Leopard Cone of the Indo-Pacific; an eight-pound specimen has been found in Hawaii.

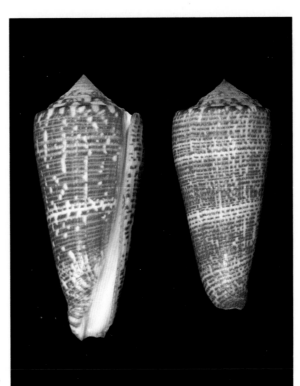

Cowries

The cowries are the jewels of the marine mollusk world. The brilliant gloss and bright colors of the shell, produced by the soft, fleshy mantle of the snail, are often thought by novices to be the product of the buffing wheel or furniture polish. Early man used these bright natural objects as ornaments and trade goods. They were used extensively in the slave trade by Arabs, by Negroes and, later, by white Europeans. National expeditions sent out in the late 1600s and early 1700s for spices, rare woods, medicinal herbs and valuable minerals came home to Europe with a large assortment of colorful cowries. In the early 1800s, there was hardly a mantelpiece in England or Holland without a cowrie.

This popular family has been avidly collected and thoroughly studied by a dozen generations of conchologists. Today, about 180 species are recognized and, surprisingly enough, a new species occasionally turns up as, for instance, Porter's Cowrie, discovered in the Philippines in 1965. The richest area is the Indo-Pacific, with the Pacific Panamanian and Caribbean areas running second and third.

The growth of cowries mystified early naturalists. Since most shells grow by the addition of new shell material onto the outer lip of the last whorl, and since cowries had a large, toothed, curled outer, and inner, lip, it did not seem possible that a cowrie could grow any larger in the conventional manner. One theory was that the soft cowrie animal deserted its shell, puffed itself up larger and then created a new shell, a process used by crustacea. But the answer is obvious when one has a growth series of a cowrie shell before him. The thin, elongate, young and immature cowrie, known as the *bulla*, is shaped like an ordinary shell, so that it can add to its size in the usual manner at the edge of the outer lip. When quite large, the shell becomes mature, thickening the outer lip into a rolled-in, toothed ledge.

The sexes are separate in cowries, and the males inject sperm into a special sac in the female where they wait until eggs are ready to be fertilized. Fifty to a hundred eggs are placed in each small, sausage-shaped capsule, the latter being laid in crowded clusters under rock ledges. The females sit on the eggs, not to incubate them but to protect them from being eaten by crabs and worms.

During the 1800s, several rare cowries were described by British and French conchologists. Most of them were based on deepwater species that had accidentally been washed into shallow water. The stomachs of fishes have been the best source of some of the rarities—Fulton's and Broderip's cowries from South Africa, Barclay's Cowrie from the Indian Ocean and the Surinam Cowrie from Brazil. The two most valuable cowries today are the Leucodon and Prince cowries. The latter, scientifically known as *Cypraea valentia*, is represented by only seven specimens. The earliest known specimen, owned by Lord Valentia, was known as "The Brindled [brownish] Cowrie of the Persian Gulf." Subsequently, the species has been accurately recorded from New Britain Island and the north shore of Guadalcanal, Solomons. It lives as deep as 180 feet and may not become readily available for some time.

The Leucodon Cowrie, described in 1828 by the British conchologist Judge W. J. Broderip, was the most sought-after cowrie in the world for more than a century and a half. A second specimen mysteriously turned up in the collection of the Boston Society of Natural History about 1880, but it may have been collected about the same time as the first. In 1965, the mystery of the authentic locality of this species was solved when a collector sent an *ex pisces* cowrie to Peter Dance at the British Museum. It was a genuine *leucodon*, and it is now on display in the Delaware Museum of Natural History.

TOP: The rare Great White-spotted Cowrie, *Cypraea guttata* Gmelin, from the southwest Pacific. × 2.
BOTTOM: Chestnut Cowrie from California. On the left is an immature specimen. × 2.

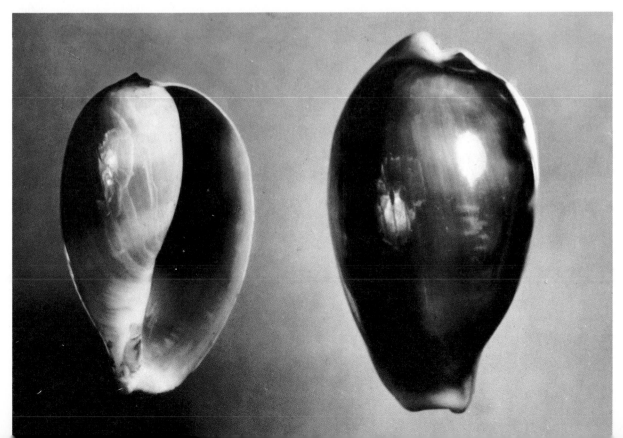

One of the handsomest of the choice collector's items is the Great White-spotted Cowrie, *Cypraea guttata*. The popular name is misleading because many cowries are white spotted. The prettiest part of *guttata* is the underside, where about two dozen dark brown raised teeth cross the whitish base. On either side of the narrow aperture is an irregular brown blotch. In the mid-1960s, a dozen were found in the Solomon Islands. Others have been found in southern Japan and the New Hebrides, but because it lives in deep water, it is not a shell likely to become very common in collections. A Malaita, Solomon Islands, specimen was sold in 1963 by a Dutch Roman Catholic priest for $2,000.

The tropical Indo-Pacific supports over 100 species of cowries, most of which are inhabitants of intertidal rock areas where old broken coral slabs offer protection. The two most widespread of the family are the Snakehead Cowrie, *Cypraea caputserpentis,* and the Eroded Cowrie, *C. erosa,* both extending from the shores of Africa to Japan, Hawaii and Tahiti. Commonest, and with almost as wide a distribution, are the two small money cowries, *Cypraea moneta* and *C. annulus.* At low tide they may be found abundantly in the grass or under small stones on the reef flat. It would be safe to say that within the last hundred years man has collected over a million pounds of these species, yet they continue to flourish.

Perhaps one of the best known of the larger, brighter shells is the Tiger Cowrie that grows to the size of an apple and sports a shell coloration of mottled spots of various shades of brown. It does not have stripes, as the name *tiger* implies. For many centuries, the shells were brought home by seafaring men, and they graced the Victorian mantelpieces of Europe and the Americas for several generations. During the early 1900s they were shipped from Zanzibar by the ton and sold at eastern American beach resorts, usually with the Lord's Prayer etched in the top surface.

The color variations of the shells of the Pacific are almost infinite, and some of them are worth detailed study. Who could deny that the delicate patterns of the Ziczac Cowrie or the Diluculum Cowrie are artistic masterpieces of nature? Or look closely with a hand lens at the small Clandestine Cowrie. What appears from a distance to be a brownish coloration turns out to be, upon magnification, the most delicate lines of brown ever set upon a cream enamel background. Or examine carefully the spots on the Ocellate Cowrie of Ceylon of southeast Asia—what perfect jet-black spots, each bounded by a rim of white, set in a sea of tawny brown! This is the secret appeal of the cowrie.

Three large, uncommon cowries of the Pacific have fascinated collectors since early times, and certainly even ordinary collections of cowries include this famous triumvirate—the Eyed, the Map and the Tortoise cowries. Living usually at depths of from ten to thirty feet of water and occurring in pairs rather than in swarms like the commoner Lynx and Arabian cowries, they are not easy to find. The distribution of these three large cowries is quite extensive, ranging from east Africa to Polynesia, which has assured a steady, although limited, supply over the years. The Eyed Cowrie, *Cypraea argus,* is extremely handsome. Its elongate buff-colored shell is adorned by numerous, often interlocking, circles of darker brown. The Map Cowrie has a sufficiently intricate, geographical design on its back to justify its name, *Cypraea mappa.* Rare color forms of this species have a beautiful salmon-red underside. The Tortoise Cowrie, largest of the three, is shaped like a cucumber and has the soft, deep browns of tortoise shell. Over this pleasant finish are sprinkled tiny specks of opaque white, as if salt had been shaken upon the surface.

Although the shells of cowries are extremely beautiful, the soft fleshy mantle that slips up over the cowrie to form the shell's colors and patterns is almost as remarkable in design. Mantles may be brilliant orange, jet black, snowy white or bedecked with soft, colorful protuberances.

Largest of the cowries is the Atlantic Deer Cowrie, *C. cervus,* which may reach a length of seven inches. Living among the coral gardens of the Florida Keys, it is a monstrous animal, covered with a great black-brown, fuzzy mantle. In contrast, some cowries rarely exceed nine millimeters in length, not much larger than a grain of cooked rice. *Cypraea microdon* and *C. irrorata* of the Pacific are probably the smallest species. The Microdon Cowrie has a brilliant carmine mantle.

The Americas are relatively poor in cowries, the

West Indies having only three common species—
C. spurca, C. zebra and *C. cinerea.* Two others are
seldom collected, one of them being the deepwater
Surinam Cowrie, the other the curious and very
distinctive Mouse Cowrie, known to Europeans for
over 300 years. Slave ships traveling from Africa
made landfall on the northern coast of South
America not only to obtain food, fresh fruit and
water but also to transfer slaves to smaller boats.

When the ships picked up slaves in Venezuela and
Colombia, the sea captains often purchased shells
at the docks, including the Mouse Cowrie that is
not uncommon in the shallow, muddy areas of that
part of the world. When the Mouse Cowries were
distributed among shell-collecting circles in the
United States, they were erroneously reported as
having been collected in Africa, thousands of miles
from the secret transfer ports of South America.

The Umbilicate False Cowrie, *Calpurnus verrucosus* (Linné), of the Pacific,
usually lives on soft coral. Its mantle and foot are heavily dotted with
black. The shell is white with a pink umbilical button at each end. × 1.

Murex shells

The murex shells are a major group of univalves known from very earliest times and characterized by their spiny ornamentation. Man's interest in this group, aside from the edible qualities of its members, was spurred by the accidental discovery that the juices from the animal could produce a very permanent and colorful rosy-purple dye. This dye, which later became known as royal tyrian purple, played a major part in the commercial enterprises of the Mediterranean ancients, from the Phoenicians to the Romans. The Roman Catholic and Episcopal churches perpetuated the reverence they inherited for this dye by using it in their ritual colors for bishops' robes and altar trappings at certain ecclesiastical seasons.

The Muricidae family is an enormous assemblage of hundreds of small genera, ranging from the true spiny *Murex* to the knobbed, wide-mouthed *Purpura* and the insignificant *Morula,* or drupe, rock shells. They are all carnivorous, usually feeding on barnacles, oysters, mussels and rarely chitons. Most members of the family are tropical, although the drills that plague oyster beds are cold-water inhabitants. A few aberrant muricid groups have become closely associated with corals and sea fans, such as *Coralliophila* and *Quoyula.*

The murex shells are probably the most underrated of the collector's items. This is probably because many of the more intricate species are difficult to identify and because the beauty of the delicate spines, frills and sculpturing is usually marred by abrasion or marine growths. A perfect specimen of a Rose-Branch Murex is much more difficult to find than a good cone or cowrie. The situation is

further complicated by the fact that the degree of webbing, frills and sculpturing on a murex is often determined by environmental conditions. A shell growing in quiet, protected waters is apt to have longer and more delicate spines than one living on the exposed, wave-dashed intertidal rocks.

Perhaps the most striking and certainly one of the oldest known collector's items in this family is the Venus Comb Murex, a spine-bedecked shell resembling the ribs of a fish picked clean. Although many collections contain this moderately common species, few can boast of a specimen with no broken spines. The most desired murex throughout the nineteenth century was the gorgeous Rose-Branch Murex, *M. palmarosae*, described in 1822 by Lamarck. Pictures of it occur in earlier, hand-painted books. In all likelihood, these specimens

came from the waters of Ceylon, where today an occasional specimen is collected by scuba divers.

One of the least known of the rare species was the Alabaster Murex, a large, winged, white shell found on the beach by the well-known collector Hugh Cuming while he was shell collecting in the Philippines from 1836 to 1839. It was seldom mentioned in the literature, and no additional specimens came to light until 1961 when Chinese fishermen began hauling them up in nets. Each of the first few specimens sold for about $100, but within a year the price, even for a good one, had dropped almost tenfold. Among the famous remaining rarities are Löbbecke's Murex, a truly exquisite, two-inch-long species known from only five or six specimens from Japan and the China Sea, and Barclay's Murex from the remote St. Bran-

OPPOSITE: Löbbecke's Murex, *Pterynotus loebbeckei* Kobelt. These rare specimens were collected in the 1800s in the China Sea. × 2.
THIS PAGE: Deerhorn Murex, *Chicoreus damicornis* Hedley, from Australia. The left one is a very rare sinistral, or left-handed, specimen. × 2.

don Islands, or the Cargados Carajos group in the Shoals of the Indian Ocean.

Although the Philippines were a source of several rare murexes, it was not until after World War II that they became relatively common in collections. Two of these were the bizarre Rota Murex with squarish clublike spines and the equally strange Clavus Murex, *Murex elongatus*. The latter has a towerlike spire with weak varices, or ridges; on its final whorl, just opposite the aperture, a single earlike webbing abruptly protrudes from the outer lip.

The largest and most attractive of the murex shells of the Americas live in the muddy areas of the west coast of Central America. At one time all five of the biggest and most colorful of the Panama murexes were abundant, but overcollecting has reduced their numbers in many places. Commonest is the Pink-mouthed Murex, a shell whose color evidently gave rise to the original concept of *shell pink*. Its aperture and surrounding shield are a brilliant, rich shell pink. Outside, the shell is handsomely adorned with short white fluted spines. In contrast, the Radish Murex is a giant, round burr covered with numerous rows of short, sharp spines of jet black. A closely related northern species, *Murex nigritus*, differs in having fewer rows of spines and in being painted with numerous black spiral lines and bands. Perhaps the handsomest is the Regal Murex, a four-inch-long shell with contrasting black-brown and pink coloration on the shield surrounding the mouth of the shell. Largest of these five well-known species is the Cabbage Murex, some six to eight inches long. It has a large, wide mouth bounded by a narrow rim of shell pink.

The Atlantic coast of the Americas is well represented in murexes. Largest is the Giant Atlantic Murex, *M. fulvescens*, of the Carolinian province. It reaches a length of six inches and may weigh over five pounds. It abounds on offshore beds, not far from shore, along the Georgia and Texas coasts particularly. In the spring these murexes swarm together for spawning and often venture into shallower water where the females lay thousands of squarish, urn-shaped egg capsules on rocks and on the shells of fellow murexes. The Apple Murex, a smaller but more colorful species, is abundant off the west coast of Florida. When they swarm, several females and males get together to form and fertilize huge mounds of egg capsules the size of basketballs. The Apple Murex has a wide range, extending from North Carolina to Brazil.

One of the most delicate and exquisitely sculptured of the Atlantic species is the deepwater Hidalgo's Murex, discovered in 1869 in the French West Indies. Twenty years later, an American deep-sea expedition dredged further specimens off Barbados and Cuba. Under a hand lens, the winglike varices of this delightful small white shell are a miraculous filigree of the most delicate crinklings of calcium carbonate ever designed by nature. Recently, enterprising Florida shrimpers have turned their skills to dredging up basketfuls of coral rubble and shells from depths off the southeast United States. They have been selling the malacological grab bags to avid shell collectors. To the astonishment of everyone, Hidalgo's Murex has been turning up at the average rate of two in every bushel of dredgings.

West Africa, with its isolated and strange fauna, is the homeland of a huge horned murex resembling a spiked native war club—*Murex cornutus*, known to Europeans since the sixteenth century and finally given a scientific name by Linnaeus in 1758. It is characterized by a long, snoutlike siphonal canal and a turnip-shaped body whorl that is encircled with two rows of strong stout spines. A similar species, *Murex haustellum*, from the Philippines, lacks the spines and has a rosy-encircled mouth. It has been known for centuries among collectors as the Snipe's Head Murex. It is found on sandy mud bottoms, usually only in pairs, at depths of from twenty to forty feet.

Australia has a large number of murexes, most of them being of Indo-Pacific origin. Two of them are renowned for having extraordinary spines. In one, the Monodon Murex from western Australia, the three or four spines on each varix are curved in a circle, sometimes bending back and touching the main part of the body whorl. It is an uncommon species, found lurking under rock ledges in fairly shallow water. Rarely, the color is a solid black or a solid white. The second unique Australian species is the Two-Forked Murex, *M. cervicornis*, whose delicate spines are forked at the ends in the manner of a serpent's tongue.

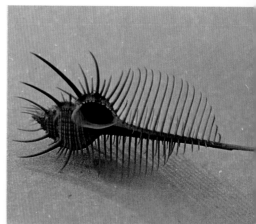

LEFT: Top view of an
undescribed species of
Latiaxis from off Taiwan. × 4.
TOP RIGHT: Venus Comb Murex,
Murex pecten Lightfoot.
BOTTOM RIGHT: *Murex
acanthostephes* Watson, of
Australia, elevates itself in
order to crawl forward. × 1.5.

Spider conchs

The most bizarre members of the family Strombidae are the *Lambis* spider conchs that are, biologically speaking, nothing but strombs with extra long, spiny protuberances on the outer lip. The soft parts are practically the same as those of other conchs. Like the strombs, they have most unusual eyes, resembling colorful round agates set at the very end of long tubular tentacles. Many species have characteristic eyes, some with red circles, others orange and a few multicolored. Typically claw-shaped, the operculum is attached to a narrow, powerful, muscular foot that pole-vaults the animal forward. The spider conchs look somewhat threatening with their curved spines, but the fact is that all members of the family are herbivorous.

The nine known species of *Lambis* run the gamut of shapes and colors. The most difficult to obtain is the Violet Spider Conch, known to Europeans in the 1700s but not described until 1821 by the English conchologist William Swainson. The lovely lavender interior and dozen somewhat flattened, yellowish spines make this a truly beautiful shell. The majority of known specimens have come from waters near Mauritius, mainly from the Cargados Carajos shoals. Sir David Barclay, a collector living on Mauritius during Queen Victoria's reign, sent back quite a number of specimens, but its relative rarity continued until about 1960.

Curiously, two of the rarest spider conchs come from the very eastern end of Polynesia. One, Pilsbry's Spider Conch, from the Marquesas Islands, is a very long spined subspecies of the widespread Orange Spider Conch. Some specimens have curved prongs, six inches in length. Equally rare is the False Scorpio Conch, *Lambis robusta*, that was a lost species for almost a hundred years. Described by Swainson in 1821 only as coming from "the Pacific," it was confused with the common Scorpio Conch, *Lambis scorpius,* and for a while believed not to exist. After World War II, several specimens turned up from the reefs of Tahiti, and the mystery of this still uncommon shell was solved.

Most abundant of the lot is the Common Spider Conch that ranges from East Africa throughout the Indian and Pacific oceans to Japan and Micronesia. It is quite variable in coloration and in the nature of its spines. In some eastern localities, particularly the Palau Islands, a marked degree of sexual differentiation is exhibited in the shell. The smaller males have very short spines. The females have long ones, but they are curled upward in the region of the oviduct. This permits the male to get close enough to inject his sperm during the mating season.

Largest of the genus is the thirteen-inch Giant Spider Conch, *Lambis truncata*. The tip of the spire of this species is flat, or truncate. Young specimens, lacking the pronged outer lip of adults, resemble the shell of other families, such as the *Ficus* figshells. In fact, one paleontologist described the young as being a new species of *Pyrula*. The Giant Spider Conch ranges from the Red Sea to Polynesia. Like many other large members of the stromb family it is eaten by native peoples and, in some areas, it is considered an aphrodisiac.

OPPOSITE: Spider Conchs of the genus *Lambis,* all from the Indo-Pacific. Top row contains *Lambis lambis* (Linné), *Lambis crocata* (Link), *Lambis digitata* (Perry). Bottom row contains *Lambis scorpius* (Linné), *Lambis violacea* (Swainson), *Lambis chiragra* (Linné).

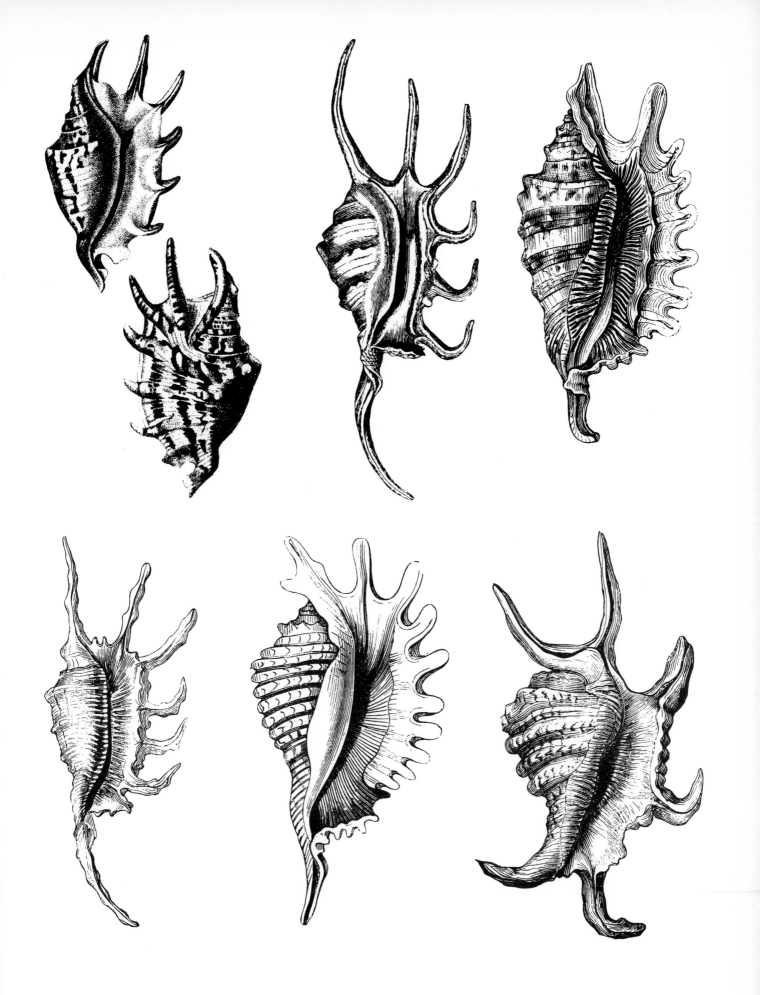

Strombus conchs

The word *conch,* of Greek origin, was adopted by the Romans to mean any large marine univalve. The study of mollusks is called *conchology,* and the romance languages use forms of this word to mean "shells," such as the Italian word *conchiglie* and the Spanish word *conchas.* To the English and Americans, the word *conch* is a generic term for any large marine snail shell, whether it be a *Busycon* whelk, a *Charonia* Triton's Trumpet or a *Cassis* helmet shell from the West Indies. In the Bahamas, the word *conch* refers to the edible Pink Conch, known scientifically as *Strombus gigas.* Today, at least among most conchologists, a conch is a member of the family Strombidae.

The Pink Conch of the West Indies, Bermuda and Florida was brought back to Europe, if not by the crew members of Christopher Columbus's ships, then certainly soon afterwards. Woodcuts of it appear as early as the sixteenth century. Throughout the Bahamas, it became a major source of protein for the early European colonists and their slaves. The huge attractive shell soon found its way back to England in large quantities during the Victorian era. Hardly a cottage doorstep was without a Pink Conch, and many fancy estates had shell grottos with fountains and dozens of conchs. Cameos were cut from the thicker portions of the shell, and pink pearls from the animal became popular as gems.

The four genera living today are the slim little *Terebellum,* the long regal *Tibia,* the true *Strombus* and the closely related spider conchs of the Indo-Pacific, *Lambis. Terebellum* is represented by a single species from the Indo-Pacific. Its slim, glossy shell is renowned for its wide variety of color patterns, ranging from oblique brown stripes to rosy tan spots. There are only six known species of *Tibia,* or shinbone strombs, all of which come from south Asia. Commonest is the Arabian Tibia, a very heavy-shelled, chunky species with a short, stout siphonal canal and with weak prongs on the outer lip. It is locally abundant in fairly shallow water from the Red Sea to India. A rare form of it has a yellow aperture.

The best known of the collector's items among the *Tibia* is the true Shinbone Tibia, *T. fusus,* which has an extraordinarily long siphonal canal. Eleven-inch specimens have a five-inch siphon. The outer lip has five or six short, delicate prongs. Known to early naturalists, the Shinbone usually brought about $100 at early auctions. Today they are more plentiful in collections, since Philippine and Taiwan fishermen now not infrequently bring them up in nets. Martin's Tibia, described in 1877, was extremely rare until the vessel *Albatross* of the United States Bureau of Fisheries dredged up thirty-five specimens in 1908. These shells remained unobtainable to private conchologists until about 1964 when Philippines fishermen found their deepwater habitat. Dealers now sell them at reasonable prices.

There are about fifty-two true *Strombus* conchs. Fortunately for collectors with modest pocketbooks, nearly all of them are common in nature and hence reasonable when purchased from a dealer. Most species live in the Indo-Pacific, the four most abundant being the Mutable, Gibbose, Plicate and Luhu conchs. The latter, also known as the Strawberry Conch, has a brilliant scarlet mouth accentuated by a jet black inner border. The strombs vary in size within the same species. Usually the males are much smaller. The smallest known species is the Maculated Conch of Polynesia, which varies from eight to twenty millimeters in length. Largest is the Goliath Conch of Brazil that reaches a length of fifteen inches.

Among today's rare conchs is the Wentletrap Conch, *Strombus scalariformis,* known from only one specimen. It was described in 1833 and has not been found since, perhaps because it is a freak. Among the most sought-after species are Bill Old's Conch from Somalia, the pretty Bull Conch from Micronesia and the handsome Thersite Conch from the South Pacific.

OPPOSITE, TOP LEFT: Original specimen of the Bull Conch, *Strombus taurus* Sowerby, that probably came from Admiralty Islands, South Pacific, about 1856. × 1. TOP RIGHT: Well-known Pink Conch, *Strombus gigas* Linné, from the West Indies. BOTTOM: A cautious Bahama Milk Conch, *Strombus costatus* Gmelin, peers out at the photographer. × 4.

Slit shells

The term *missing link* is misused in most popular accounts of evolution and biology. What it generally means is that for a very long time the average scientist has been aware that a certain family or genus of animals has been extinct for millions of years and that, suddenly, to everyone's surprise and to the dismay or delight of the expert, a living specimen has been discovered. It is not that people haven't looked in the right place before this, it is really a case of a monumental discovery—and is usually dubbed a "missing link" to make the public take note.

Nevertheless, the family Pleurotomariidae was well known by several hundred species of European fossils going back to the Upper Cambrian, practically to the dawn of the mollusks. It was an ancient stock of univalves that gave rise to the modern trochid and turban snails. It was extinct and long since laid to rest in geology textbooks. In the far away French West Indies in November of 1855, marine Commandant Beau obtained the first living representative of this family. It was a recently dead specimen brought by a hermit crab into a fisherman's pot set at a great depth between the islands of Marie-Galante and Dominica. Beau, who had already had many species named after him, sent the specimen to the leading French conchologists in Paris, Paul Fischer and A. Bernardi. They named

it *Pleurotomaria quoyana*. Needless to say, this discovery shook the conchological world.

The slit shells take their name from the deep, narrow slit that occurs naturally on the middle of the last whorl, behind the outer lip. The length of the slit and its exact position varies from one species to another. As the animal grows, it fills in the slit at the bottom, leaving a scar running around the middle of the previous whorls. The slit serves the important function of allowing waste water to be quickly expelled from the mantle cavity. Because the primitive slit shells have two plumelike gills rather than only one as do more highly evolved families, this rapid flushing is necessary.

The shells of the slit shells are simple and top shaped. The shell material is relatively thin. The exterior color is usually cream, reddish or brown, but the interior surface is a beautiful iridescent mother-of-pearl. Some species, belonging to the subgenus *Entemnotrochus*, have a very deep umbilical hole on the underside. There are fifteen known species living today, nine of which have been found in the Atlantic. There are four species in Japan. The most common is Hirase's Slit Shell, sometimes referred to as the Emperor's Top in honor of His Majesty, Emperor Hirohito, who is a trained marine biologist and ardent shell collector.

Largest of the slit shells is Rumphius's Slit Shell of eastern Asia that grows to a length of eight inches. It was named in 1879 in honor of the sixteenth-century Dutch naturalist who lived in Indonesia. For years it was known only from a rather colorless specimen residing in a public museum in Amsterdam. Today it is known from several dozen handsome, live-taken specimens from the straits lying between Taiwan and the mainland of China. Most of the slit shells may continue to be considered rare collector's items because of the difficulty in collecting them. They live on vertical cliffs or under overhangs at a depth ranging from about 180 to 350 feet. This puts them beyond the reach of the average scuba diver and certainly prevents them from being dredged. So far as is known, these vegetarians would not respond to baited traps.

The two most remarkable of the Atlantic species are Adanson's Slit Shell, a vividly painted species with a very long slit, and the King Midas Slit Shell, the latter being discovered as recently as 1965. It has a curiously "pushed-down" apex, giving the shoulders of the whorls a keeled, or carinate, appearance like the prow of a ship. Smallest of the species is the Jewel Slit Shell, *Pleurotomaria gemma*, a two-inch-long shell coming from Barbados.

OPPOSITE: The underside view of the rare Japanese slit shell, *Pleurotomaria beyrichii* Hilgendorf. X 2. ABOVE, LEFT: *Pleurotomaria africana* Tomlin, from off South Africa. RIGHT: *Pleurotomaria beyrichii* Hilgendorf. X 1.

Harp shells

For those who are newly exposed to shells, it is difficult to believe that the fabulously sculptured, brilliant harp shells, with their intricate color patterns and hard, sharp, glossy ribs are made by a soft-bodied animal. For those who have had the privilege of collecting a live specimen, the wonderment over this mollusk merely increases. The curious, arrow-shaped forefoot and the great long back foot, to say nothing of the mantle and siphon, are as bizarrely colored as the shell.

The harp shells of the Indo-Pacific have a very advanced form of carnivorous feeding. Normally, they plow through the sand or just at the surface of the bottom, invariably at night, in search of shrimps and crabs, dead or alive. The large box crab is, in its own way, a voracious feeder of mollusks. Should it come by a harp, it reaches out and grabs at the foot of the snail. The harp has

an autonomous segment of its foot which it can sacrifice, much in the same manner as does a salamander or chameleon. The crab finds that it has a dainty morsel to work upon. Meanwhile, the harp turns around and emits an enormous amount of mucus, at the same time shoveling up a mound of sand over the crab. In a few moments, the crab is helplessly enrolled in a compact ball of sand. Then the harp protrudes its proboscis down through the sand and shell of the crab and into the soft flesh of its victim. The strong radular teeth of the snail soon rasp out the vital muscles and organs of the crab. This is clearly a case in which the intended victim, the harp, has sacrificed a bit of himself as bait and turned his adversary into a meal.

The harp shells are an advanced family related to the volutes. During the early Tertiary period, 40 million years ago, they were fairly well represented

throughout most tropical seas of the world. In Recent times, geologically speaking, they have dwindled in numbers, so that today there are fewer than a dozen species. There are none living in the Caribbean or Mediterranean seas.

Most famous of the harps among connoisseur collectors is the Imperial Harp, *Harpa costata*, which has always brought high prices at auctions. Its value was enhanced by the mystery of its origin and by the fact that it stands unique among the harps for its golden yellow aperture and more than forty crowded ribs. It generally brought about $100 at auctions and maintained that price among private collectors until about 1940. Captain William Bligh, of H.M.S. *Bounty* fame, brought a specimen back from Mauritius in about 1810, thus establishing the correct provenance of this rare species. Despite the fact that numerous shell collectors in Mauritius

collect and export this glorious shell, it remains a difficult shell to acquire for one's collection, and, if anything, overcollecting will increase its scarcity and value in the years to come.

Rarer than the Imperial Harp, but not as attractive, are the small, slender *Harpa gracilis* from eastern Polynesia and the strange, deep-sea Punctate Harp from South Australia. The most abundant species, collected by the thousands in the Philippines, is the Common Pacific Harp, *Harpa harpa*. The most widely distributed is the common Minor Harp, a somewhat drab, two-inch-long species from the Indo-Pacific. Most unexpectedly, there is a large, daintily patterned species from the Gulf of California and the Pacific side of Central America, *Harpa crenata*, more popularly known as the Tortoise Harp. A similar species with a reddish cast, the Rosy Harp, lives along the west coast of Africa.

Vase shells

The family Turbinellidae that includes the vase and chank shells has less than thirty species, yet it has had a marked influence not only upon generations of ardent shell collectors but also upon millions of devout Hindus who consider one of the species sacred. Shells since the dawn of civilization have been entwined in superstitions and early religions. When the Indian god Vishnu set out to rescue the sacred writings that the devil had hidden in the sea, he found them in a left-handed specimen of *Turbinella pyrum*, the Sacred Chank of India.

This heavy, white, turnip-shaped chank is characterized by three strong, spiral ridges on the inner lip. Some specimens are marked with spiral rows of bluish gray spots. The species live abundantly in the region of southern India and Ceylon, where it is collected annually by the thousands of tons, sliced up into women's wrist bangles and sold to Indians. Left-handed, or sinistrally coiled, specimens are very rare, but several had reached Europe by the early 1700s. One of them, illustrated by Martini in 1770, is now on display in the zoological museum in Copenhagen. A second specimen was owned by the famous shell collector Margaret Bentinck, second duchess of Portland. Her specimen was sold at auction in 1786, and several hands later it became the property of a Boston collector, Mrs. Fiske-Warren. Just before her death she donated it to Harvard University. There are several dozen genuine left-handed chanks in private hands in India, but most of them are in temples. In Fiji and East Africa, where there are large Indian populations, left-handed Lightning Whelks of Florida are often circulated as sacred chanks.

There are only two other chanks living today, both being found in the western Atlantic. Largest of these is the West Indian Chank, a foot-long, heavy, yellowish shell covered with a thick brown outer periostracum. It ranges from Panama to Yucatan, Mexico, and is also found in the Bahamas and on the north shore of Cuba. It is possible that the two latter localities were seeded with specimens brought from Yucatan by Carib Indians or early European explorers. A second, smaller chank, the Brazilian Chank, is found only in northeast Brazil. Chanks lay chains of large, circular, leathery egg capsules. When the young hatch, they are quite large and are unable to swim to new territories as can some other mollusks with free-swimming veliger stages.

The most spectacular member of the family is Flinder's Vase, a large, pastel pink, spiny shell dredged off the coast of South Australia. It was first discovered by the intrepid Australian collector Sir Joseph Verco, who used his own yacht to dredge for shells. It remained a rare shell until several specimens came up in fish pots off western Australia during the 1950s. A similar, smaller, and not uncommon, species, also a member of the subgenus *Altivasum*, comes from the West Indies. This two-inch-long, brownish shell is known as the Spiny Caribbean Vase.

Two strange vases turned up in western Atlantic waters in rather recent times. The first was Nutting's Vase, a curious ball-shaped shell with a pinkish brown mouth. It is found only in the Lesser Antilles, West Indies, and is common in an extremely limited area. In contrast to its globular shape, the other new species, described by Harald Rehder and me in 1952, has a very elongate shape, a narrow aperture and a rather long siphonal canal. Because it had more the shape of a *Fusinus* or *Latirus*, we

named it the Latirus-shaped Vase. It is only two inches in length, bright peach in color and a deep-water inhabitant of the Gulf of Mexico. I have had the privilege of naming two other new vases, one being the Zanzibar Tudicula, with a peach aperture and long black spines on the whorl, and the Polished-mouth Tudicula, a charming and uncommon shell that is found off the coast of Queensland, Australia.

Rarest of all the vase shells is *Vasum crosseanum*, described from the Seychelles Islands in the Indian Ocean in 1875. Only two or three have been found, and someday some lucky collector will discover their optimum habitat. The Zanzibar Vase, known from only six specimens, was originally collected in 1957 by Alfred J. Ostheimer III, a wealthy private collector from Philadelphia and Hawaii. The most abundant vase is the well-known Common Pacific Vase that lives in shallow waters from Africa to Polynesia. It is a chunky, top-shaped shell with strong spines on the shoulder, and it is well represented in most private collections.

ABOVE: Second known specimen of Crosse's Vase, *Vasum crosseanum* Souverbie, collected in the Seychelles, Indian Ocean; now in the National Museum of Wales. × 2.

Thorny oysters

Second only to the true scallops to which they are related, the *Spondylus* thorny oysters have attracted collectors of showy bivalves. They have appealed more for their unusual flowerlike beauty than for their interest as conchological items, mainly because of the infinite variations and the constant confusion as to what constitutes a species in this group. Estimates of the number of different living species run from a dozen to a hundred. Members of this genus are readily identifiable by their peculiar ball-and-socket type of hinge, a characteristic absent in the similarly ornamented *Chama*.

About four or five species are readily recognizable, the most showy of which is *Spondylus americanus* that reaches its climax of growth and beauty in Florida waters at depths of 100 to 150 feet. These six-inch-long delicately spined bivalves are appropriately called chrysanthemum shells. In color they vary from snowy white, yellow, pink and purple to lovely mottled and red-speckled combinations of these shades. Curiously, these outer colors are not visible when the shell is living because the entire outer shell is covered with a heavy growth of sponges, algae and other marine creatures. Scuba divers collecting these shells look for the colorful mantle curtain within. The orange and white flesh is quite vivid on a wall of coralline and algal growths. Touch a live *Spondylus* and it will snap shut and disappear from view. This species used to bring about $100 for a large and perfect specimen, but recent scuba collecting methods resulting in many more shells being made available have reduced its value considerably.

An equally beautiful species, *Spondylus princeps*, lives in the Pacific waters of Central America. It differs in having broader and stouter spines that lie flatter against the main shell. It is unique in having among its various color phases a solid brick-red form. Although this is a moderately common species, it can be collected only by diving for it. The third most distinctive species is Wright's Spondylus from the tropical waters of Australia. It has probably the longest spines of any thorny oyster, although the central part of the valves is relatively small. The shell is usually white in color, and the long spines few in number.

Best known of the thorny oysters is the "Regal Spondyle," as it was called by early European collectors who prized it highly. It is said that the duke of Orleans paid the equivalent of about $200, sometime before 1698, for a specimen. It turned up for auction on several occasions, usually bringing large sums. The French conchologist and physician J. C. Chenu relates a tale concerning the well-known botanist and shell collector Louis Richard, who could not resist the spell of an unusually fine specimen that was up for sale at a price far beyond his means. Richard contrived to exchange some of his wife's best silver plate for the specimen. He replaced it with tin substitutes, but while he was away making the trade, his wife discovered the deception and gave him a furious reception upon his return. She berated him so severely that the poor man accidentally sat on the specimen, breaking off two of the spines. He became so melancholy over this horrifying turn of events that the good Madame Richard ceased to complain and, instead, attempted to console him.

The Regal Spondylus was well-enough known to have been first described in 1758 by Linnaeus. The shell is characterized by six or seven main rows of sparsely spaced long reddish spines. Between the rows, the shell surface is finely sculptured with numerous very fine radial lines of microscopic prickles. It is a deepwater species of the tropical waters of the southwest Pacific. Early specimens were probably brought up accidentally with rocks entangled in ships' anchors.

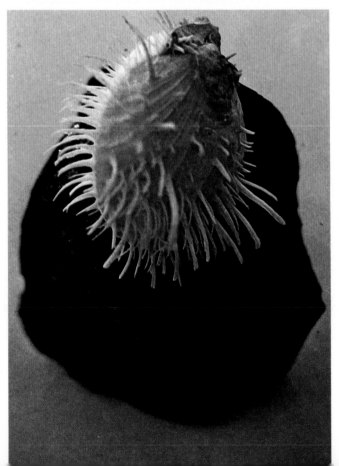

ABOVE: Two handsome specimens of *Spondylus americanus* Hermann, collected at 100 feet off east Florida. Both have been cleaned of marine growths. LEFT: A specimen recently collected in a marine cave on Cozumel Island, Mexico, and now mounted on a piece of glass slag. × 0.5.

Scallop shells

For several curious reasons the bivalves have never appealed to shell collectors to the extent that the univalves have entranced the acquisitive type of conchologist. Perhaps part of the reason is that bivalves come in two pieces, which makes collecting good specimens and displaying them more bothersome. Also, there are relatively few families of bivalves that can be considered beautiful or that are unusually interesting in sculpture, shape or color patterns. A third possible reason lies in the fact that the study of the bivalves has been neglected and that there are not many comprehensive monographs or books that can help the amateur to identify his specimens.

One of the great exceptions to the rule that bivalves are unpopular among collectors is the regal and aristocratic family of scallops. This family has received the accolades of gourmets for centuries, has been used as inspiration by artists, architects and sculptors for thousands of years and has truly stood among the most favored of shell collectors' trophies. The Lion's Paw of Florida, with its gorgeous colors and entrancing gnarled sculpturing, has out-

shone the reputation of the most handsome of volutes, vases and cones. Even the common Bay Scallop of Massachusetts has a prominent place in the showcases of many private collections, for one could look far to find more brilliant orange, yellow and red variations than are found in this common species.

Scallops are not only renowned because of their cheerful colors and delicate sculpturing, but they are popular because they show a very wide range in general shapes and types. There are about 400 living species, and scientists have been attempting to classify them, somewhat unsuccessfully, into various generic groups. There are flat scallops; there are fat ones. There are strongly ribbed scallops; there are smooth ones. There are glassy, transparent scallops; there are richly colored opaque ones. The varieties of scallops are legion. It would take a lifetime for a man to accumulate a good, representative collection of this remarkable family.

The moon scallops are a primitive group, represented by about a dozen worldwide species and characterized by their extremely smooth, almost

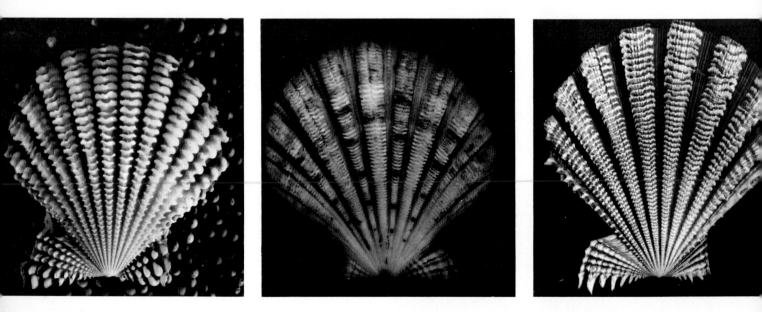

flat and almost circular shells. They are so flat that the muscle holding the valves together is of little commercial food value. The best known of this group was the Asian Moon, *Amusium pleuronectes,* described and illustrated numerous times in eighteenth-century literature. A close relative of it, Ballot's Scallop, comes from Australia. Generally, the lower valve is white or cream and the upper valve colored. There are two American representatives of this group that are occasionally brought up in shrimp nets from a depth of several fathoms— Laurent's Moon Scallop and the Paper Moon Scallop, both fairly common in the Gulf of Mexico and Caribbean.

The true *Pecten* scallops are characterized by a very deep, dishlike lower valve and a much flattened upper valve. The well-known Jacob's Scallop from Europe is a member of this group. So, too, is the edible Zigzag Scallop of Bermuda, Florida and the West Indies. The only representative on the Pacific coast of the United States is the San Diego Scallop, *Pecten diegensis,* a rather uncommon shell. In Japan, the remarkable Puncticulate Scallop has a very deep lower valve and a concave upper valve. Like other members of *Pecten,* it has typical radiating, strong ribs on both valves. These scallops are free-swimmers.

Among the nonswimming scallops are the *Chlamys* type, in which both valves are about the same thickness but one of the "ears," or projections on the hinge end, has been reduced to almost nothing. These scallops, such as the Sentis of Florida and the Imbricate of the Caribbean, spend most of their lives under boulders, attached to the bottom by means of a byssus.

The most bizarre of the scallop family is the Giant Rock Scallop of California, *Hinnites.* In its early life, when it is less than an inch in size, it looks and acts like a typical *Chlamys* scallop. But soon it begins to transform in shape and size, as if it were the Dr. Jekyll and Mr. Hyde of the bivalve world. It anchors itself to the bottom and grows into a monstrous, heavy, crude, oysterlike bivalve. Only by carefully examining an adult in the region of the hinge can one discern the early scalloplike nature of this rock-clinging scallop.

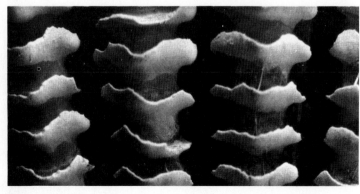

LEFT to RIGHT: Scallops from the central Pacific—*Gloripallium pallium* (Linné), *Excellichlamys spectabilis* (Reeve), *Gloripallium spiniferum* (Sowerby), *Chlamys coruscans* (Hinds), all × 1, and a magnified view of the rib scales. × 8.

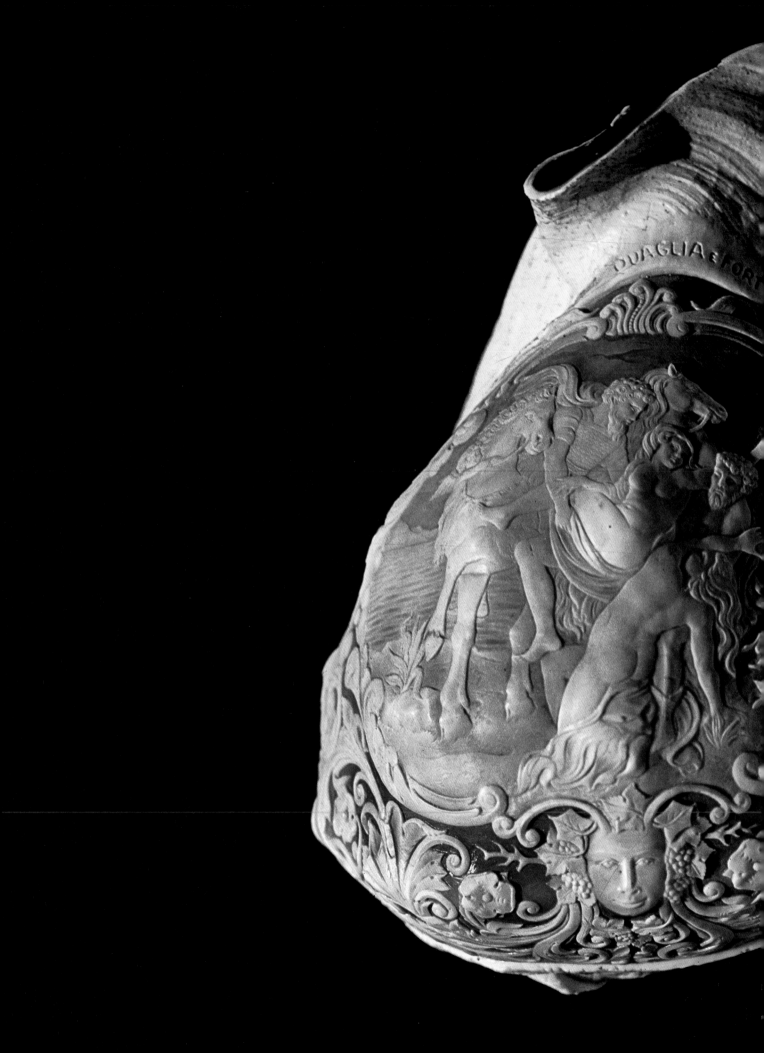

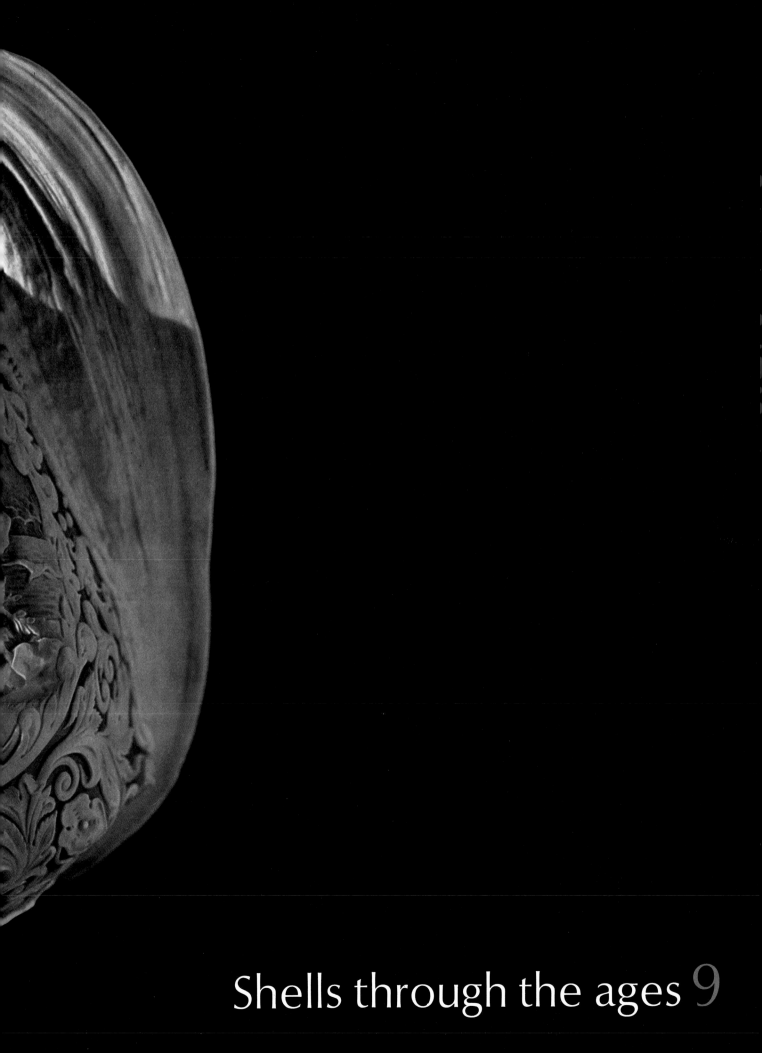

Shells and primitive man

As he was just beginning to learn the use of tools and weapons and scarcely experienced in the use of fire, it was natural for prehistoric man to have become familiar with such simple and readily available forms of food as snails, oysters and clams. He undoubtedly admired and collected colorful objects, such as minerals, feathers and shells. From the excavations of Neolithic man and his grave sites, it is obvious that he used mollusks as food when they were available. Kitchen middens throughout all continents, including the more recent North American sites, contain vast quantities of oyster, clam and univalve shells, the latter showing signs of having been roasted or boiled.

Large univalve shells were used as pots and ladles. Among people living in areas where hard stone and metal were unavailable, such as Barbados and the low coral islands of the South Pacific, large pieces of shells were used as scrapers, hoe blades and arrowheads. In areas where clay was not available nor the art of pottery manufacture mastered, large shells, such as the giant clams and cut helmet shells, were used as food receptacles.

One of man's ancient uses of shells was as trumpets or horns. Throughout the Mediterranean area, many centuries before Christ, the large marine triton shell *Charonia nodifera*, was commonly used as a horn for religious and for nautical purposes. In the Neolithic caves of Liguria Triton's Trumpets have been unearthed that have had their tops ground off, presumably so that they could be blown. The early Minoan culture of Crete produced clay seals, having representations of triton shells, that were evidently used in their religious ceremonies. One of these seals depicts a woman sounding the shell of a triton before the sacred altar. The Greek god Triton, who was one of Neptune's trumpeters, has been depicted with a large conch shell in his hand with which he convened the river deities around their monarch. The coins of Agrigentum, Sicily, (before 406 B.C.) show Triton holding and blowing into a large conch.

Shells other than the tritons were used by primitive peoples. In Borneo the large helmet shell *Cassis cornuta* was used for calling buffaloes. Large *Bursa* frog shells and tritons were used as horns by the natives of Papua and New Guinea. In this area, the piercing of the trumpet shell was done on the side of one of the upper whorls. In eastern Asia and Japan, the apex of the shell was ground off and sometimes a metal mouthpiece added at the tip end. There the blowing of the conch was used for calling to arms, for frightening away evil spirits and for the ritual of initiation in sacred rites. In Fiji and the New Hebrides, the conch shell was blown in connection with sacred drinking ceremonies. In Tonga, they were blown only at the funerals of chiefs, while in the Society Islands, they were blown when warriors marched to battle or when processions were made to temples.

PRECEDING PAGES: Cameo carved in Florence, Italy, from the West Indian Emperor Helmet, *Cassis madagascariensis* Lamarck. ABOVE: British Columbian Indian blanket decorated with bits of freshwater pearly clams.

ABOVE: Mayan figures carved in olive shells.
BELOW: California *Tivela* clam and abalone,
sources of Indian shell beads. RIGHT: A Triton's
Trumpet, commonly used in the Pacific as a bugle.

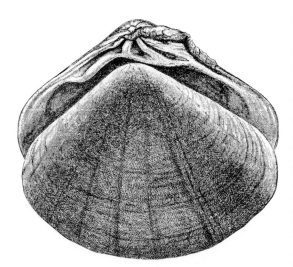

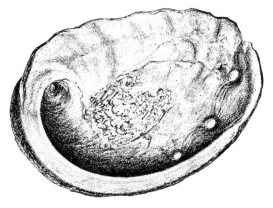

Even in the New World, trumpets made of shells were used extensively. The Indians of Peru blew a *Strombus* conch, ornamented with locks of human hair and leather straps of exquisite workmanship, to announce the arrival of important visitors. The Portuguese writer Suarez de Sousa reported, in 1589, the use of a very large conch in Brazil as a trumpet shell. It was undoubtedly the well-known, endemic Goliath Conch. In the ruins of the Hopi settlements in Casa Grande, in southern Arizona, large conchs, with their apical ends ground off and perforated for blowing, were commonly excavated at the turn of this century. In some areas of central Mexico, Aztec ruins have revealed a combination of Pacific and Atlantic species. These prehistoric sites have brought forth both the West Indian Chank, *Turbinella angulata,* and the Eastern Pacific Horse Conch, *Pleuroploca gigantea,* from the same graves, indicating that Aztec trade was carried on with both coasts. When the Spanish explorer De Soto made his way through the wilds of Florida in 1539, the Chickasaw Indians were aroused to action by horns made from *Busycon, Strombus* and *Cassis* shells.

Conservation was something practiced by even primitive peoples, one classic example having been carried out by the Central American Indians on the west coast, from Nicaragua and Costa Rica to Panama. During the sixteenth and seventeenth centuries, before the influence of the white man, the coastal Indians of that region produced a superior cloth woven from agave fiber and dyed a deep rich purple color that they obtained from the seashell *Purpura patula.* The Indians had produced the dyed cloth long before the advent of the Spaniards, perhaps, as some ethnologists claim, under the direction of wandering Phoenicians who were well versed in this then-important industry. By 1648, according to the early traveler Thomas Gage, the Indians were producing purple-dyed cloth in Salinas and Nicoya, both in Costa Rica, for export to the wealthy classes of Spain.

With the increased demand for this molluscan purple dye, the Indians began to practice conservation. Instead of dumping the snails into a cauldron and crushing them in order to extract the dye—the method used by the Phoenicians—the Indians learned that if they plucked the snail off the rocks and gently blew upon the animal, it would exude its dye in the form of a viscous liquid, which was collected in a calabash gourd bowl. The snail was then returned to the same place on the rocks, and the Indians would paddle off in their canoes, continuing their milking operations as they went. On the return trip, the Indians would again milk the snails, obtaining more of the dye from each rested individual. During this canoe voyage, the women passengers would draw the agave threads through the precious mucus liquid, one by one. When the threads were laid in the sun to dry, the color would begin to change from yellow to blue and then to a rich magenta.

Purple-dyed yarns have been found in pre-Columbian textiles in Mexico and Peru. Ancient codex paintings of Mexico are illustrated in this purple dye, showing women of rank in purple skirts and numerous chieftains with fringed waistcloths and capes of purple.

Since earliest time, man has admired and used mother-of-pearl and pearls as symbols of purity, beauty and nobility. Marine pearl shells have been found in the earliest Egyptian graves, usually in the form of bracelets and pendants. Freshwater pearly mussels were used by almost all early tribes in Egypt and Greece, by the early Britons and extensively by the prehistoric Indians of North America. The custom of using iridescent shells has continued throughout the ages, perhaps reaching its climax during the Victorian era when inlaid boxes, lamp shades and room screens were in vogue.

Pearl shells were cut into sharp, hooked pieces and used for catching fish by most of the Polynesian and Melanesian tribes. Usually these hooks were adorned with feathers, much like our modern fish lures. When used for fishing octopus, the pearl hook was surmounted with a Tiger Cowrie to attract the creature. The New Zealand Maoris used pieces of the iridescent paua, or Iris Abalone, as a substitute for the flashing nacre of the pearl oyster. Pearl shells were used extensively as breast ornaments by many Melanesian islanders and are still made by the natives of the British Solomon Islands. The prehistoric mound builders of the areas now known as Ohio and Indiana made beads from the pearly freshwater mussels of the Mississippi and Ohio rivers.

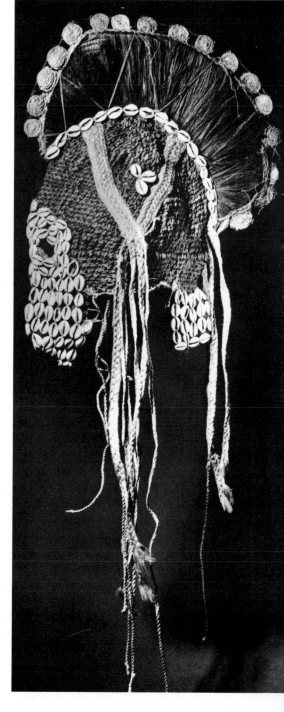

TOP: Native dancers of central Africa adorn themselves with belts
of cowries. RIGHT: Headdress of Mali witch doctor has money cowrie,
Cypraea moneta Linné, from the Indian Ocean. ABOVE: Prehistoric
Mediterranean urn is decorated with likeness of an octopus.

Shells as money

Evidence from the burial sites of prehistoric man indicates that the first good-luck charms and the earliest forms of currency were cowrie shells. Evidently, minerals, glass and metallic objects came into similar use soon after or possibly about the same time. The most extensively used species were the Money Cowrie, *Cypraea moneta*, and the Gold-Ring Cowrie, *C. annulus,* also referred to as a money cowrie. Their small, uniform size, the beauty of their shape and glossy enamel finish and their abundance rendered them ideal as objects of exchange. They could be easily cleaned at their source and used in their natural state.

The term *cowrie* is derived from a Greek word meaning "little pig," a name undoubtedly chosen because many kinds of cowries resemble a pig's back. The Romans called them *porci* or *porculi*, from which the word *porcelain* is derived. It is believed that cowries were used as money in China as early as 2000 B.C. and that this monetary use lasted until about 600 B.C., when the first metal coins, shaped like small cowries or beans, were introduced.

Money cowries live abundantly in many parts of the Indo-Pacific region. The leading sources were East Africa, especially Mozambique, Kenya and Zanzibar, the Maldive Islands south of India, the Philippines and Malaya. The very earliest graves found in Egypt, dating long before the building of the pyramids, contained numerous species of cowries. The largest ones were perforated near the end and probably used as pendants. The Gold-Ring Cowrie was found in large numbers in a grave at Abydos, a predynastic Egyptian settlement. Similar caches have been found in prehistoric cemeteries on the northern slopes of the Caucasus Mountains near the Caspian Sea, in western and northern Germany and in pagan burial urns of Lithuania.

In some of the interior parts of Africa, particularly in Uganda, cowries were extensively used as money as late as the nineteenth century. The standard of currency among the Baganda tribe was set by the value of the cow, which sold for 2,500 cowrie shells. A goat was worth 500; a chicken, 25; an ivory tusk weighing sixty-two pounds, 1,000; and a tobacco pipe, from 50 to 100 shells. Drumsticks made from human arm bones were ornamented with them. In the Congo and Lake Tanganyika regions, *Cypraea moneta* was used extensively during the time of Livingstone's and Stanley's visits (1871–1876). The Hottentots used the shells for ornaments.

The farther a people lived from the natural source of the money cowrie, the more extensively it was used and valued. The chief area of circulation was in the western Sudan and on the Atlantic coast of Guinea, where both the Money Cowrie and the Gold-Ring Cowrie did not live. In the seventeenth and eighteenth centuries, cowries were commonly used in the slave trade.

Prior to the time of Alexander the Great, money cowries were used extensively as currency throughout various parts of India, particularly in Bengal where they were exchanged for rice from the Maldive Islands. In 1740, the Indian rupee exchanged for

2,400 cowries; in 1756, for 2,560 cowries and in 1845, for 6,500 cowries. Shells were brought into Dacca by the boatload, usually fifty tons per boat. In the early 1800s, a gentleman in Cuttack paid several million in cowries for the construction of his bungalow. *Cypraea moneta* was also used as small-change currency in Thailand and Burma in the middle of the eighteenth century.

The British used these cowries for the barter of goods with the blacks of western Africa. In 1848, 60 tons and, in 1849, 300 tons were brought to the port of Liverpool from the East Indies for redistribution to the Guinea coast. Cowries were being imported into England as late as 1873. In that year, a four-masted bark, the *Glendowra,* homeward bound from Manila with a cargo of 600 bags of money cowries, went aground in the fog near Seascale, along the coast of Cumberland. For many years these shells could be picked up in good condition on the English beaches.

In the Melanesian islands, particularly the Solomons, where money cowries are very common, other shells were used for money. Round disks, three to five inches across, with holes in the centers were carved from the Giant Tridacna Clam. Even to this day in Malaita, women from Langa Langa lagoon manufacture money from the *Chama* bivalves that their men gather. Small, pierced beads, resembling the wampum of the northeastern American Indians, are strung into bridal belts, each worth from $20 to $100 in 1971. Red beads are worth ten times the value of the white ones.

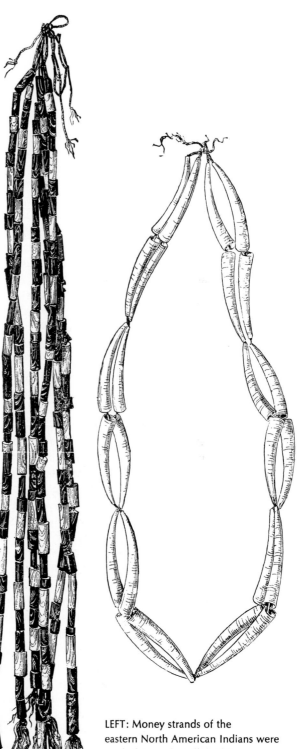

LEFT: Money strands of the eastern North American Indians were made from columellae of *Busycon* whelks. RIGHT: Northwestern Indians used *Dentalium* tusk shells.

179

North American shell money

When Europeans first came to the shores of North America, they found that the Indians of both the Pacific and the Atlantic coasts used shells as money. Excavations of prehistoric sites throughout the United States indicate that both freshwater and marine shells had also been long in use as good-luck charms, religious symbols and ornaments. Although early trade routes in the southwestern part of the United States brought shells together from both the Gulf of Mexico and the Gulf of California, there apparently was nothing in common between the shell currency of the Pacific and the Atlantic.

Wampum was made by the Indian tribes living along the coast stretching from New England to Virginia. The black wampum came from the small purple section of the Hard-shelled Clam, or quahog, *Mercenaria mercenaria*. A common inshore species living in shallow water, this was, next to oysters, the most popular seafood among the Indians as well as the Europeans. The beads, usually one-third inch in diameter, one-eighth inch in length, were drilled through the center so that they could be strung. The white wampum, worth two or three times less than the black, was usually made from the whelk *Busycon*, generally from the thicker parts of the central column, or columella. Sometimes these beads were larger and of a cylindrical shape, about a half-inch in length, but of the same diameter as the black wampum.

The Indians first used wampum as ornaments and, in the form of long, wide belts, to record treaties, declarations and important transactions between various Indian nations. The wampum was dyed various colors and shades so that very intricate designs and patterns could be woven into these wampum belts. Soon after the coming of white man, wampum was used as currency, together with beaver skins, musket balls and coins. Early colonists also used wampum as currency, a six-foot strand being worth about five shillings. In the early 1700s, it could even be used on the Brooklyn ferry as fare.

Two enterprising Scotchmen then set up a wampum factory in northern New Jersey, which flourished for several years. However, wampum was finally outlawed as a form of currency when the market became flooded with counterfeits in the early 1800s.

The Indians of the northwest United States, British Columbia and Alaska used the tusk shell, *Dentalium*, as a form of currency before the coming of the Russians and English. The center of fisheries for these white, two-inch-long, hollow tusks was in Puget Sound, where the Indians fished them by jabbing special multipronged clumps of sticks into the ocean bottom, impaling the mud-dwelling *Dentalium* upon them in the process. The tusks were used for ornaments and placed, as a decoration, in a hole pierced through the nose. *Hi-qua*, as it was called, was strung end to end in strands of about six feet in length. The longer the individual shells, the greater the value. The strands were used to buy slaves, canoes and squaws. After Hudson's Bay Company's introduction of blankets as a medium of exchange, *hi-qua* gradually lost its use. Toward the middle of the 1800s, European specimens of the more common *Dentalium entale* were brought in by Europeans, further undermining the value of this form of currency. In northern California, a six-foot-long strand of *hi-qua* called *allicochick* was originally worth about fifty dollars in gold.

Shell money was used to some extent by the interior tribes, but it originated among the coastal nations. Shell buttons from both the *Glycymeris* and abalone snails came from the Gulf of California, and strands of *Olivella biplicata*, a glossy, purple snail shell, came from the sand flats of the West coast. In the late eighteenth century, the Hudson's Bay Company brought quantities of money cowries into northern Canada. Although they were never very popular, thousands of them made their way south, from tribe to tribe, and some of this shell money has been recently unearthed from some midwestern Indian burial sites.

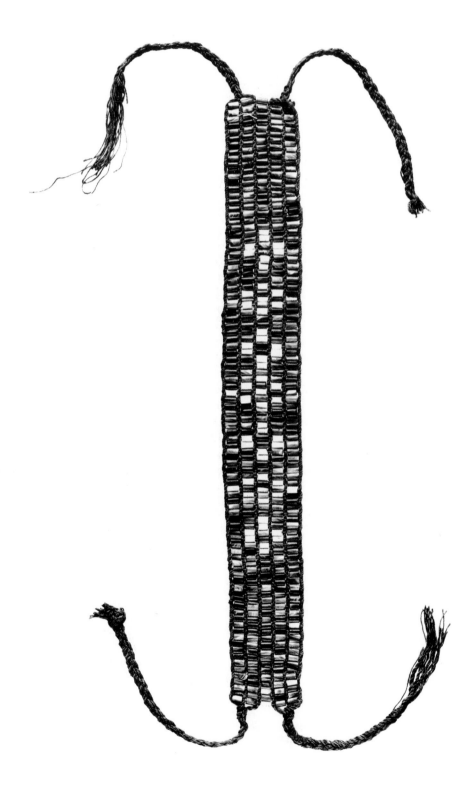

Wampum belts, such as this Iroquois piece, were made of shell beads
from *Mercenaria* clams and *Busycon* whelks. Some beads were dyed. The belts
were used in sealing bargains and recording treaties.

Royal tyrian purple

The most famous and influential of dyes produced by the ancients was a purple coloring obtained from members of the murex family. Although the dye was probably known to and used by Neolithic man, the earliest evidence of its use points to the Mediterranean island of Crete at least as early as 1600 B.C. Almost every shell collector who has collected live *Purpura* or *Nucella* rock shells has noted that the mucous juices from the snails stain the cloth collecting bags and fingers a deep magenta purple. Early man could not have overlooked this fact. The legendary story of the dye's being discovered by a Greek shepherd whose dog had stained its mouth when breaking a shell on the seashore is probably apocryphal.

The earliest authentic accounts of the preparation of the dye were given by Aristotle and later by Pliny. There were two species of *Murex* and one *Thais* used in the Mediterranean by the Minoans and later by the Phoenicians, who perfected the manufacture of the dye and maintained a monopoly for several centuries from about 300 B.C. to A.D. 150. Pliny's description is quite accurate in view of what is known today about the physiology of the snail and the properties of this organic dye. The liquid was obtained from a transparent branching vessel (the hypobranchial gland on the roof of the mantle) behind the neck of the animal. At first the liquid was the color and consistency of thick cream (it is a yellowish mucous fluid that, in the presence of direct sunlight, gradually—in a matter of ten minutes—turns to greenish, then bluish and finally purple red). Small shells were crushed in rock mortars, while larger shells were broken with a cleaver, in order to extract the entire soft parts. The slimy bodies were steeped in salted water for three days and then set to boil in vessels of tin or lead. Skeins of wool or cotton threads were continuously dipped into the fluid over a period of five hours and later dried and carded. Redipping produced darker shades.

Evidently the Phoenicians of Tyre and Sidon (now in Lebanon) used two different dye baths, one made from the juices of *Murex brandaris,* the other from *Thais haemastoma.* Their dyed wool was very highly esteemed, and during the reign of the Roman Augustus, a pound of dyed wool sold for 1,000 denarii, a sum now roughly calculated to equal $150. The dye itself was very costly, since it took many thousands of hours to collect the shells, each of which

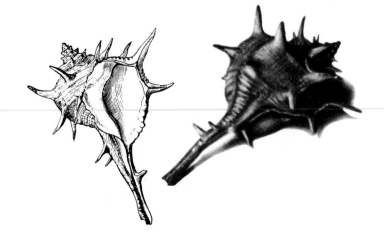

yields just a few drops. For fifty pounds of wool, the ancients used no less than 300 pounds of liquid dye.

The dye was very fast and did not fade for many years. When Alexander the Great took possession of Susa, he discovered among the treasures of Darius over 5,000 pounds of purple cloth still bright and fresh after 180 years of storage. Some museums today possess mummy wrappings dyed with molluscan purple that still show strong coloration after thousands of years.

Tyrian purple cloth was always considered an article of luxury and was usually reserved for the hangings of temples, the robes of priests or the garb of princes and kings. Purple cloth is mentioned several times in the Old Testament. Earlier, the Babylonians used it to dress their idols. The Romans used it extensively, and during the reign of Nero, it was reserved, on pain of death, for only the emperor himself. Later, with the advent of the Christian era, purple coloring, usually from other sources, was used in the church for bishops' robes and altar drapes. The most extravagant use of it was made by

Antony and Cleopatra in the battle of Actium, in which their ship was distinguished by having all sails colored in royal tyrian purple.

The Phoenicians spread out well beyond the Mediterranean in search of new beds of murex shells. They circumnavigated Africa and got as far as the British Isles. Archaeological digs have uncovered huge mounds of murex shells that were used in giant dyeworks in over thirty centers throughout the Mediterranean.

Mounds found in Ireland, dating back to 1000 B.C., contain enormous numbers of *Nucella lapillus,* a snail used as a source of purple dye as late as the nineteenth century in England and Scotland. The Phoenicians are recorded to have obtained a "black purple" from the British Isles, which historians believe must have come from *Nucella.* The dye from this source was used to paint illuminated manuscripts, long before the advent of printing. In northeast Europe, and later to a limited extent in New England, *Nucella* was used as a convenient, cheap and effective way to mark laundry.

OPPOSITE: The common Mediterranean snail, *Murex brandaris* Linné, was the main source of royal tyrian purple dye during ancient times.
ABOVE: The sails of royal Egyptian ships were dyed purple.

Pinna and the Golden Fleece

The pen shells of the bivalve genus *Pinna* were well known to the ancients of the Mediterranean world not only as a source of a very rare golden silk but also as a prime example of commensalism among marine creatures. Aristotle's studies included an investigation of the small, pea-sized crab that lives inside the mantle cavity of the pen shell.

There are about seventeen living species of *Pinna* pen shells, ranging from the extremely thin and narrow Incurved Pen of the East Indies to the heavily frilled, husky, two-foot-long Noble Pen of Mediterranean fame. Because of their shape, they are sometimes called fan shells or wing shells. The pen shell lives with its narrow end deeply buried in the sandy bottom. In order to prevent currents and underwater swells from uprooting it, the pen shell has developed an enormous tuft of silklike byssus filaments that anchor the clam safely to the bottom. Buried as it is, with the sandy or gravel bottom covering most of the shell, the bivalve is constantly being bombarded by foreign objects that could clog its gills or actually fill up its shell. To cope with this, the clam has a long fingerlike organ that it can manipulate to shove bits of broken shell and gravel out into the open. Finer sand is driven out along two fleshy gutters well endowed with flagellating cilia that set up strong currents.

Nearly all species of *Pinna* have small crabs or shrimp living inside the mantle cavity. Usually there is only a pair per bivalve. The ancients were familiar with the commensal association of the *Pinnotheres* crab and the Noble Pen of the Mediterranean, but they fancied that the very small, soft crab that sought protection within the *Pinna*'s shell served as a food gatherer and a lookout. They believed that when the crab returned from a foray, it would tap on the shell with its claw so that the bivalve would open and let it in. They also thought that the crab would warn its bivalve host of the approach of enemies. Modern biologists have found, though, that the crab rarely, if ever, leaves the mantle cavity and that the *Pinna* receives no benefits from this association.

The byssus of the Noble Pen was used by the ancients and by Sicilians as late as the nineteenth century in the manufacture of specialty clothing items, such as gloves, stockings, caps and collars. The threads, spun by the foot of the *Pinna*, are fine, strong and of a deep, bronze gold color. Fishermen gathered the pen shells by using long-handled tongs, sometimes twenty feet in length. The byssal tufts were washed in soap and water, dried in the shade, combed and finally carded. A pound of byssus would produce only three ounces of high-grade threads. In 1754, a pair of sea-silk stockings was presented to Pope Benedict XV. Queen Victoria is said to have worn a pair made in Taranto, Italy. Some historians have suggested that the Golden Fleece, sought by the legendary Greek Jason, was a piece of cloth made from *Pinna* silk. Its elusive qualities may stem from the fact that the material is readily destroyed by clothes moths. Early illuminated manuscripts of the fourteenth and fifteenth centuries show kings wearing collars of Golden Fleece resembling *Pinna* silk.

Today, the manufacture of this silk cloth has evidently disappeared. Pen shells, however, serve as a source of food in parts of Japan—the muscle disk of the Caribbean species is as tasty as that of scallops. Pearls of gem quality are sometimes found in the large *Atrina vexillum* of the Indo-Pacific. Their thick shells are sometimes used as platters for food service and as bases for various kinds of decorative carved articles in Polynesia.

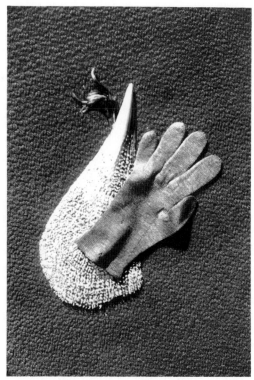

LEFT: Since medieval times, Italians fished the pen shell, *Pinna nobilis* Linné, with this type of pole grasper.
ABOVE: This glove was woven from *Pinna* byssal threads. The manufacture of this type of cloth ceased after World War I.

Shells in religion

In prehistoric times, before man had developed sophisticated religions, shells played an important part among primitive tribes as amulets, or good-luck charms, and as symbols for love, fertility and life eternal. The large cowries, probably *Cypraea tigris* and *C. pantherina*, symbolized sex among peoples bordering the Indian Ocean and Red Sea. Anthropologists claim that this came about because of the resemblance of the underside of a living cowrie to the female genitalia. This speculative explanation seems quite plausible in view of the archaeological and historical evidence found in the Mediterranean region.

The cowrie was called the "Concha Venerea"—the shell of Venus—by the ancients. The scientific name for the genus *Cypraea* arose from *Cyprus* or *Cyprian,* the island where the worship of Aphrodite, or Venus, began. Other legends, and Renaissance paintings, depict Venus's being born from a seashell, usually a scallop. The cowrie was worn by the women of Pompeii to prevent sterility, and even today in the Ryukyu Islands, a woman giving birth to a child holds a Tiger Cowrie clenched in each hand to assure easy delivery. In Japan this cowrie is called the *Koyasu-gai,* or "easy-delivery shell." Cowries were worn as girdle and breast ornaments by women of many tribes, and these shells have been found associated with skeletons of women of Cro-Magnon caves, Saxon graves in Germany and pit-dwellers of prehistoric sites in England and in predynastic Egypt.

Shells served as fetishes and were worshiped by Africans and North American Indians. The eyes of Congolese wooden images were made of cowrie shells with the apertures facing outward. The Algonquin tribe of the Ojibwa in Canada maintained a Grand Medicine Society in which the sacred emblem was a shell. The sacred shell, in some cases a cowrie originating from very early European traders, was taken on national hunts and consulted as an oracle before wars. A similar use was made of the cowrie shell in the Human Leopard Society of the Sierra Leone cannibals during the nineteenth century. The Aztecs of ancient Mexico also used shells in their religion. Tlaloc, the rain god, is depicted as emerging from a conch shell, and in some areas of Mexico the god of food supplies was preceded by a priest blowing a *Strombus* or *Pleuroploca* conch shell.

The chank shell, *Turbinella pyrum,* particularly in its rare sinistral form, is even today considered sacred by Indian Hindus. The god Vishnu and his many incarnations are associated with the chank. He is supposed to have dived into the sea during a great flood to rescue sacred writings that had been hidden in a chank by the Devil. In the daily liturgy of the Brahmans, the following prayer is said while a *Turbinella* is held in the left hand:

At the mouth of this shell is the God of the Moon. . . . In this chank is the chief of the Brahmans. This is why we worship the sacred chank. Glory to thee, sacred shell, blessed by all the gods, born in the sea, and formerly held by Vishnu in his hand. We adore the sacred chank and meditate upon it. May we be filled with joy!

Indians making religious treks to southeast India today obtain blessed bangles cut from the chank shell. Neolithic and early Iron Age sites on the Tungabhadra River, fifty-three miles west of Bellary, India, have contained ancient bangles made from chanks as well as from cowries.

In both Egypt and China the cowrie was used in connection with burials. Mummies sometimes had eyes of cowries to ensure good sight in the afterlife. In pre-Christian times in China, the mouth of the Son of Heaven (the emperor) was stuffed with nine cowries, that of a feudal lord with seven, that of a high officer with five and that of an ordinary official with three. Common people usually had their mouths stuffed with rice, but if they were of some wealth, the last molar tooth on each side of the jaw was supported with a small money cowrie. This wishful and symbolic gesture was made in an effort to ensure that the deceased would have plenty to eat and plenty to spend in the unknown world of the hereafter.

TOP: The rarest of the seven-inch-long sacred chanks of India coils sinistrally, in the direction opposite to that shown in this normal—dextral, or right-handed— sacred specimen of *Turbinella pyrum* (Linné). Brahmans of India use the sinistrally coiled shell in religious ceremonies. LOWER: A favorite motif of ancient Greek terra-cotta work was Aphrodite being born from a scallop shell.

Shells in ancient art

It is to be expected that shells would have been depicted in the early carvings and paintings of man, since the cowrie, conch shells and scallops were used as symbols in sex and religion. In addition, many forms of shellfish were considered aphrodisiacs and also used as a main food. For these reasons, shells are commonly found in early forms of art, particularly as minor embellishments for more important central themes.

Since many shells were extremely colorful and attractive, they were used extensively in the decorative arts. Pearl shell pendants and sculpturings in wood and ivory inlaid with shell were commonplace in the world of primitive art. Even in South America, thousands of years before Christ, the Indians were using shells in their art, evidently independent of any Mediterranean influences. In the Taltal region of Chile, in association with arrowheads of the hunting peoples of about 3000 B.C., scallop shells have been found that showed evidence of having been used in the decorative arts. Vases, dating back to 900 B.C., were made in Peru to resemble the thorny oyster, *Spondylus*. Exquisite examples of pottery vases of the Mochica culture of Peru, about A.D. 600, depict *Cardium* cockles and the scallop *Argopecten purpuratus*. The later Chimu culture used shell motifs on gold beakers and pottery vases.

The Mayans of Mexico depicted shells on their public buildings. The temple of Quetzalcoatl has numerous bivalves and conch shells carved in the walls. One Mayan stone block shows a man wearing shells suspended from a necklace of beads. The scallop and *Spondylus* appear in the art of the Mayans and Aztecs. Many of their goddesses are shown arising from a shell. An Atlantic Lion's Paw Scallop from an Aztec site was evidently used as a pendant. The characteristic hollow nodes on the ribs of the shell were ground open and stuffed with oblong pieces of gold.

In the ancient world of the Mediterranean, the theme of Aphrodite's (Venus's) arising in birth from the scallop repeated itself in figurines and wall paintings and on vases at least as early as 400 B.C. and on through medieval times. A two-handled jar created about 370 B.C. in a Greek town on the Aegean Sea depicts Aphrodite emerging from a scallop. The same theme was used in the manufacture of cheap terra-cotta figures that were sold to tourists near the shrines of Athens and Corinth in the third century B.C. They usually show a well-proportioned female figure kneeling on two open scallop valves.

Shell grottos, originally designed as altarlike

shrines for one's ancestors, came into being in the first century B.C. Usually the semidomed topping was in the form of a stylized scallop. The theme persists in architecture from the Herculaneum period of Rome down to the creation in England of the Queen Ann shell porch. Mosaic floors and walls depicting scallops have been found in many Roman sites, including Pompeii. Roman lead coffins frequently bore the design of scallops. Ancient Phoenician coins distributed throughout the Mediterranean world are sculptured with the likeness of the scallop as well as that of the *Murex* and *Charonia* shells. Although shells undoubtedly were used for simple, decorative purposes, in many instances they were also adopted as symbols of religion|and often as symbols of mysticism and of sex.

OPPOSITE: A scallop shape was used in this early Roman perfume flask fashioned in blown glass. ABOVE: The story of the birth of the love goddess, Aphrodite, is depicted on this Grecian burial urn dating from about 370 B.C.

Shells in medieval art

The Middle Ages of Europe inherited the wide-spread Roman use of the scallop design as an ornament on furniture, public buildings, coffins and coins, but the most famous use of this bivalve was as a pilgrim badge. During the early life of the Roman Catholic Church, the religious practices of financial penance, self-imposed exiles and long pilgrimages on foot came into great vogue. Rome was one of the chief meccas where sinners could go to pay symbolically for their sins. Shrines and sanctuaries sprang up throughout western Europe, partly for religious purposes and partly as tourist attractions. One could avoid the rigors of a pilgrimage by paying off the local courts, and in the Low Countries in 1100 one could avoid a trip to Rome for £12 and a voyage to São Thomé in Portuguese India for £60.

About this time a story arose surrounding St. James the Greater, one of Christ's apostles who spent several fruitless years evangelizing in Spain. When he returned to Jerusalem, he was beheaded by Herod Agrippa. A legend of the eighth century says that St. James's disciples rescued his remains and took them by boat to Iria, now Padron, at the northwest corner of Spain. The legend was known throughout France and as far away as Rome by the ninth century. St. James's grave was rediscovered in a place called Saint James of Compostela, later reduced to the Spanish name of Santiago. Pilgrimages to Santiago gradually became popular, especially for Catholics in France and Spain, despite harassment from Rome, including the excommunica-

tion of the bishop of Santiago in 1049 for excessive indulgences and elaborate titles. Special travel booklets were published to assist the pilgrim travelers. Most of the routes to Santiago followed the old Roman roads.

At some point, some enterprising salesman in Santiago, finding piles of empty scallops brought in sixteen miles from the sea for food purposes, began to sell the shells as pilgrimage souvenirs. This led to extravagant tales being circulated during the 1500s that associated St. James with scallop shells. The basis of these tales involved a horseman's arising out of the sea and finding himself and his horse miraculously covered with scallops. Some versions make the horseman a reincarnation of St. James; other variations have the miracle created by the ghost of St. James.

The scallop and its art renditions spread rapidly throughout the Christian world. It appeared on almost all stained glass windows of cathedrals, was added to the statues of St. James, together with a pilgrim hat, and appeared on the walls of Catholic church buildings. The business of selling scallop shells became so brisk that specimens had to be imported to Spain from other countries. It finally became so commercialized that one of the popes stepped in and forbade the sale of shells anywhere near the town. Santiago, however, continued for many centuries to be a pilgrimage of great popularity, being third only to Rome and Jerusalem. No other object or symbol served to represent a pilgrimage more than the scallop *Pecten jacobaeus*.

LEFT: The scallop shown on St. James's staff reoccurred many times in medieval art. It symbolized the penitents' journeys to the saint's grave in Spain. BELOW: In 1687, Martin Lister republished Rembrandt's 1650 etching of a Marble Cone, this time properly making it a dextrally coiled specimen.

Shells in the Renaissance

Shells did not take a major place in the various art forms of the Renaissance, although the use of the scallop motif still continued. Early Dutch, French and English masters, particularly when doing portraits of naturalists and explorers, occasionally depicted shells in their work. The influence of the rigid aspects of the Christian church was beginning to wane. The scallop and triton were now used to illustrate pagan legends. Among the most famous of such representations was Sandro Botticelli's *Birth of Venus,* painted in 1478 and now at the Uffizi in Florence, Italy. The masterpiece depicts Venus's being wafted ashore aboard the lower valve of the Mediterranean Great Scallop. About 1520, Titian painted his naked *Venus Anadyomene* with the symbolic floating scallop shell in the lower left corner of the painting.

The shells depicted in sixteenth-century family portraits, particularly of naturalists, are interesting clues to the extent of explorations of the day. The Italian canvas *The Treasures of the Sea,* created by Jacopo del Zucchi about 1562, depicts nude women by the seashore, admiring seashells being brought in by divers. In the foreground are about fifteen species of shells, including a Mediterranean *Cardium* cockle, the Portuguese Pelican's Foot (*Aporrhais*), ten times as large as it should be, a Venus Comb Murex from the Indian Ocean and nondescript oysters bearing precious pearls the size of walnuts.

A portrait, painted about 1645 by Emmanuel de Critz, of John Tradescant, Jr., an avaricious collector of shells and plants, shows a jumbled pile of common shells, including a polished *Turbo marmoratus* from southeast Asia, a West Indian *Cittarium* top shell and many Indo-Pacific species, including the magnificent large Triton's Trumpet, a *Cypraecassis rufa* helmet, a spider conch and a Marble Cone. The oil painting is now in the Ashmolean Museum at Oxford University, England.

One of the better shell paintings, done in oils by Balthasar van der Ast about 1620, portrays a very unusual group of about twenty species of shells tastefully scattered about on a cloth-covered table. A sprig of autumn cherry leaves, a cluster of currants and a passing butterfly add superb contrast. The shells are so accurately painted that each of the species is scientifically identifiable. The collection contains a *Liguus* and a *Polymita* land snail from the eastern end of Cuba. From the Philippines must have come the murex shells and possibly the Tiger Cowrie and Marble Cone. An unusual turrid shell, *Turris babylonia,* is shown in the forefront. This elongate, spotted shell probably does not appear in any other Renaissance painting.

It is curious that Rembrandt, so far as is known, did not depict shells in his oil paintings. However, among many of his hundreds of etchings on metal plates, one, executed in 1650, carries a fairly good representation of the Marble Cone, *Conus marmoreus,* of the Indo-Pacific. He etched the shell, as he saw it, directly on the plate. The resulting print was, of course, a mirror image, thus causing the normally dextrally coiled cone shell to be printed erroneously as a sinistral specimen. Rembrandt was careful to etch his name in mirror image but failed to reverse the shell. Apparently this offended Susanna Lister, daughter of the famous seventeenth-century physician Martin Lister. While she was preparing the drawings for her father's monumental work *Historiae Conchyliorum,* published in 1687, she pointedly copied a Dutch print in her possession but reversed the shell so that, at last, the shell looked normal. Under her superior rendition, she gave due credit: ad explar. Rambr. V. ryn. [from an example of Rembrandt van Rijn].

To some extent, shells were featured in other objects of art, however, during the Renaissance period. During the seventeenth century very ornate cups and chalices were expensively produced in the shape of shells by artists and metal craftsmen. The chambered nautilus, especially when polished, lent itself to very ornate productions. The shell was usually carved or bejeweled and mounted on graceful statues of Triton. Benvenuto Cellini frequently used the scallop motif as the basis for his cuplike gold chalices.

OPPOSITE: Famous eighteenth-century goldsmiths created elaborate chalices by adorning the chambered nautilus with metal scallops. This one is carried on the head of Triton, god of the sea. ABOVE: Nürnberg eggs, as these early German watches were called, were protected by a case shaped like a scallop.

The scallop in heraldry

Early man undoubtedly identified the family groups and tribes to which he belonged by the use of a common color of clothing, an ornament of some sort or a badge worn in the hair or on the body. In times of battle, a simple identification to mark one's friends and foes was a necessity. Cults, even today, are advertised by their practitioners through the use of a peculiar garb or hair style. In medieval Europe, the practice of heraldry, or armory, as the experts call it, blossomed overnight during the middle of the twelfth century. This craze among the military-minded nobles came about possibly because of the need to identify horsemen hidden behind great shields and armored suits. It was also a romantic time, and one in which royal lines and the exclusiveness of nobility were developing. Mystical symbols appealed to the medieval eye.

Of the thousands of arms invented and used in modified form by succeeding generations, only a few decorated them with the scallop motif, perhaps only four or five in every hundred. Lions, unicorns, swords and castles were much more popular. The whelk shell was used very seldom. The escallop, the heraldic term for *scallop,* was probably used in decorations and possibly in association with families long before the crusades but seems to have become more popular just after the thirteenth-century wars with the Saracens. The earliest coat of arms appearing in the official roles of the College of Arms of 1280 depicts a blue shield with a rearing (*rampant,* as armory students say) lion among a scattering of gold symbolic escallops. It was the intention of the medieval artist to emphasize the features of the scallop, so that most renditions show only a few bold, curved ribs and a narrow, flaring beak or ear section of the scallop.

Many knights returning from the crusades wore the traditional badge of St. James—the deep valve of *Pecten maximus.* Very commonly, this scallop shell was hung around the neck or laced to cords encircling the horse. For this purpose, two holes were drilled through the beak area of the scallop. In many heraldic renditions, the escallop shows these two slits, or "eyes," as a signal that the knight had been to war in search of the Holy Grail, the cup supposedly used at Christ's last supper.

Many family names developed before heraldic symbols and arms were invented. The scallop was probably chosen to represent certain surnames for whimsical reasons or as pictorial puns. For instance, both the escallop and the whelk appear on the crests of two of the families of Shelley. Robert de Scales (his name is etymologically close to the Anglo-Saxon word *skal* and the Dutch word *schelp,* both meaning "shell"), who was a knight at the siege of Caerlaverock in 1300, had a shield of red bearing six silver escallops. Among the surnames of thirteenth-century knights using the escallop in their arms were Chamberlain, Langley, Tracy, Danyell, Prychard, Crombe and Fitz Nichol. Many of the Knights of the Garter, a noble order founded in 1348 and still in existence, used the escallop. Among the gentlemen recently raised to this order is Sir Winston Churchill, with six silver scallops.

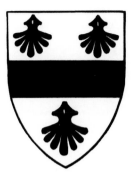

Many heraldic arms of the thirteenth century in England used scallop shells for various reasons, including reference to Roman Catholic ancestors who participated in either pilgrimages to Spain or the holy wars in the Near East.

The uses of shells today 10

The edible oyster

The oyster has been man's favorite edible mollusk since prehistoric times. The ancient kitchen middens—huge garbage dumps—found throughout the cooler parts of the world, attest to their popularity. The ancient Greeks and Romans used them as a main dish, and their taste for them encouraged the development of artificial oyster beds a century before Christ. Some enterprising Roman merchants discovered that oysters could be packed and shipped in ice and snow obtained from the north side of high mountains, and there are records of oysters being shipped for hundreds of miles to special banquets. Our earliest colonists found that the maritime Indian tribes were great oyster eaters and that when meager land crops failed, oysters supplied the necessary proteins to carry them over the hard winters.

There are about a dozen species of edible oysters, belonging to the genera *Ostrea* and *Crassostrea*, that supply 90 percent of the world's harvest of oyster meats. It would be difficult to estimate the annual world consumption, but fisheries' records show that countries having advanced shell fisheries, such as those in Europe, Japan and the United States, produce well over a billion pounds of oyster meat each year. In the eastern United States, the production has been gradually declining from an annual high of about 160 million pounds during the early 1900s to about one-third that amount today. The eastern industry is based upon the Virginia oyster, *Crassostrea virginica*, a brackish-water species that extends from southern Canada to Mexico.

In Europe, a similar species, *Crassostrea angulata*, is very popular, but the main species is *Ostrea edulis*. It differs in that it lives in clearer waters of higher salinity. It retains its fertilized eggs within its mantle cavity until they hatch into free-swimming veligers. In the *Crassostrea* forms, which live in brackish water, both the eggs and sperm are shed into the open water.

On the Pacific coast of North America, the small, native *Ostrea lurida* was at one time extremely abundant, particularly in the state of Washington. By 1906, most of the beds from San Francisco to British Columbia had been exhausted. Modern culture methods, including the annual importation since 1922 of the young of the large Japanese Oyster, have revived the industry to the extent of a harvest of over 10 million pounds of meat each year in Washington alone. Mariculture—the farming of sea creatures under controlled conditions—is a relatively new approach in the Americas and holds promise of furnishing an adequate supply of shellfish. The northern oyster normally takes from three to four years to reach edible size, but when the species is raised on special rafts in ponds and given special nutrients, the growing time can be reduced to a year or two.

Oysters are harvested in a variety of ways, depending upon the bottom conditions and the depths at which they grow. In some areas, such as North and South Carolina, they grow in large clumps on reefs that are exposed at low tide. In the Chesapeake and Delaware bays, hand grappling from small boats is still employed. The oystermen use a long-handled, scissorlike pair of tongs to pull clumps of oysters aboard their small two-man boats. In Connecticut and Massachusetts, modern trawlers with motor-driven winches and dredges harvest huge quantities. In all these operations it is necessary to maintain proper growing bottoms by taking the mountains of shucked oyster shells back out to sea. In some areas, hatcheries are used to rear young oysters, called *spat*. Chemicals are used to control the serious pests of oysters, such as starfish, crabs and oyster drill snails.

The production of oysters varies from year to year. Hurricanes may wipe out natural seed or spat production for several years. Epidemic diseases of the oysters themselves, such as MSX, a disease protozoan called *Minchinia nelsoni*, and a fungus disease, *Dermocystidium*, may decimate oyster beds for several years.

PRECEDING PAGES: This modern mosaic of shells, patterned after a Victorian sailor's valentine, contains more than 10,000 undyed, natural shells. It is on exhibit at the Delaware Museum of Natural History.

TOP: Primitive harvesting methods, using hand tongs, are still used by oystermen in the eastern United States. LEFT: In New England powered dredges are used. ABOVE RIGHT: New methods of raising and farming oysters are being developed.

199

The edible clams

A billion pounds of clam meat are harvested annually throughout the world, and, next to the oyster, it has been a major source of food since prehistoric days. The word *clam* covers a host of species, ranging from the quahogs in the family Veneridae and the razor clam in the family Solenidae to the Soft-shelled Clam in the Myacidae. Each country has its major and its minor commercial clam species. Japan and the United States account for about 70 percent of the world's production.

In the eastern United States there are three major clam industries. One is based upon the *Mercenaria mercenaria*, commercially known as the quahog or chowder clam when it is large and the littleneck or cherrystone when it is the size of a half-dollar. It ranges from the Gulf of St. Lawrence to the Gulf of Mexico, although from Virginia southward it lives not in estuarine waters but in more marine conditions and is considered the subspecies *campechiensis*. It is the most valuable, although not the most productive, clam in eastern America, bringing in about $10 million a year. The major producing states are New York, Virginia, Rhode Island and New Jersey.

The northern quahog becomes sexually mature at one year and of commercial cherrystone, or on-the-half-shell, size at two or three years. A large specimen, six inches in size, will weigh two and a half pounds, but the meat will be so tough that it must be finely diced and used in chowder. Hard-shelled Clams live in sand, buried just below the surface. In the north they occur in protected lagoons and bays where the water is slightly brackish and from one to twenty feet deep. In New England, and also Florida, they occur in intertidal zones and can be readily dug manually with hoes or long-tined rakes during low tide. Elsewhere they are grappled from the bottom by long-handled tongs or dredged by larger vessels using power winches and large steel-mesh bags.

New methods are being developed for the artificial culture and propagation of this species. Of considerable importance are new methods to cleanse these clams of pollutant bacteria and viruses that might endanger the public's health. By 1970, almost half of the natural beds of these clams had to be put off limits because of sewage contamination from overpopulated eastern cities.

Second in value to the quahog is the Soft-shelled Clam, *Mya arenaria*, also known as the "steamer" or Nanny-nose. Like the quahog, it was extensively used by eastern American Indians and was well known to the early colonists. It was favored over the quahog because it was much more tender and sweet. The clam lives very deep in black, mucky sand, with its fused siphons extending up to the surface of the mud. Adults range from two to four inches in length and have a rather fragile white or grayish shell. In New England, they are collected at low tide by means of hand diggers. When one stamps on the sand beside a clam's hole, a jet of water squirts up, revealing the clam's presence.

The New England Soft-shelled Clam industry underwent a spectacular decline from 1940 to 1955, due in part to the predation by the green crab. The largest quantities of *Mya* clams are now harvested in the shallow waters of Chesapeake Bay by means of boats rigged with an escalator that digs and delivers the washed clams to the surface. They operate to a depth of forty feet but are limited by present law to forty bushels per boat per day. This species is popular for fried clam dinners, and it has for generations been a favorite when steamed in its own broth or baked in fire pits under mounds of wet seaweed. About $3 million worth of Soft-shelled Clams are harvested a year.

Throughout the world seafood is becoming an increasingly valuable source of protein. Clams, lobster, two varieties of shrimp and red snapper combine in this handsome and delicious Zarzuela de Mariscos—a popular Spanish seafood stew.

Curiously, the largest clam fishery in the world is the least known to the public. It is based upon the so-called Surf Clam (that rarely lives in the surf), *Spisula solidissima*, a five- to seven-inch-long clam living in depths from the low-tide zone to about 100 feet. The fishery is confined to a limited area off New Jersey and adjacent states. Each year about 40 million pounds of meat are landed there.

The Surf Clam was known to the Indians and early colonists but was rarely eaten because it was caught in the surf and was usually loaded with sand. Since World War II modern technological improvements in fishing gear have permitted huge offshore beds, at depths of thirty to ninety feet, to be exploited. A hydraulic dredge, equipped with water jets, a digging blade and an enormous chain bag, can deliver 400 huge bags of clams to the boat above in a matter of a few hours. The clam is then shucked, steamed, cleansed and canned in the clam factories of New Jersey and New York. It is the main ingredient in cans of chopped clams and New England clam chowder.

As the supply of the Surf Clam has somewhat dwindled, another clam living in deep water has been used in the eastern clam industry. Known variously as the Arctic Clam, the Ocean Quahog and the Mahogany Clam, *Arctica islandica* has become of increasing importance to fishermen who can dredge from fifteen to eighty fathoms in depth. Other eastern clams of lesser importance not as yet profitable commercially are the razor clam, *Ensis*, of superb culinary qualities, and the *Tagelus* clam, now being brought up and discarded during the fishing operations for the *Mya* Soft-shelled Clam. A relative newcomer to the eastern shores of the United States is the *Rangia* clam, a thick-shelled, three-inch-long, gray clam that was formerly restricted to the Gulf of Mexico. In the last thirty years it has spread northward from Florida to Delaware and is so prolific that it can be collected by the ton with little effort. It is quite edible and is now canned in combination with quahog meats.

Two clams new to the commercial field in the Atlantic are the Venus Sunray Clam, *Macrocallista nimbosa*, and the Calico Clam, *Macrocallista maculata*. The former, beautiful seven-inch-long clams, are being experimentally fished in the Gulf of Mexico off Florida, but the area in which they are concentrated is probably too limited to permit extensive fisheries. Bermuda has recently been invaded by the smaller Calico Clam, thousands of which have been collected by private individuals for "cherrystone" clams on the half shell. They are sweeter and more tender than young quahogs.

On the Pacific coast of the United States, there is a relatively small clam industry. The clam there is of more importance to the sportsman and private individual than it is to industry. Among the Pacific coast species are the razor clam, *Siliqua patula* (about 10 million are harvested per year); the famous Pismo Clam, *Tivela stultorum*, which has suffered a drastic decimation due to overcollecting; the *Saxidomus* butter clam (about 1 million pounds per year) and the littleneck *Protothaca* clam. Some species are now very uncommon, such as the geoduck, *Panopea generosa*, a soft-shelled clam growing to a weight of eight pounds and living in deep, soft mud. Because its catch is limited to only a few specimens per person per week, it is of recreational rather than commercial importance.

Next to the United States, Japan is the largest producer of clams. While a large proportion of its catch is locally consumed, a great many tons are smoked and canned in oil for foreign export. A unique clam industry exists in Malaya, where there is an annual catch of over 25 million pounds of ark shell meats from the *Anadara* clams. Cockles are still extensively harvested in northwest Europe and in Malaysia, with a worldwide annual harvest of about 74 million pounds.

TOP: The favorite American clam is the soft shell
or steamer clam, *Mya arenaria* Linné. In the Chesapeake
Bay, they are harvested with the aid of this
escalator. LEFT and ABOVE: The Surf Clam, *Spisula
solidissima* Dillwyn, occurring off the coast of New
Jersey, is the source of most canned clams.

The edible scallop

Although by no means as abundant as the oyster or the clam, the scallop has held a high place among the choicest of shellfish. Gourmets prefer the delicate sweet muscle of the scallop to the meat of any other mollusk when it comes to preparing a particularly tasty seafood dish. Some of the holiest of gourmet recipes have been built around the plump, pearly white body of the scallop, with the roes, shaped like scarlet cockscombs, containing the delicate, granular eggs. Scallops excel the tougher crustaceans and the coarser clams in taste. Among the practitioners of gastronomy, the cult of the scallop is revered and universal.

The world production of scallops is reported to be about 300 million pounds of meat each year, with the United States producing 41 percent, Japan 20 percent, Australia and Western Europe each about 10 percent. In the Mediterranean region, the shells are saved, cleaned and packed for export to foreign countries where they are used for baking dishes. In most places, only the adductor muscle is eaten, probably because of past histories of paralytic shellfish poisoning resulting from eating the mantle and gills.

The most-often-eaten scallops in the Americas are the Deep-Sea Scallop, *Placopecten magellanicus,* of the northeast United States and, to a lesser extent, the Alaskan *Pecten caurinus,* both large, flat, rather smooth-shelled scallops with shells measuring from six to eleven inches across. From these come the edible portion, a round disk of white muscle about the size of a half-dollar. The eastern species lives in large colonies at depths of 60 to 150 feet, on gravel bottoms, from Nova Scotia to off Cape Hatteras, with the major industrial concentrations being on the Georges Bank and the Gulf of Maine. They are capable of swimming for short distances.

Catches worth as much as $13 million have been landed in one year. Today they remain one of the most expensive seafoods, largely because of the scarcity of the product and the expense in fishing them with deep-sea trawlers. The industry has thrived since the 1880s off the coast of New England, but the United States is now taking second place to the efforts of the Canadians, who are working new beds off the mid-Atlantic coast and Georges Bank. Large diesel-powered vessels scrape the bottom with two large scallop dredges, usually on a twenty-four-hour basis, with hauls being made about every half-hour. The cruises last about ten days, with the shucking of the scallops being done immediately. The muscle meats are frozen aboard in forty-pound bags.

Two other kinds of scallops are fished on the east coast of the United States—the very small Bay Scallop, *Argopecten irradians,* a once very popular item in early America, and the Calico Scallop. The Bay Scallop is readily fished in shallow water in New England and in New Jersey from grassy bottoms in two to twenty feet of water. The muscle is small but very tasty. About 2 million pounds are landed each year, which means that about 20 million specimens are collected annually. Shucking is a "cottage industry," with the live scallops being taken by truck to the small scallop factories for processing. The Calico Scallop, *Argopecten gibbus,* a southern species, has recently come into its own in the Carolinas. The development of efficient shucking and eviscerating machinery has made harvesting this small two-inch-long shell an economically feasible operation. Scallops are also extensively fished in southern Australia and Japan. Minor fisheries exist in almost all of the cool-water areas throughout the world.

The scallop reigns supreme among the molluscan table delicacies and is
prepared in many ways, from simple sautéed scallops to much more elaborate
dishes, such as this broiled, buttered, cheesed and sauced Bay Scallops Mornay.

Other edible mollusks

When we consider the number of miscellaneous kinds of minor molluscan shellfish used throughout the world, we can conclude that man has eaten almost every marine species of worthy size. In areas not affected by algal poisonings, the common blue mussels of the genus *Mytilus* are cultivated in huge numbers for the table. The world annual production is about 500 million pounds, with the Netherlands and France farming about 40 percent of the supply. Chile, which has had a tradition of mussel fishing since the Spanish arrived in the 1600s, leads among the South American countries.

Mytilus edulis is the most abundant shellfish in New England, but it has never gained the popularity that it has in France, where tons are eaten. A small fishery in New England produces about a million pounds of meat and shells, but they are distributed mainly to large cities where there are people of French and Italian extraction. Mussels are not generally eaten to any great extent on the Pacific coast of the United States, mainly because of the dangers of paralytic mussel poisoning at certain seasons.

The leading gastropod fishery in the United States involves several large species of *Haliotis* abalones found in commercial sizes and quantity only on the Pacific coast. Each year about a million pounds of meat are marketed. Its wholesale value exceeds that of the 23 million pounds of squid caught annually in United States waters.

The abalone fishery goes back into Indian days, long before the advent of white man. Overfishing and the return of the sea otter have reduced this fishery in recent years. Formerly, helmet divers, and now, scuba divers, obtained the abalones in commercial quantities.

The most important species is the large Red Abalone, which reaches a size of about ten inches. It customarily lives attached to rocks, where it grazes on algae at a depth of twenty to fifty feet, and is particularly abundant along the coast of central California. The other ten species of Pacific coast abalones are rarely exploited commercially because

of their smaller size and increasing rarity. Sportsmen obtain large quantities, but strict California fisheries laws reduce the catch by size restrictions and limitation of the manner in which they may be collected. Eventually, these species may come back to their former abundance. Abalones are also extensively fished in Japan, South Africa and South Australia. The foot, when pounded to make it tender, tastes not unlike scallop. The remainder of the soft parts is discarded.

Throughout the West Indies, and particularly in the Bahamas, the nearly foot-long Pink Conch, *Strombus gigas,* has been a mainstay meat for the natives for many centuries. At its height, the stromb fishery in the Bahamas was worth nearly a quarter of a million dollars a year. The huge piles of dead shells seen almost everywhere throughout the Bahamas attest to their use as a food. Supplies are dwindling, and in the Lower Florida Keys adult specimens are now rarely found. The large muscular foot is used in chowders, fritters and, when pounded, sliced and diced, is used raw in conch cocktails and seafood salads.

In the eastern United States, the *Busycon* whelks, or conchs, were popular with the Indians, and in recent times, largely because of Italian tastes, a large fishery is developing from Massachusetts to Virginia. The conchs, of which there are three main species, reach a shell length of six to ten inches. They are gathered by hand or dredged in shallow water. Many are sent alive to fish markets; others are sent to large canning operations in New Jersey and New York. From one-half to one million pounds are landed each year. Some are ground up and dumped into the water to serve as bait for sport fishing.

In England, Ireland and to a limited extent in New England, the Common European Periwinkle is gathered along the rocky shores by hand and sent alive to market in baskets. Before being eaten, the small snails are boiled and sometimes soaked in vinegar or dipped in hot garlic butter. About 50,000 pounds were harvested in New England in 1967, but an amount many hundred times that is annually consumed in northwest Europe. To a lesser extent, and mostly by picnickers visiting the seashore, the *Nucella* dogwinkles are eaten, either roasted over open fires or boiled.

OPPOSITE: Many thousands of pounds of conch are prepared for market each year in southern Florida and the West Indies. The foot is served in salads, fritters and chowders. ABOVE: The "Nanny-Nose," or Soft-shell Clam, *Mya arenaria,* of eastern United States, supplies the fried clam market.

Edible cephalopods

The thought of eating squid and octopus is not particularly appealing to Americans and northern Europeans, despite the fact that they are fond of fish and many other shellfish. Yet the cephalopods, from a worldwide standpoint, are second only to the oysters in annual catch. The Japanese land and eat over a billion pounds of squid a year, and the Spanish annually catch over 17 million pounds of *Sepia* squid, which they can in the squid's black ink and export to foreign countries. A mere 200,000 pounds of *Octopus* are caught and eaten each year by the Japanese, and throughout the East Indies and South Seas, women make nightly trips to the reef to catch the next day's meal of octopus. However, over 8,000 tons of squid are annually sold in the fish markets of California, Oregon, Washington and New York City. Modern supermarkets in most parts of the United States now sell five-pound packages of frozen squid. In the west, they are eaten mainly by people of Chinese and Japanese extraction, and in the east by Italians, Spaniards and Puerto Ricans.

The canning of huge quantities of squid for export has been thriving in California for more than fifty years. In 1946, some 30 million cans of squid were sold to Mediterranean and Far Eastern countries. For many years, in Monterey, squid were slit open, hung on open racks and sun-cured for future shipment to the Orient.

Squid are caught by jigging, a procedure used to attract and ensnare the squid. One fisherman may sometimes land squid at the rate of 1,200 an hour. Nets, traps and creels are also used in many parts of the world. Octopuses are sometimes caught by baiting them into jars lowered to the bottom of the sea. Off Naples, Italy, a basket similar to a lobster pot is used, from which the octopus cannot escape. Squid are sometimes caught in large numbers, occasionally as many as 16,000 bushels in a single evening off the coast of Maine.

The main squid fishery of eastern America is centered about Newfoundland, where *Illex illecebrosus* is a seasonal migrant from July to September. The annual catch fluctuates radically, but in good years as many as 20 million pounds may be landed, frozen and sold in Norway and Portugal for use as codfish bait. Near Newfoundland and to Cape Cod and Cape Hatteras, North Carolina, the bait squid, *Loligo pealei,* is commonly trawled in large numbers, usually about 1,500 metric tons per year. Many of them are sold to Spanish canners.

The Philippines produce, for internal consumption, meat from the chambered nautilus. The shells are saved and sold to a ready overseas seashell market. About a hundred thousand *Nautilus* are fished each year in this area.

The *Sepia* squids of the Mediterranean produce an internal, calcareous cuttlefish bone which is commercially harvested by the ton and exported for use in the manufacture of toothpaste and as "bones" for pet cage-birds. In Roman times, the soft, lightweight cuttlebones were ground to a powder, tinted with purple dye and used as a cosmetic rouge. Yearly, several hundred tons are collected along the southern shores of the Mediterranean and sold to wholesalers.

For many centuries, the ink from the sacs of the *Sepia* cuttlefish of the Mediterranean was a major source of brown coloring matter. It was used also as a writing ink. Its use has now been replaced by aniline dyes because sepia fades in light and will not mix well in oils.

OPPOSITE: Squid are caught and marketed by the millions of pounds each year. This freshly caught load of *Loligo* squid from Newfoundland will be frozen and shipped to Europe for food and for fish bait.

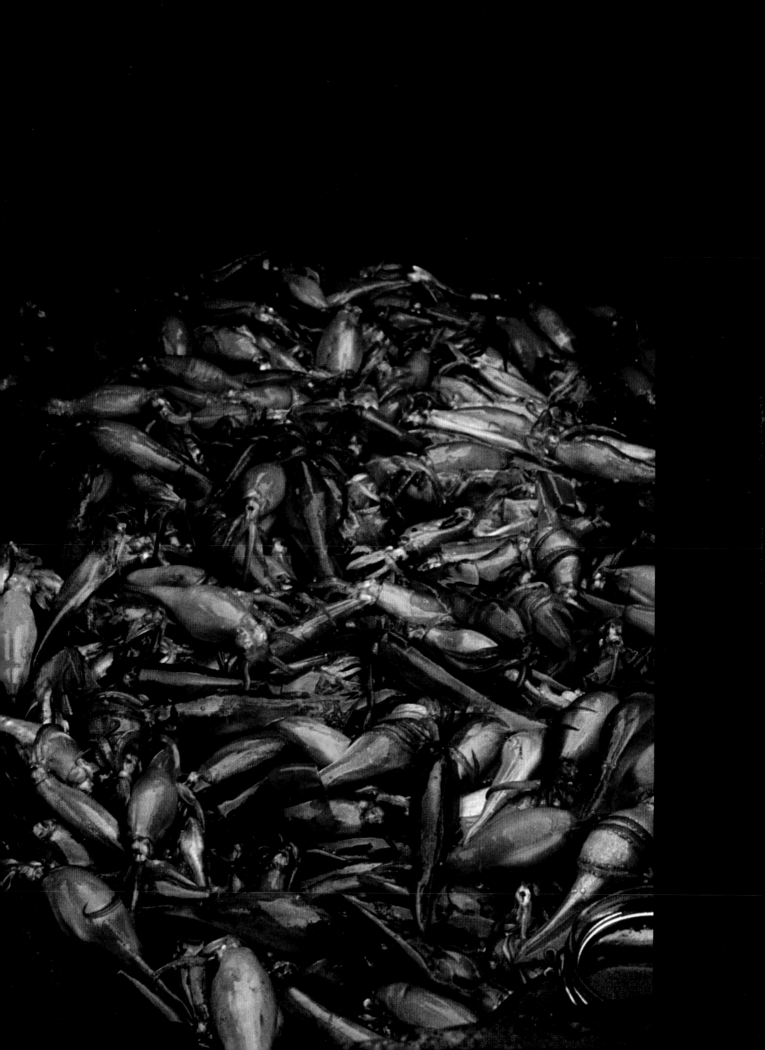

The early story of the pearl

TOP LEFT: Japanese ama girls with their glass-bottomed buckets prepare to dive for pearl oysters. BOTTOM LEFT: Japan is the cultured-pearl center of the world. ABOVE: A cultured pearl is ready for harvest.

As early as 1500 B.C., Egyptian women used pearls in their necklaces and pendants. After the Persian conquest in the fifth century B.C., pearls—both marine from the Persian Gulf and freshwater ones from the Nile—came into common use among the wealthy. The ancient Greeks and Romans often referred in their writings to the extensive pearl fisheries that began over 2,000 years ago in the Persian Gulf. Throughout northern Asia Minor, pearls were buried in tombs with the dead. The Greeks called them *margaritae,* a word adopted by the Romans and made synonymous with *beauty.* The Romans used pearls lavishly on their clothing, furniture and favorite animals. Both Persian nobles and Grecian men of rank wore a pearl earring in the right ear, while the women wore a pearl in each ear or attached one to a ring through the left nostril.

In India and Ceylon, pearl fisheries flourished many centuries before Christ. Ancient Indian deities were adorned with necklaces and crowns made of pearls. As early as 500 B.C., pearls were used as good-luck charms for bestowing long life and prosperity upon young Brahmanical disciples. In addition to the well-known pearl from the *Pinctada* pearl oyster, there were two other kinds of pearls rather extensively fished in the Madras area of India. One of these was greenish in color and came from the estuarine mussel, *Mytilus smaragdinus;* the other was a small, iridescent, soft pearl coming from the so-called Window Pane Shell, *Placuna placenta.* Pearls from the latter were powdered and used extensively as chunam, a popular lime powder mixed with the betel nut for chewing. Marco Polo, more than 650 years ago, noted that the middle class placed these pearls in the mouths of their dead. The poorer classes used rice, and the very wealthy used *Pinctada* pearls.

Curiously, the Chinese were evidently not familiar with the pearl until traders arrived from the Persian Gulf region about the seventh century B.C. About the fifth century B.C., Red Sea merchantmen, bringing pearls and pearl shell, began to use Hangchou and more northern stations. As the demand for pearls increased in China, the natives began to search their own waters but succeeded only in establishing moderately good fisheries on the west coast of the island of Hainan, in southern China. For centuries the Chinese used pearls as medicine; unpierced ones were usually used. Besides being used to promote fertility in the male, they were ground, mixed with the blood of a cockscomb and inserted in the eyes of a patient to recall lost speech.

Freshwater pearls were used in the burial rites of man at very early periods. Although they were inferior to the marine ones, they were greatly coveted even during the Roman days. It is said that one of the motives of Caesar's expedition to Britain in 55 B.C. was to obtain its freshwater pearls. These came from the freshwater mussel *Margaritana margaritifera,* which are believed to have been common in the rivers of north Wales at that time. Freshwater pearl fisheries were fairly extensive in medieval times, mostly in France, Germany, Austria, Norway and Sweden. The Chinese took to freshwater pearling not long after the Arabs had introduced them to pearls in the seventh century B.C. The North American Indians were using freshwater pearls before the coming of Europeans. In 1847, an archaeological dig uncovered more than 50,000 pierced mussel pearls in the Indian mounds near Madisonville, Indiana. When the explorer De Soto traveled through Florida in 1539, he obtained fourteen bushels of mussel pearls from one Indian burial site. The tombs of the chiefs were decorated with pearls, and beside the embalmed corpses small baskets of pearls were set.

Marine pearls were highly appreciated by the Central American Aztecs. In 1513 and 1522, the Spanish explorers Cortez and Balboa recorded pearl fisheries in both the Gulf of Panama and the Gulf of Mexico. The Incas of Peru, who believed that pearls were the eggs of the pearl oyster, used them for decorating their temples and palaces.

Biology of the pearl

Probably every kind of shelled mollusk is capable of producing a pearl. Even the shell-less sea hare, *Aplysia,* produces pearls. A pearl is merely an isolated concentration of shelly material made by the glandular mantle, that same fleshy organ that produces the main shell of the mollusk itself. It follows, therefore, that if a pearl is formed in a nacreous shell, it too will be nacreous. The pearl of a porcelaneous, dull white shell, such as that of the Hardshelled Clam or the edible oyster, will have color, luster and nature similar to that of its maker. In the northern quahog, which is partially purple in color, pearls are very often solidly or partially shaded in purple.

The creation of a pearl may be considered an accident of nature. Not normally produced by healthy mollusks, they are formed only when some foreign body or substance becomes embedded in the mantle tissue. Unless the foreign object can be ejected by the mollusk within a few days, it will be covered over by succeeding layers of shelly material.

Pearls are rarely perfectly round. Very often they are merely misshapen blisters appearing on the inner surface of the shell. In many clams and oysters, it is not uncommon to find irregularities on the inner side of the valves, usually because numerous sand grains or bits of seaweed have become wedged between the living mantle and the old shell. There have been cases in which a small shrimp or an inch-long fish has flitted into a large pearl oyster for protection, but instead of entering the mantle cavity, it unfortunately wiggled in between the shell and the mantle curtain and, unable to extricate itself, became entombed by layer after layer of mother-of-pearl. The outline of the shrimp or the fish was readily visible.

Pearls formed attached to the oyster shell are called blister pearls. Baroque pearls are large, badly misshapen free pearls, not attached. Some pearls are dumbbell-shaped, others elongate and others disk-shaped. Most of the perfect pearls were begun by the invasion of a very small marine organism, such as a microscopic egg of a marine nematode,

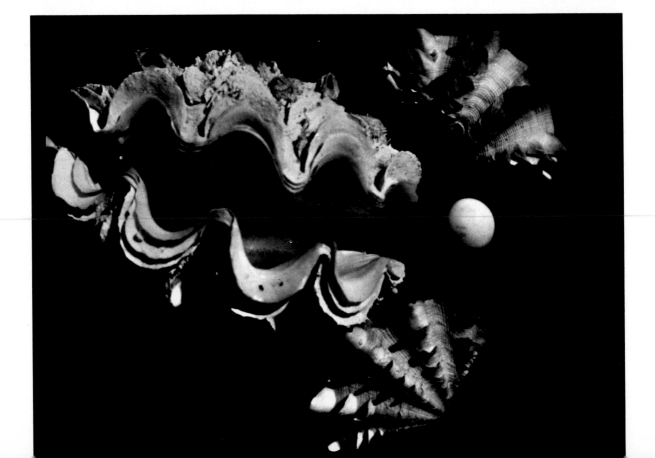

trematode or cestode. Sometimes a single grain of sand may serve as a stimulant for the gradual production of a pearl.

Pearls are about 91 percent calcium carbonate, 6 percent organic conchiolin material and 3 percent water. Growth may vary according to the species producing them and the temperature of the water. A pearl produced by a giant *Tridacna* clam may take as long as ten years to reach the size of a golf ball. Pearls of gem quality from the mother-of-pearl oyster take from six to eight years to reach a diameter of ten millimeters.

This type of gem pearl is made up of the aragonite form of calcium carbonate, in which the nacreous structure is characterized by thin leaves, all of the same thickness and equidistant, being separated by equally thin leaves of organic conchiolin substance. The leaves, which are always placed in the horizontal plane, have a thickness of 0.001 millimeter. This combination of structures produces an iridescent, nacreous refraction. The various shades of pearls, such as pink, cream, bluish and black, are due to the nature of the organic layers and the introduction of certain pigments into the aragonite.

Pearls of gem quality have been found in many mollusks other than *Pinctada,* the genus of pearl oysters. The Pink Conch, *Strombus gigas,* can produce a beautiful pink pearl as large as a grape; one such pearl half that size has a 1971 value of about a hundred dollars. Abalone pearls are relatively common, but most of them are large and misshapen. A beautiful black pearl is occasionally formed in *Pinna* and *Atrina vexillum* of the Indo-Pacific. Large pearly wing oysters of the genus *Pteria* sometimes produce a pearl that can hardly be distinguished from the true *Pinctada* gem pearl. Pearls of gem quality coming from freshwater mussels were very popular and expensive in Europe during the nineteenth century. The literature is replete with tales of enormous pearls in the possession of royalty and various wealthy people. The famous "La Peregrina" pearl, 250 carats in weight (one-tenth of a pound), was brought from Panama in 1560 by Don Diego de Temes, who presented it to Philip II of Spain. In 1779, a pearl in the shape of a sleeping lion and weighing one-fifth of a pound sold in India for £4,500.

OPPOSITE: Giant *Tridacna* clams sometimes produce pearls the size of a golf ball. They are alabaster white like the interior of the clam shell. ABOVE: When shrimp and worms are trapped under the mantle of a pearl oyster, they are entombed in mother-of-pearl.

Cultured pearls

It was only a matter of time before the ingenuity of man developed both an artificial and a cultured pearl. Glass or clay beads, covered with minute iridescent fish scales or ground mother-of-pearl shells, were the first artificial pearls. But man dreamed of and sought methods, over the centuries, of inducing the oyster and the mussel to produce pearls in quantities. The Greek philosopher Apollonius of Rhodes, in the second century B.C., expressed this long-held goal of man by describing in very unscientific terms how the pearl fishermen of the Persian Gulf made "cultured pearls." First, they would render the sea smooth by flooding it with oil, a procedure that today would not seem necessary, considering the large number of perfectly calm days per year on the Persian Gulf. They then dived into the sea, and by holding out a small container of the aromatic herb myrrh as bait, they would

ABOVE: Liqueur cups and household drinking implements are made from mother-of-pearl coming from abalone, trochids and pearl oysters. RIGHT: Chinese once cultured pearl Buddha figures in river clams.

214

induce the oyster to gape. Into the opening, they would insert a long hollow pin and draw off the pearl-making liquid, which was then placed in iron molds where it would solidify into pearls.

The Chinese first developed the techniques for producing cultured pearls in freshwater mussels. The originator, Ye-jin-yang, lived in the years between 1200 and 1300. The art was practiced in central China where, in the spring, large quantities of big, eight-inch-long mussels were obtained from Lake Tahu in Kiangsu and placed in bamboo cages. By means of a forked bamboo stick, small pellets of hardened clay and small outlines of Buddha made of tin were placed either in the center of the mussel or between the inner shell and the mantle. The cages of live mussels were left dangling in canals and pools for about a year, after which they were opened and the pearl objects removed. The tiny pearly raised Buddhas were sawed off the shell, hung on necklace strands and sold in the temple markets.

It was the Japanese in the early part of this century, however, who mastered the technology of producing cultured pearls. The earliest pioneers included Tokichi Nishikawa and Kikutaro Konishi. Later, entrepreneurs, such as Kokichi Mikimoto, put the industry on a businesslike basis and skyrocketed Japan into the leadership of pearl production. Although some Japanese developed laboratory methods of inducing pearls by using microscopic nuclei —either introduced parasite eggs or certain irritating globules of oil—this method has always proved too lengthy and chancy for worthwhile commercial rewards. Through trial-and-error methods, the research workers discovered that large beads, from two to seven millimeters in diameter, made from the freshwater mussels of the Mississippi River, were the least likely to be rejected by the oyster. Two-year-old oysters can handle beads two to three millimeters in diameter, and four-year-olds can cover beads up to seven millimeters. Today, most of these beads are made in Osaka and sold in varying sizes to the pearl cultivators.

Baskets of pearl oysters (*Pinctada martensi*) are removed from the water and placed in the shade for thirty minutes or so until they gape open far enough to allow the careful insertion of a large plug of wood. A shell bead, together with a one-eighth-inch square of mantle tissue from a "donor oyster," is then pushed inside each gaping oyster, usually near the gonad or the stomach. The tissues are then smoothed back into place and the oysters allowed to close. Finally they are transferred to baskets and lowered into the bay. Some procedures call for tying the oysters to a long, tarred rope by means of nylon strings. These strands of oysters are dangled into the sea from floating bamboo rafts. The oysters must be pulled from the ocean about once every month so that dead individuals may be removed and excessive sponge growths cleaned from the outer shells of those still alive. The pearls are harvested after the second, third or, rarely, fourth year, depending upon the size desired. Older pearls are likely to be rejected by the oyster and lost. Rapid dips in temperature in the winter, typhoons, planktonic "red tides" and swarms of eels are a few of the natural catastrophes that may befall a raft of seeded oysters. Only about 40 percent of the entire pearl harvest has some marketable value, and fewer than 10 percent are of gem quality.

The production of cultured bead pearls is watched over by the Japanese government to prevent poor-quality specimens from being sold. Intricate methods are used to grade the pearls according to size, color, luster and weight. Bead pearls, with the parallel layers of the freshwater shell nucleus, can be distinguished by x-ray or with a very strong light from pearls that were started from a microscopic nucleus. The latter pearls have concentric layers throughout the gem.

Harmful and medicinal mollusks

On the whole, marine mollusks have caused relatively few deaths among man. The main dangers come from the venomous Indo-Pacific cones—they have caused only 9 or 10 deaths—from the octopus that on rare occasions inflicts a fatal bite and from bivalves that carry paralytic shellfish poisoning, responsible for more than 200 deaths. Numerous outbreaks of infectious hepatitis and typhoid have been directly attributed to clams and oysters that were collected near sewer outlets.

Freshwater snails of Egypt, Venezuela, the Philippines and China have indirectly caused the deaths of hundreds of thousands of people because they are the intermediate hosts of the fatal blood fluke disease schistosomiasis, or bilharziasis. The larval stages of the guilty trematode worm must spend several weeks developing and multiplying inside certain species of snails before they can attack and infect man. There have been no cases of this disease in Canada or mainland United States.

Of more serious concern to seashore residents of North America is the possibility of becoming paralyzed and possibly dying from eating clams and mussels that are carriers of paralytic shellfish poisoning. In this day of "back-to-nature" and economic food hunting, caution should be exercised when eating raw or cooked clams and blue mussels taken from either of our coasts. Fortunately the infected areas are limited, the infectious season short and the deaths not many. The bivalves become poisonous because they ingest the microscopic marine algae *Gonyaulax*. This dinoflagellate "blooms" in great quantities when the temperature of the water exceeds 10°C. The causative agent on the Pacific coast is *G. acatenella;* on the Atlantic coast, it is *G. tamarensis*. Within historic medical times, there have been 957 cases of bivalve paralytic poisoning, 222 of which have resulted in death. These figures do not include cases of severe allergic reactions to eating shellfish. Mussel poisonings, including deaths, have also been recorded from Scotland, Wales, Belgium, Ireland, France, Australia, New Zealand, South Africa and Japan.

On the Atlantic coast there have been about 100 poisonings and three deaths. The areas affected were the Bay of Fundy between New Brunswick and Nova Scotia and the Gaspé Peninsula in Quebec. Bivalves carrying the poison are the mussels *Mytilus edulis* and *Modiolus modiolus,* the Soft-shelled Clam *Mya,* the Surf Clam *Spisula solidissima* and the razor clam *Ensis*. Poisonings occur between June 4 and October 11, with the peaks being in August and September. Ordinary cooking reduces but by no means eliminates the poison. There is a wide range in the degree of human susceptibility—some people, especially those who do not normally eat shellfish, are very sensitive. Cats and chickens die very quickly when fed infected clams or even the "rims," or trimmings, of scallops. The muscles of scallops are not infected and therefore safe to eat.

Within five minutes of chewing an infected bivalve, the victim begins to feel a stinging, tingling and numbness of the lips, tongue and throat. In the case of severe poisonings, when five to twenty bivalves have been eaten, there will be, within fifteen to thirty minutes, a numbness of the fingers and toes that may spread to the knees, then hips. The face, arms and neck may become paralyzed. Death ensues when the paralysis affects the respiratory muscles. The effects usually last from eight to forty-eight hours, depending upon the dose.

The Pacific coast has had more trouble with this than the Atlantic. The earliest recorded cases occurred on June 15, 1793, when one death and four illnesses took place among Captain George Vancouver's men, who had eaten toxic mussels in British Columbia. According to historians, in 1799 the Russian Baranoff expedition lost about one hundred men near Sitka, Alaska, from eating infected mussels. The Pacific infections are recorded from eleven species of edible bivalves, including the venerid clams and *Mytilus* mussels.

Any carnivore that eats an infected bivalve will also carry this infection. For instance, whelks and moon snails, which often feed upon clams, may also be toxic when eaten.

LEFT: Although the blue mussel, *Mytilus edulis* Linné, is farmed and extensively eaten in Europe, in eastern Canada they are dangerous to eat at certain seasons.
ABOVE: Pacific cones have stung and killed at least ten people. This is *Conus ammiralis* Linné, a potentially dangerous species from the Indo-Pacific.

Early man used every edible plant and animal at one time or another for medicinal purposes. Many plants and animals were adopted as medicines for superstitious reasons or simply because they resembled the shape of some organ of the human body. A heart-shaped leaf or cockle clam was supposedly good for heart trouble. Mollusks stood high among the foods that were considered an aid to sexual activities. The belief is still prevalent that oysters are good for one's sex life. Automobile bumper stickers in the eastern United States and signs in seafood restaurants proclaim Eat Oysters, Love Longer, a slogan undoubtedly invented by the public relations firm representing the oyster industry. Lord Byron's Don Juan claimed that "Oysters are amatory food." It is reported that some diners at Roman feasts consumed several hundred at one sitting. As if to prove this point, a Joe Garcia of Melbourne, Australia, appears to have broken the record in 1955 by eating 480 in sixty minutes!

For many centuries, and even today in China, pearls ground into a powder and dispensed with milk and various herbs have been considered cures for stomach troubles. Snails were used throughout the ages as a medicine, generally for treating bad colds and for consumption. There are at least two stories about snails having been introduced to other countries by some distinguished person for the benefit of his consumptive wife. One case involved Sir Kenelm Digby, who introduced *Helix pomatia* to England; the other involved the governor of Madagascar, who in 1800 introduced the Giant African Snail to his palace gardens for the benefit of his sick wife. In the sixteenth century, it was thought that convulsions resulting from high fever could be forestalled by "beating snales which be in shell with bay salt and mallowes, and laid to the bottomes of your feet and to the wristes of your

hands." A popular Spanish cure for headache was to "Make a poultice of bruised snails. They must be broken up with their shells and put into a piece of linen folden 4 times as to make it thick, dip it in brandy, and squeeze it tolerably dry; then apply it to the forehead." The thought is enough to give moderns a headache!

Pliny recommended that raw mollusks be used to cure sore throats and coughs. There seems to be some scientific basis for this cure. In the 1960s it was discovered that extracts of the Hard-shelled Clam, later called mercenine, was a strong growth-inhibitor of experimental cancers in mice. Subsequent work by Drs. C. F. Li and Benjamin Prescott at the National Institutes of Health in Washington, D.C., found that one active fraction of raw abalone juice was very effective against penicillin-resistant strains of *Staphylococcus aureus, Streptococcus pyogenes, Salmonella typhi* and paratyphoid A and B. The new substance was called paolin. Experiments have demonstrated that the juices from oysters also have antiviral properties.

OPPOSITE: The venom injected into the flesh of a human being by this small Australian octopus, *Hapalochlaena lunulata* (Quoy and Gaimard), can cause death within a few hours. × 0.5. ABOVE: The venomous cone, *Conus omaria* Hwass, extends its siphon (left) and dangerous proboscis. × 2.

Mollusks and pollution

Several years ago a malacologist asked an official of a large American railroad why he didn't take the precaution of protecting the wooden pilings of a train causeway that passed over a salty marsh. It was common knowledge, at least to biologists and malacologists, that the shipworm clam can thrive in such an environment and, by boring into the wood, reduce the causeway to rubble within a few years. The executive laughed and explained that there was no danger and that there was no need to spend millions of dollars impregnating the pilings with creosote. There already was a "natural" cure. Pollution of the water, the filth and oily refuse from nearby industries, was so strong in that marine marsh that no *Teredo* shipworms or boring crustacea could possibly survive. One biological wag once facetiously said that if a magician could suddenly clean up our harbors and estuaries without cost, the shipping and railroad companies would go broke trying to save the wharves and bridges from being destroyed by reinvading marine organisms.

The absence of certain mollusks is an excellent indicator of pollution and other abnormal environmental conditions. Despite all the expensive precautions that many enlightened manufacturers take, there is no way of predicting the effect of sewage through chemical and temperature measurements. The delicate organisms of the area are the best barometers and will soon give warnings if biological disaster is ahead.

Certain sensitive species die off first. When the Florida Everglades were being drained excessively by artificial canals into the lagoons and bays of east Florida, particularly Boynton Inlet, the cowries, tun shells and *Strombus* conchs were the first to succumb to the sudden drop in water salinity. The more tolerant estuarine species, such as *Cerithidea*, *Neritina* and *Littorina*, suddenly blossomed and took over the environment. But when sulfides and oil pollutants are added, even these species disappear.

Oil spills in excess of a thousand gallons are very destructive to mollusks, especially to the bivalves, whose microscopic breathing cilia are paralyzed by oil that eventually sinks to the bottom in intertidal areas. A new threat to the open expanses of the salt marshes, where there are billions of mussels and snails serving as potential nutrients for offshore fisheries, are the huge nuclear plants that give off millions of tons of heated water. A rise of only a few degrees, particularly during the higher temperatures of summer, often makes deserts of marshes. Fortunately, remedial steps are well on their way toward solving this man-made imbalance.

The introduction by man, either accidentally or purposely, of foreign mollusks is a very old form of

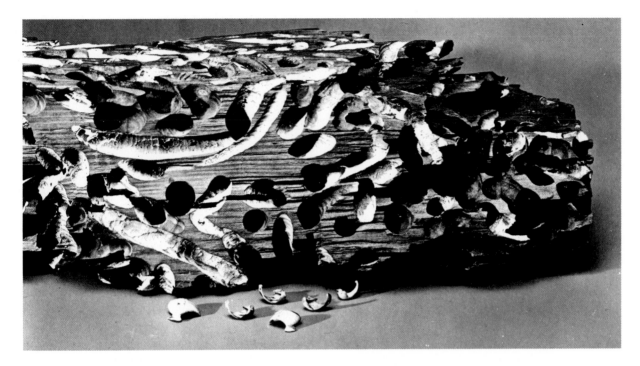

pollution. A foreign species introduced to a new environment usually has no natural enemies to keep it in check. Furthermore, it may find the new habitat particularly rich in foods not available in its homeland. If the introduced mollusk multiplies rapidly and becomes a pest by destroying beneficial mollusks or crowding out useful native species, it becomes as much a factor of pollution as chemicals or excessive temperatures.

An outstanding example of unwanted introduction is the American Slipper Shell, *Crepidula fornicata,* which was accidentally introduced to England at the end of the nineteenth century. It soon began to choke the oyster beds by its sheer numbers. Today, sea bottoms must be dredged to remove the pests so that the oysters will have room to settle. A number of snail drills were brought in with oyster seeds from Japan to the Pacific coast of the United States many years ago, and they still constitute an expensive menace. The latest, most drastic introduction was the Chinese freshwater clam *Corbicula* which has invaded and almost completely clogged the irrigation ditches of California. It is now so abundant in midwestern rivers that cement can no longer be made with the gravel contaminated by these soft shells.

OPPOSITE: Abandoned wrecks are eventually weathered away and, if made of wood, may be eaten down by bivalve shipworms. ABOVE: *Teredo* shipworms riddled this plank within a few months.

Shells and psychiatry

There is a popular saying, "You don't have to be crazy to be a shell collector, but it certainly helps!" that is most often made by people who have a very strong, abiding interest in shells but who feel somewhat guilty that their preoccupation is shining above the priorities of their spouses, their children or their normal circles of friends. Hobbies are, however, very necessary things for many people, and many depressed, bored or cynical individuals might be satisfied, fulfilled, deeply interested and productive if they had a hobby to use as a medium for self-expression. "Shells don't talk back to me!" is a statement I have heard from several professional malacological scientists. They were each really saying, "I find life's problems tough and I like to seclude myself occasionally among my shells and concentrate on them so that I can solve simple problems, one by one, without someone's frustrating me."

The psychological benefits of shell collecting and shell studying are no more extensive than those of any other interest or hobby that allows the individual to forget himself and his problems for a while, enabling him to "recharge his batteries" in order to return to the humdrum life of business or housework.

Shells in themselves have no special psychiatric charm for normal people and, indeed, may represent a menace or a real frustration. In my thirty years of experience as an editor of several scientific journals, I have seen several examples of excessive interest in shells. "Every time I pick up my pen to work on the so-and-so family, I feel a wave of physical nausea and revulsion. I am sorry, but I cannot complete my project that I promised you. I have worked on it so long that I am sick of it" are the sentiments of individuals who have had "too much of one thing" to the exclusion of other interests. Even a malacologist, reveling in shells all day and being paid for it, needs normal diversions.

One of the earliest works dealing with beneficial results of studying and admiring shells was that of the Italian Jesuit priest Philippo Buonanni, who produced, in 1681, the first extensively illustrated book on shells. His title—*Recreation for the Eyes and the Mind . . . through the Study of Shells*—was a psychiatric one. It was an introduction to the study of conchology and suggested that some degree of peace of mind could be found in pursuing such problems as the way in which colors are produced in shells, the way that spiral gastropods obtained their form and the ways in which mollusks are useful to man. Although his treatise was interwoven with some degree of mysticism and a nonscientific approach to the biblical flood and existing fossils, his woodcuts of foreign shells brought to central Rome from far away were useful references for scientists, such as Linnaeus, for many years to come.

A leading Boston psychiatrist, who later gave his life in World War II while helping battle-fatigued soldiers, once wrote a fifteen-page article for the *American Imago*, explaining why he liked shells. He was of the Freudian school, so after simply stating that he studied conchology because he enjoyed it, he went on to say that during his early days his father had sent him shells that he enjoyed playing with and that during his later years a stranger had sent his mother a green turban shell that reminded the psychiatrist of her beautiful face. However, he did mention a number of feelings and procedures that pleased him about shell collecting. They are familiar to most shell enthusiasts:

(1) I collected shells—actually hunted them up and searched them out. (2) Then I cleaned, sorted, classified, labeled and studied them. (3) I gave away or swapped duplicates for other shells. (4) I showed them to people who were interested, which made me feel important. (5) People gave me shells. (6) I began to collect a library about shells and thus . . . studied geography and natural history. (7) Gradually I began to get the feel for general science and logic. (8) Shells were an emotional outlet and a help in adjusting to the natural restrictions of my early home and school life. (9) Last (or first) I believe that the study of shells, as a sublimation, aided me in my unconscious efforts to deal with my inner drives. Shells probably represented things I wanted but could not have at that time.

Psychiatrists, who deal with sane people more often than with insane people, find that simple psychotherapy in the form of shell collecting is ideal for certain people suffering from mental strain, nervous fatigue or mild psychoneurosis. It is especially useful in the case of men plunged into retirement who have no hobby cushion or challenging avocation. Shell collecting is also recognized as being a cooperative venture that allows several members of a family to participate, bringing about better understanding among them.

A Jesuit priest, Philippo Buonanni, in 1681 published this treatise, *Recreation for the Eyes and the Mind . . . through the Study of Shells*. He extolled the virtues of conchology as a hobby.

Shells and the connoisseur 11

Early shell art

PRECEDING PAGES: The study desk of a true connoisseur of mollusks. ABOVE: An artistic attempt by a shell lover of the 1600s. OPPOSITE, TOP: A shell cameo of exquisite detail, made in Italy about 1890. BOTTOM: Nineteenth-century whalers made valentines from colorful shells.

The original use of shells in artistic designs and decorations is undoubtedly lost in the unrecorded history of early man. It would be inconceivable to think that the first peoples to show any signs of appreciation of beauty and art did not arrange pretty shells on the sand beach to amuse themselves. Some of the early surviving examples of pottery and ceramics in Europe have shells buried in the clay. The primitive mound-building Indians of Mississippi used ground mother-of-pearl shell to enhance the beauty of their pottery.

During the Renaissance, when collections of shells from foreign lands came into vogue, specimens were placed in drawers in cabinets. Since a scientific classification had not yet been developed, the owners arranged their shells in various kinds of designs, some taking the outlines of traditional wreaths, others resembling faces of animals or persons.

During the Elizabethan era and on through the early Victorian period, the creation of huge shell grottos became fashionable on English estates. They were roomlike retreats, usually supplied with a fountain bearing a giant clam, where lovers could find moments of privacy. During those times large supplies of pretty clams and conchs from the New World tropics were being brought to English ports. It was not uncommon to see more than three or four hundred West Indian Fighting Conchs, *Strombus pugilis,* cemented to the roofs of alcoves. Small and quite delicate floral bouquets of shells also became popular, but they were placed under glass domes to protect them from dust and to prevent the rusting of wires.

The first great producers of shell books usually reserved a section in the back of their encyclopedias for illustrating especially outstanding examples of shell arrangements. Among these were Buonanni (1638–1725), who advocated making shell arrangements as a recreation; Albert Seba, the Amsterdam druggist (1665–1736), who depicted the heads of monsters with shells and sold his collection to Peter the Great in 1717; and G. W. Knorr, who wrote a colorful lexicon (1760–1773) entitled *The Delights of the Eyes and the Soul, or a general collection of shells*. Auguste II, king of Poland, decorated his shell room with complicated murals made entirely of shells. The wall monogram of the king was surrounded by two bouquets of flowers and two platters of fruit, all formed of shells.

In France and the United States, about the time of the American Revolution, the art of using shells to make glazed ceramic towers, each about two feet tall, came into vogue. Some of the surviving pieces in museums and private collections have shells that are readily identifiable as being from the Caribbean. Most royal collections of shells in Europe had their share of shell bouquets and mosaics made by the ladies of the court.

While whaling was at its height during the middle of the nineteenth century, the art of producing sailor's valentines came into being. These were fashioned from a pair of octagonal shadow boxes, outlined with polished wooden frames, covered with glass and hinged so that they would open like a book. Within the boxes were intricately designed scenes and floral arrangements made of shells. Most of the sailor's valentines were made of West Indian shells. It is said that a moderately good business existed in Barbados and other West Indian ports where local Negro women made elaborate valentines to sell to sailors who had dissipated their time aboard ship playing cards.

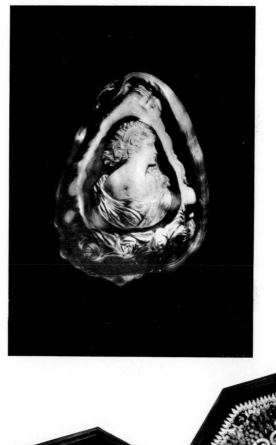

Today's shell art and jewelry

Shellcraft and shell art of today are as varied in subject matter, medium of expression and quality as are the more conventional forms of pictorial art. What one person considers attractive and tasteful may, indeed, be offensive and gauche to another. There are some schools that prefer to work in shells in natural color, despising the creations of those who dye and disfigure their shells. Some very delicately dyed shells have, however, been effectively and tastefully used in some of the most graceful of shell art and shellcraft.

A number of artists, mainly women, have revived the Victorian art of making flowers of natural-colored seashells. Their creations over recent years have had to meet the standards of some of the most famous shell shows in America. As a result, there has arisen an aristocracy of shell art, superior in many respects to its Victorian counterpart.

The zenith of today's shell art is reached in the exquisite, life-size bouquets of flowers made entirely of natural shells. This enchanting pursuit calls for an inborn ability in artistry and handicraft, a blending of knowledge of botany and floral arranging, a bit of conchological science and a beachcomber's endurance for shell collecting. Certain species of cleaned, undyed shells are chosen to make various kinds of flowers. Buttercups, for instance, are made of five bright yellow cupped valves of the Common Jingle, *Anomia simplex*. *Janthina* purple sea snails are used to make the bell-shaped violet flowers in the erect spike of Canterbury bells. Carnations are beautifully represented by thin valves of the Kitten's Paw Shell, *Plicatula gibbosa*, especially specimens that have dentate, or toothed, margins and dark hairlines at the edges. Among the genera used most frequently for petals are *Tellina, Macoma, Mytilus, Argopecten*, the freshwater mussel *Elliptio, Donax* and *Laevicardium*. The tiny baby *Busycon* whelks found in egg capsules

Jewelry featuring shells has been created by man since early Egyptian days, but today's height in grace and charm has been reached by Marguerite Stix of New York.

228

TOP and LEFT: Floral arrangements
made from undyed, natural shells,
created by Helen K. Krauss.
CENTER RIGHT: Modern carving done
by Taiwan artisans on the
polished surface of the Green
Turbo, *Turbo marmoratus* Linné.

are used in the centers of flowers with their narrow ends pointed either up or down, depending upon the flower.

Shadow boxes to display shell arrangements are made of deep picture frames that have been covered with glass and bounded by a wooden or metal frame. They are deep enough, say from two to four inches, to permit the use of a ceramic vase as a base for arrangements of shell bouquets. The arrangement becomes a sort of bas-relief with the flowers all turning toward the viewer. The background may be a smooth, pastel-shaded cloth or it may be lightly tinted with paint. Shadow boxes also lend themselves well to mosaics, which are geometrically arranged patterns of clumps of flowers interspersed with ovals, triangles and diamonds, all made of various colors and species of shells. Some very intricate works may incorporate as many as 10,000 specimens. Many shadow boxes are constructed to resemble underwater scenes, in which case objects other than shells are introduced to simulate the graceful life of the watery reefs. Bits of coral, sea fans and mounted seaweeds and starfish are sparingly and tastefully employed.

Montages, or three-dimensional panels, are made of shells and other forms of sea life that are raised enough to cast a shadow. Although these arrangements are not usually glassed in, they are often seen in deep shadow boxes. Today, such open creations are lightly sprayed with clear plastic so that they can be easily cleaned.

Perhaps the most exquisite and intricate of glassed-in shadow-box art are the miniature oval creations made of tiny, almost microscopic shells. These are usually made in pairs, one being the mirror image of the other. In a good miniature frame—less than three or four inches to a side—there may be more than 1,000 individual shells, arranged to represent a bouquet of flowers, with perhaps a shell hummingbird, butterfly or snail added to give additional charm. None of the shells in these miniatures is larger than a grain of rice.

Artistic standards for other objects made of shell material are equally demanding. Animals, dolls and jewelry made from shells are studies in themselves, and, alas, it is only the soul of an artist, the hand of a craftsman, the judgment of a connoisseur, the patience of Job and the heart of a saint that can create the perfect piece.

Some of man's great triumphs in the field of shell artistry have been in his creations of cameos and other jewelry. These creations require artistic talent, skill, patience and knowledge not only of the raw material but of the art form itself. Some of the greatest cameo creations were born of the labors of a team of experts—the art designer, the craftsman who executed the carving and the shell buyer. The professional designer of jewelry, when creating a piece, selects a subject that appeals to his sensibilities and portrays some emotion, personality or event. Then by tasteful selection of the perfect shells in combination with supporting metal edgings and matrices, gemstone borders and beads, the artist fashions an inspiring piece of jewelry. Sheer simplicity may give a stunning grandeur to some pieces, such as a single rosé pearl, twelve millimeters in diameter, hanging delicately from a thin, gold chain.

Cameo carving is an ancient art, usually employing snail shells or, rarely, hard chalcedony gemstone. A cameo is engraved through several layers of differently colored shell material to give a shallow relief. The engraver obtains a great sense of natural depth by having his subject, in the upper pale-colored layers, highlighted and contrasted by the darker layers below. Shell cameos are shaped by hand, with the aid of steel tools, gouges and points, and finished with files and abrasive powders. The better pieces are beautifully finished so that even under a hand lens one cannot readily detect scratches or "overshoots" caused by slips of the engraving tool. Four species of large shells are used in cameo making, the most common of which is the Red Helmet, *Cypraecassis rufa*, a thick five- to eight-inch-long shell from the Indian Ocean. The smaller and thicker male shells make better cameos. The layers range in color from light whitish orange to a deep brownish orange. Cameos made from this species are rarely more than two inches in size.

Other cameo shells include the large *Cassis madagascariensis* of the Caribbean. In the gemstone trade they are called the Black Helmets. The upper layers are alabaster to cream white in color, while the lower levels are dark brown to blackish. Because of the large size, this species is used for carving large artistic scenes. The pictorial cameos are not removed from the shell. The Sardonyx Helmet, *Cassis tuberosa,* of the West Indies, is used for small, brown-and-white cameos, and the Pink Conch, *Strombus gigas,* so abundant in the Bahamas, makes a thin, pink-and-white cameo, which is not particularly popular because the colors soon fade. Florence and Torre del Greco, near Naples, are the great Italian centers of shell cameo manufacture.

The nautilus shell is so thin that it is used as a medium for black-stained scrimshaw work or for delicate filigree carving. Small bits of polished shell are used in inlay work. A large, silvery blue *coque de perles* is obtained by removing a section of the inner whorl, cutting it off flat and filling it with wax or cement. The result resembles a large blister pearl. Small carvings are made from abalone shell, but traditionally these shells have been used for inlay work in metal goblets, snuff boxes and wooden panels. *Haliotis rufescens,* the Red Abalone, and *H. fulgens,* the Green Abalone, both of California,

are the most popular, mainly because of their size.

The bright, glossy, green cat's-eye that serves as an opercular trapdoor for the Pacific Tapestry Turban, *Turbo petholatus,* is used extensively in pendants and bracelets or mounted in its natural state. Pearl shell engravings, figures and small utensils are made from the shells of two large pearl oysters—*Pinctada margaritifera,* the Black-Lip Pearl Oyster of the Indo-Pacific, and the Gold-Lip Pearl Oyster, *P. maxima,* of the southwest Pacific. Carvings and engravings are made by Oriental artists in two species of heavy, pearly snail shells from the tropical Pacific—the Green Turban, *Turbo marmoratus,* a ten-inch shell from southeast Asia that lends itself to large, deep engraving, and the Commercial Top Shell, *Trochus niloticus,* a smaller shell abundantly fished in the Palau Islands, the Andaman Sea and northern Australia. The latter is used mainly for buttons and small pearly trinkets.

A large scallop shell, hinged and bound in gold, has been used to fashion a woman's compact, its striations far handsomer than man-made decoration.

Voyages for shells

The earliest voyages for shells were undertaken by the ancient Phoenicians, who traveled as far as the British Isles and circumnavigated Africa in search of new beds of dye-producing murex shells. Other commercial voyages involved the quest for pearl shells and money cowries. But scientific voyages for natural history specimens, and for mollusks in particular, were long in coming. In fact, most of the great voyages of exploration of the eighteenth and nineteenth centuries were flag-planting excursions in search of new sources of minerals, spices, rare woods and medicinal herbs. Nonetheless, many of them resulted in very important shell collections and in very impressive published volumes. The three voyages of Captain James Cook between 1768 and 1779 to the South Seas resulted in such profitable natural history collections that other nations soon followed with their own naturalistic voyages.

The first large scientific expedition to the New World was financed and organized by the great German naturalist Alexander von Humboldt in 1799. He and the botanist Aimé Bonpland spent five profitable years scouring the unexplored regions of northern South America. This was followed by

Alcide d'Orbigny's 1826 expedition for the Paris Museum to southern South America, a trip that resulted in a huge work on mollusks. Between 1826 and 1829, Quoy and Gaimard collected many molluscan novelties during the global travels of the *Astrolabe*. They published hundreds of exquisite colored paintings of living mollusks, together with pictures of their internal anatomy. Of almost equal splendor were the results of the twin voyages of the *Astrolabe* and the *Zelée*, published from 1842 to 1854 by Louis Rousseau, Jacques Hombron and Charles Jacquinot.

The British sponsored small expeditions during this period, including the voyage of the *Blossom* under Captain F. W. Beechey from 1825 to 1828, the *Sulphur* under Captain Edward Belcher from 1836 to 1842 and the *Samarang,* from 1843 to 1846. The latter voyage brought back great conchological treasures that were described by the ship's surgeon, Arthur Adams. Not to be outdone, the Americans, in 1837, mounted their United States Exploring Expedition to the Pacific. The expedition, under a nonnaturalist commander, did not fare well, and the somewhat poor catch of mollusks was unreported upon until about ten years later when the results were published by A. A. Gould.

With the coming of the steam engine and steel cables, attention was given to exploring deeper waters. The advent of dredging inspired many government-sponsored voyages, beginning in the 1860s. The British vessels *Lightning* and *Porcupine* worked bottom dredges at depths of 650 to 2,000 fathoms. One of the greatest scientific deep-sea expeditions was carried out under the direction of Sir Wyville Thompson aboard the *Challenger*. From 1872 to 1876, the expedition covered 69,000 miles and obtained the astonishing number of 1,900

OPPOSITE: Hundreds of voyages sponsored by private collectors have increased our knowledge of shells.
ABOVE: Pioneer voyage of the deep-sea investigations was made by the British corvette *Challenger* from 1872 to 1876.

species, some from as deep as 2,900 fathoms. Other great deep-sea voyages followed—the American *Blake* (1877–1880); the U.S. Fish Commission steamer *Albatross* (1887–1906); the German *Valdivia* (1898–1899); the Dutch *Siboga* (1899–1900); the Danish *Galathea* (1950–1952) and the Russian *Vitjaz* (1960s).

Many smaller privately sponsored voyages, almost too numerous to list, have been undertaken by enthusiastic amateur conchologists. There was Hugh Cuming's *Discoverer* in Polynesia (1827–1830); Sir Joseph Verco's *Adonis* and steamboat *Mermaid* in South Australia (1890–1914); John B. Henderson's yacht, the *Eolis,* that made seven cruises off Florida from 1910 to 1915; Alfred J. Ostheimer III's *Gloria Maris,* that, between 1955 and 1962, doubled the size of the marine collection at the Academy of Natural Sciences of Philadelphia and Mrs. Mariel King's motor launch, *Pele,* that in the 1960s stimulated interest in the various kinds of Hawaiian and western Australian mollusks.

Famous shell collectors

Of the many hundreds of truly outstanding collectors in the annals of conchology, four or five individuals stand out as unqualified successes in accumulating significant collections. There were undoubtedly many collectors in ancient and medieval times whose collections have long since been lost or destroyed, such as those of the Roman consuls Laelius and Scipio of the second century B.C. Many royal families amassed shell collections, some of which became the nuclei of national scientific museum collections. Among the royal collectors have been Louis XIII of France; Empress Catherine II and Peter the Great of Russia; Christian VI of Denmark; Cosimo III, the grand duke of Tuscany; Empress Maria Theresa of Austria; Queen Louisa Ulrica of Sweden and, today, Emperor Hirohito of Japan, whose excellent training as a marine biologist enhances his interest in collecting.

The earliest of the outstanding scientific collectors was George Eberhard Rumpf, more often referred to as Rumphius, since that is his Latin name appearing on the title page of his classic chronicle of shell observations, *Amboinsche Rariteitkamer.* Born in Holland in 1627, Rumphius was sent to Amboina in the East Indies to be the representative of the Dutch East India Company. There he amassed an enormous amount of material on the mollusks of the Indo-Pacific, which he put down in the first extensive written account of their natural history. He originated most of the names of the common Pacific shells as we know them today, such as *Cassis cornuta,* and was the first to report upon the fatal bites of cone shells. Although Rumphius became blind in the middle part of his life, he continued his work for years. He lost his wife and his first set of manuscript drawings in the Amboina fire of 1687. One set of his text was lost at sea, and by the time a second set reached Holland to be published, in 1705, Rumphius had been dead for three years. He became known as the "Pliny of the East Indies," and his work has been frequently quoted by

every subsequent generation of conchologists.

Whereas Rumphius was a field collector, the second duchess of Portland was a drawing-room collector. Born in England in 1714, Margaret Cavendish Bentinck was an attractive, wealthy lady who had an insatiable taste for collecting shells. Among the distinguished people to be entertained at either of her two mansions were King George III, the French botanist Rousseau, Captain James Cook, Sir Joseph Banks, the shell dealer George Humphrey and the shell artist Thomas Martyn. She employed Daniel Solander, the knowledgeable conchologist and student of Linnaeus, to curate and prepare a catalog of her huge, growing collection. Solander died before publishing the results, and three years

ABOVE: Most famous of yesterday's collectors were the Englishman Hugh Cuming (1791–1865) and the Belgian Philippe Dautzenberg (1849–1935).
OPPOSITE: Before the days of Linnaeus and modern classification, seventeenth-century shell collections were artistically arranged in drawers.

later the duchess died but not before exhausting her fortune, largely on shells and objects of art. A public auction, in 1786, of her 4,000 lots of shells lasted almost a month and fetched more than £11,000 (about $100,000 today). Most of the higher-priced shells were purchased by the duke of Calonne, the prerevolutionary minister of finance of France.

Hugh Cuming (1791–1865) was to conchology as Henry Ford was to the automobile industry. No man has ever equaled the amount of material he personally acquired nor discovered a larger number of new species. Cuming, a sailmaker who had made his fortune in Chile, built himself a yacht and christened it the *Discoverer*. From 1827 to 1831, he sailed among the Polynesian Islands and up and down the Pacific coast of South and Central America. When he returned to London, the great scientists of Europe clamored to examine his new species; in the years that followed, nearly 2,000 species discovered by Cuming were described by the Sowerbys, Reeve, Pfeiffer, Deshayes, P. P. Car-

penter, Henry Adams, Dunker, Pease and Philippi, to mention but a few great conchologists. Cuming's greatest expedition, which lasted from 1836 to 1840, was to the Philippines. There he collected great stocks—including 3,000 species of shells, 3,400 different plants and 1,200 birds—that he used later for selling and trading. The remainder of his collection is in the British Museum of Natural History in London.

Probably the greatest twentieth-century collector and, indeed, an outstanding conchologist in his own right was Philippe Dautzenberg, a Belgian born in 1849 and later heir to a fortune from the carpet industry. He spent the early part of his life collecting in European waters, and at the same time he accumulated rarities and old collections by purchase. By the age of sixty-five, he had acquired more than 30,000 species and a magnificent library. Fortunately, his well-documented collection, including such rarities as *Conus gloriamaris* and *Cypraea valentia,* is preserved in the Institut Royal des Sciences Naturelles in Brussels.

Famous malacologists

The study of mollusks is called either conchology or malacology, terms originally meaning the same thing but in recent years somewhat polarized into *conchology* to mean the study of shells, particularly by amateurs, and *malacology* to mean the study of mollusks, their shells and their biology. Both terms have been in use for over 200 years as have the alternate spellings, *mollusc* and *mollusk*. The latter, used in the nineteenth century in England, is still the one more frequently used, particularly in America.

Early malacologists were usually physicians who knew anatomy and looked upon shells as being the external skeletons of living animals. In their spare time, physicians often collected, observed and published works concerning their personal interests, which in many cases were mollusks, insects or plants. Dr. Martin Lister, physician to Queen Anne of England, was an ardent student of mollusks. He not only collected and dissected many species but he also traveled throughout Europe to inspect and and in some cases borrow specimens for study. He published two books, one in 1678 and one in 1685, on the shells of the British Isles. His great work *Historia Conchyliorum,* consisting of a thousand engraved plates of worldwide species, was for years the only reliable source of illustration for most species. It was the first scientific attempt to arrange the mollusks in related systematic categories. Other early malacologists who had an appreciation of mollusks as living organisms were Argenville of France, Poli of Italy and Michel Adanson, also of France.

One of the most industrious and competent malacologists of the late 1700s was a Danish clergyman, Johann Chemnitz, who wrote eight enormous volumes on the shells of the world. His beautiful colored plates, long and accurate descriptions, attention to locality data when he had it and classification were a great stimulus to others in the field. He was followed by another producer of excellent encyclopedias, Jean G. Bruguière, a Frenchman who had a masterly sense of speciation and kept accurate locality data as well as original notes taken during his travels to the South Seas.

Malacology did not come of age until some years after the Swedish botanist Linnaeus had published, in 1758, his system of binomial, or two-name, nomenclature. Once this was accepted, distinguished zoologists of France—Georges Cuvier (1769–1832); H. M. de Blainville (1777–1850), who popularized the term *malacology* in 1832; Comte de Lamarck (1744–1829) and his disciple G. B. Deshayes (1796–1875)—launched modern malacology on its way. France's great contributions to malacology continued until World War I through the efforts of Paul Fischer (1835–1893), J. C. H. Crosse (1826–1898) and anatomist-biologist Paul Pelseneer (1863–1928).

Meanwhile, England was languishing scientifically under the influence of drawing-room shell collectors and the species-mongering, or the overdescribing of new species, of G. B. Sowerby II and III, Lovell Reeve and James Cosmo Melvill. The first and last of the true malacologists at the British Museum was Edgar Albert Smith (1847–1916), a scientist who contributed many outstanding research works in all fields of mollusks while at the same time taking care of the museum's enormous and chaotic collection.

At this time, August A. Gould (1805–1866) and W. G. Binney (1833–1909) in Boston and George W. Tryon (1838–1888) in Philadelphia helped to keep malacology in America alive. Later on, the two giants in America were William Healy Dall (1845–1927), a broad zoologist and paleontologist working for the U.S. Geological Survey, and Henry August Pilsbry (1862–1957), who produced superior research for seventy-five years at the Academy of Natural Sciences of Philadelphia. He described over 3,000 species and genera and for some time also served as editor of the *Nautilus,* America's oldest scientific mollusk journal.

Thomas Say (1787–1834), malacologist and entomologist, was considered the father of American conchology. Born in Philadelphia, he later founded the Academy of Natural Sciences of Philadelphia. He explored many parts of North America and described several hundred Recent and fossil mollusks of the United States.

Charles Hedley (1862–1926), Australian marine zoologist, put Australian malacology on a firm scientific footing. He contributed greatly to the knowledge of the marine molluscan provinces surrounding that diverse continent. He was the curator of the mollusk collection at the Australian Museum in Sydney.

Otto A. L. Mörch (1828–1878), a productive conchologist of Denmark, specialized in vermetid gastropods and published numerous catalogs of local collections. He described many new species of mollusks from the Danish West Indies, particularly the Virgin Islands. Many new genera were proposed by him in his *Yoldi Catalogue*.

Henry A. Pilsbry (1862–1957), American malacologist and acknowledged world dean of malacology, described more than 3,000 mollusks during sixty years of work. He revolutionized the classification of land mollusks and produced many volumes of the *Manual of Conchology*. He was also an expert in marine mollusks and barnacles.

ABOVE: Four of many notable students of mollusks who have contributed to the science of malacology over the last 200 years.

Famous shell books

Over 4,000 books and nearly 91,000 shorter articles and monographs dealing exclusively with mollusks have been published since the invention of the printing press. Amid this great mass of literature, many works stand out for one reason or another—some because of their beauty, others for their scientific significance and a few because of rarity or curious circumstances. Some books with only small sections dealing with shells have had great influence, such as Aristotle's *History of Animals* (322 B.C.), Pliny's *Natural History* (A.D. 79) and Linnaeus's tenth edition of the *Systema Naturae* (1758).

The first printed book devoted exclusively to shells was produced in Rome in 1681 by the Italian Jesuit priest Philippo Buonanni. Its title translates as *Recreation for the Eyes and the Mind.* It extolls the virtues of shell collecting and illustrates many hundreds of worldwide species. In 1685 in England, this was followed by Martin Lister's huge, well-illustrated *Historia Conchyliorum,* a book of woodcuts that was used mainly for identification. The earliest multivolume work using beautifully hand-painted woodcuts was Georg W. Knorr's *Delights of the Eyes and the Soul* (1760–1773). It was issued originally in six parts. Knorr was a Nuremberg painter, not a conchologist, and had to borrow specimens from Dutch, French and German collectors to use as models. In 1769, the Hamburg physician Friedrich Martini began the first scientific iconography of shells, *New Systematic Conchological*

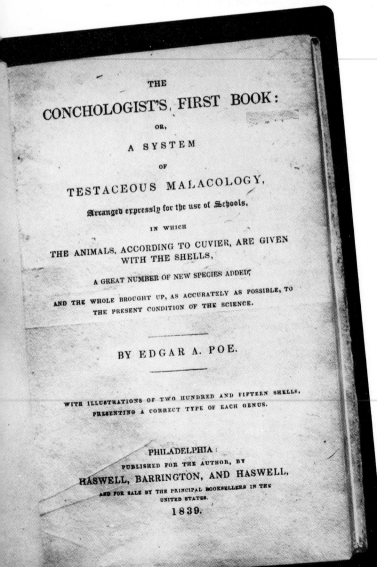

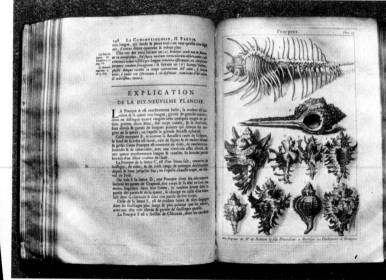

Cabinet. It unfortunately did not follow Linnaeus's binomial system of nomenclature.

In the nineteenth century, as the popularity of conchology increased and the state of its science improved, several large iconographs were launched. The Germans began Heinrich Küster's _Conchylien-Cabinet_ in 1839. The project continued sporadically until 1920, at which time it consisted of nearly a hundred parts with over 4,000 plates, most in color. In France, Louis Kiener—beginning the work in 1834 and ending, with the help of his successor, Paul Fischer, in 1879—produced ten volumes of exquisite illustrations. This work, _Iconograph of the Living Shells,_ and J. C. Chenu's _Conchological Illustrations,_ produced from 1843 to 1853, are probably the finest engraved works in the field of conchology. The English produced two great iconographs, the most extensive one being Lovell Reeve's _Conchologia Iconica,_ which was a twenty-volume work published from 1843 to 1878. It contained descriptions of thousands of new species. The other great work, by the G. B. Sowerbys—grandfather, father and son—was the five-volume _Thesaurus Conchyliorum,_ published from 1842 to 1887. In the United States, George W. Tryon launched his _Manual of Conchology_ in 1879. The first seventeen volumes dealt with marine mollusks. The succeeding twenty-eight volumes, on land mollusks, were completed by Henry A. Pilsbry in 1935.

The day of the great iconographs came and went and in its place came attempts to sum up the field in the form of textbooks and manuals. These were biological and classificatory in nature rather than descriptive. Blainville produced his manual on malacology in 1825, S. P. Woodward his _Manual of the Mollusca_ in 1851 and R. A. Philippi his handbook of conchology in 1853. Finally, the most influential and complete textbook, Paul Fischer's manual of conchology, was published in 1887.

There have been several infamous books in the history of conchology, including some of modern vintage. In 1811, George Perry produced a large folio book called _Conchology._ It contained sixty-one hand-colored plates and introduced numerous new genera and species. The paintings were so bizarre and nightmarish that the conchologists of the day attempted to rule out his "absurd names and pantomimic display of figures." Of equal anguish to modern scientists was the acceptance of a sales catalog published in 1798 by P. F. Röding. In it the author proposed numerous new species simply by referring to the figures in Martini's _Conchylien-Cabinet._ The book was overlooked until 1915, when the American malacologist W. H. Dall resurrected a copy and began to suppress many of Lamarck's well-known generic and specific names.

Edgar Allan Poe, the American poet, once "authored" a book, in 1839, entitled _The Conchologist's First Book._ Later editions appeared in 1843 and 1845. The book was almost a verbatim reprint of Thomas Brown's _The Conchologist's Textbook,_ published in England in 1833. Poe had innocently agreed to write a short foreword to the book so that good sales of the American edition would be assured. The publisher, however, later heralded the book as a Poe production, and the literary world rose up in rage to accuse the poet of blatant plagiarism, although he was innocent.

OPPOSITE, LEFT: The American poet Edgar Allan Poe claimed "authorship" of a book written by an Englishman, Thomas Brown, and caused a literary scandal. RIGHT: The first extensive semipopular book on conchology was written in 1742 by Argenville. ABOVE: The famous _Amboina Cabinet of Rarities_ of 1705 was written by G. E. Rumphius, who was blind.

Shell auctions

The first shell auctions were held in Holland during the early 1700s. They attracted purchasers from London, Paris and Copenhagen. One of the first English sales, that of the collection of Commodore Lisle, took place on February 21, 1753, at Longford's in London. A Precious Wentletrap, *Epitonium scalare*, brought £115, the equivalent today of $500. The next auction took place in 1777, opposite Slaughter's Coffee-house in London, and contained "a magnificent collection of shells, being the genuine and intire [sic] cabinet of a lady going abroad." One of the chief purchasers was George Humphrey (1745–1830), an intrepid and knowledgeable dealer who seems to have had his finger in every conchological pie of any importance for the best part of half a century. He obtained a lion's share of the collection of the duchess of Portland, which was auctioned off in 1786. It contained many rarities collected by James Cook, Sir Joseph Banks and Admiral Byron (grandfather of the poet). Another heavy purchaser at that auction was the representative of the prince of Calonne, also France's minister of finance. Eleven years later these shells, and the rest of the prince's collection, were brought back to England and auctioned off by Humphrey. Humphrey was also in charge of the auctioning of the famous Ashton Lever–James Parkinson collection of shells.

The nineteenth century was dotted with famous auctions, many offering unique specimens upon which the original scientific descriptions had been based. A rich Australian collection, assembled by G. F. Angus, took eight days to sell in 1821. The following year the collection of the widow of Captain William Bligh, of *Bounty* fame, was auctioned in three days by Dubois of Covent Garden.

By World War I, the death knell of famous shell auctions had sounded. Except for a few fund-raising donation auctions by various shell clubs, there were no further public auctions until they were revived by Elizabeth Wistar of Chestnut Hill, Pennsylvania. From 1956 to 1960, many thousands of dollars' worth of shells fell to the auctioneer's hammer. For several years after that, a spirited annual auction was held in New York under the auspices of the ardent shell collector Nick Katsaras. Sotheby and Company, famous auctioneers of London, also revived limited shell auctions in the late 1960s and early 1970s. They got together several dozen rarities, illustrated them handsomely in their catalog and auctioned off such choice items as *Cypraea guttata*, *Strombus listeri* and *Conus gloriamaris* and *C. bengalensis* at prices far above their going market values. Although there is a general rule that rare marine shells become more common as time goes on and as explorations continue, shell auctions will undoubtedly continue to be held as long as the practice of collecting shells is popular.

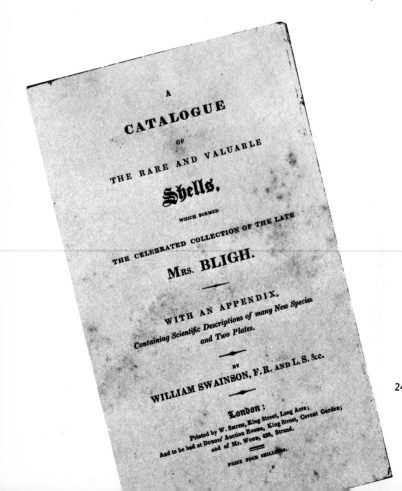

240 Early European explorers, such as Adm. William Bligh, brought many rare shells back to their homelands. Eventually they were passed on to following generations, as often as not through public auctions.

Shell shows

The exhibition of shells is a practice almost as old as the science of conchology. In the early days the museums and the meetings of local natural history clubs offered opportunities to display collections. The great international expositions of the nineteenth century in Paris, Brussels, Chicago and St. Louis had large exhibits of shells brought by various countries. The famous Quadras and Moellendorff collection of Philippine shells was a hit of the 1893 World's Fair in Chicago.

True shell shows, mainly an American innovation, began informally in Florida at the turn of the century, when enthusiastic shellers on Sanibel Island displayed their winter season's spoils on long tables set up on the veranda of the Island Inn. By the 1930s, this custom had expanded into a more formal shell show in which prize ribbons were given for the outstanding displays. Attendance by tourists increased each year, and soon shows were organized elsewhere with the cooperation of the local chambers of commerce and shell clubs. In 1942, the duchess of Windsor opened the first shell show, in Nassau, of the Bahama Conchological Society. In 1948, the Smithsonian Institution offered a top award for the annual participants of the show at St. Petersburg, Florida, at that time the largest show in the world. Today, more than twenty-five huge shows, each consisting of hundreds of entries in various classes, are held in Hawaii, California, Oregon, Texas and Florida. Attendance at a south Texas show has been as high as 12,000 people in one day. These shows have stimulated interest in shells among the public and among students just entering the field of marine biology. Conservation and antipollution themes are not uncommon in many exhibits, while instruction in biology, art and history are featured in others.

Shell shows were created for the enjoyment of participating shell enthusiasts, for the furthering of community activities and education and in some cases for the increased opportunity to sell shells, shell handicrafts and books on shells. These shows are operated on a voluntary basis, usually by members of a local club. The proceeds from entrance fees or the lottery of rare shells and shell tables is sometimes a considerable sum, usually used to help finance community projects in education and conservation. A successful show requires, among many other factors, an adequate exhibit area near ample parking facilities; sympathetic but strict, fair judging; several months' previous publication and distribution of uniform rules and types of entry classes; an orderly processing of entry applications; an allotment of adequate space and plenty of time to set up exhibits prior to judging and, above all, a desire by everyone concerned to consider the interests of the show as a whole, disregarding personal entries and interests.

It is best to have three judges, none of whom is a member of the club. Committees formed to organize and run a shell show are generally energetic "do-ers" capable of withstanding criticism and sustaining an unusual amount of patience

Rules for judging shell shows are fairly standard, although many are modified to meet special local conditions and interests. The entry classes are usually separated into three main divisions: (1) collections, (2) shellcraft, (3) children. The latter division is for exhibitors under seventeen years of age. Where competition may appear to be unequal, the children are divided into two age groups—under thirteen years old and from thirteen to sixteen years old. The number of points awarded varies from one class to another, but in general the percentage of points for, say, a worldwide collection would be divided as follows: attractiveness and arrangement, thirty points; quality and choice of species, forty points; accuracy of labeling, fifteen points; educational value of exhibit, five points; apparent amount of work on exhibit, ten points.

Some of the main types of entries in divisions 1 (collections) and 3 (children) are:

Worldwide collection: Not more than 200 species; limited to twenty square feet in size; specimens obtained personally or by purchase or gift.

Regional collection: Species collected from one region—for example, West Indies or Hawaii or Great Lakes. Not more than 400 species.

Local collection: Limited to a specific area defined by the show committee, usually a local island or lake or county.

Adult beginner's collection: Exhibitor must not have been maintaining a shell collection more than eleven months prior to show.

Commercial collection: Exhibitor must be a commercial dealer or consider himself in the business of selling shells. Limited to fifty specimens, with prices. Selling during the show is prohibited.

Family or genus collection: Group of labeled species belonging to one specific family (Conidae; Cypraeidae, etc.) or genus (*Voluta, Mitra, Cypraea,* etc.). The show committee usually has to set the taxonomic limits of the groups prior to the show.

Specialized collection: Includes freaks, albinos, growth series, examples of shell repair, etc.

Miniature shells: Micromounts or groups displayed under glass. Specimens may be adults or juveniles, but none may be over three-quarters inch in size.

Sea life: Nonmollusks, such as starfish, seaweeds, sponges, etc.

Division 3 (Shellcraft) is usually judged by those very familiar with art and handicraft. The main classes are floral arrangements, shell jewelry, shell tables, shell trays, and a class covering miscellaneous shell handicraft.

Earliest of the shell shows were sponsored by major museums, as shown here in a 1719 drawing of a European museum of natural history. [From Levin Vincent's *Elenchus Tabularum.*]

Guide to the seashell literature

This is a selective bibliography giving the more interesting references that will lead the student into the fascinating world of shell publications. In some of the categories, the books are appropriately arranged by date of publication while in others they are listed alphabetically by author.

Art, History and Literature

Cox, Ian. *The Scallop.* London: Shell Transport and Trading Co., 1957. Studies of a shell and its influences on mankind.

Dance, S. Peter. *Shell Collecting: An Illustrated History.* Berkeley: University of California Press, 1966. Excellent account of the early history of conchology.

Dance, S. Peter. *Rare Shells.* London: Faber and Faber, 1969. Contains color illustrations of fifty species with their histories.

Ehrhardt, A. *Muscheln und Schnecken.* Hamburg, 1941. A photographic study.

Hoare, Sarah. *Poems on Conchology and Botany.* London, 1831.

Jutting, Tera. *"Gloria Maris" Shells of the Malaysian Seas.* Amsterdam, 1952. A photographic study.

Krauss, H. K. *Shell Art.* New York: Hearthside Press, 1965.

Ritchie, Carson I. A. *Carving Shells and Cameos.* New York: A. S. Barnes and Co., 1970.

Robert, P. A. *Kunstgebilde des Meeres.* Bern: Iris, 1936. Fifteen colored plates suitable for framing.

Stix, Hugh and Marguerite and Abbott, R. Tucker. *The Shell: Five Hundred Million Years of Inspired Design.* New York: Harry N. Abrams, 1968.

Travers, L. A. *The Romance of Shells in Nature and Art.* New York: M. Barrows, 1962.

Early Books on Seashells

322 B.C. Aristotle. *History of Animals.* In this book, this great philosopher introduces the word *mollusk,* deals with mollusks' life habits and uses and first proposes the names *Tellina, Nerita, Purpura* and *Solen.*

77–79 A.D. Pliny the Elder. *Natural History.* An account of the way in which royal tyrian purple dye was discovered and made from *Murex.*

1558. Gesner, Conrad. *Historiae Animalium. Liber 4.* The account of a Swiss naturalist who formed what was probably the first shell collection along scientific lines.

1681. Buonanni, Philippo. *Ricreatione dell' òcchio e della mente.* This Italian Jesuit priest wrote the first large book extolling the virtues of shell collecting, *Recreation for the Eyes and Mind.*

1685. Lister, Martin. *Historia Conchyliorum.* A huge book, illustrated with woodcuts done by his wife and daughter. Lister was physician to Queen Anne of England.

1742. Argenville, A. J. D. *L'Histoire Naturelle . . . La Conchyliologie.* This and subsequent editions revised by the conchologist Favanne were the main conchology texts in eighteenth-century France.

1757. Adanson, Michel. *Histoire Naturelle du Sénégal: Coquillages.* The first comprehensive study of the anatomy and life history of mollusks, far ahead of its time.

Major Monographic Works

1769–95. Martini, F. H. W., and Chemnitz, J. H. *Neues systematisches Conchylien-Cabinet.* 11 vols. Nuremburg. The second series, 1837–1920, was continued by Küster, Kobelt and others.

1834–79. Kiener, L. C. *Spécies Général et Iconographie des Coquilles Vivantes.* 11 vols. Paris. A series of monographs with magnificently colored illustrations.

1842–87. Sowerby, G. B. *Thesaurus Conchyliorum, or Monographs of Genera of Shells.* 5 vols. London. Numerous small, hand-colored illustrations.

1843–78. Reeve, Lovell A., and Sowerby, G. B. *Conchologia Iconica,* 20 vols. London. A series of large, handsomely illustrated monographs.

1879–98. Tryon, G. W., and Pilsbry, H. A. *Manual of Conchology* (marine series). 17 vols. Philadelphia.

1941–current. Boss, K. J., ed. *Johnsonia.* 4 vols. Cambridge, Mass.: Museum of Comparative Zoology. Monographs of the marine mollusks of the Atlantic by Clench, Turner, Abbott, Boss and others.

1959–current. Abbott, R. Tucker, ed. *Indo-Pacific Mollusca.* Delaware Museum of Natural History. Monographs of the marine mollusks of the world with emphasis on the Indo-Pacific by Abbott, Powell, Rosewater and others. Colorplates.

Malacological Textbooks

1825. de Blainville, H. M. *Manuel de Malacologie et de Conchyliologie.* Paris. The first of the so-called modern textbooks.

1850. Johnston, G. *An Introduction to Conchology.* London. An excellent account with well-documented historical notes.

1851. Woodward, S. P. *A Manual of the Mollusca.* London.

1853. Philippi, R. A. *Handbuch der Conchyliologie und Malacozoologie.* Halle. The first German textbook.

1859. Chenu, J. C. *Manuel de Conchyliologie et de Paléontologie Conchyliologique.* 2 vols. Paris.

1880. Fischer, P. *Manuel de Conchyliologie et Paléontologie Conchyliologique.* Paris.

1882. Tryon, G. W. *Structural and Systematic Conchology.* 3 vols. Philadelphia.

1895. Cooke, A. H. *Mollusca.* Cambridge Natural History Series, vol. 3. London.

1906. Pelseneer, Paul. *Mollusca.* A Treatise on

Zoology, edited by Edwin Ray Lankester, vol 5. London. (Amsterdam: Asher and Co., 1964.)

1929. Thiele, J. *Handbuch der systematischen Weichtierkunde.* 4 vols. Jena. A standard reference on classification.

1938. Wenz, W. *Handbuch der Paläozoologie: Gastropoda.* Vol. 6 in 7 parts. Berlin. Gives modern higher classification.

1964. Wilbur, K. M., and Yonge, C. M. *Physiology of Mollusca.* New York: Academic Press.

1967. Hyman, L. H. *The Invertebrates.* Mollusca I, vol. 6. New York: McGraw-Hill.

1968. Purchon, R. D. *The Biology of the Mollusca.* Oxford and New York: Pergamon Press.

Popular Conchology (1815–1967)

1815. Brookes, S. *An Introduction to the Study of Conchology.* London. The first of many small nineteenth-century introductory books.

1821–34. Swainson, W. *Exotic Conchology.* London. A rare collection of forty-eight colorplates. Reproduced by the Delaware Museum of Natural History, 1968. Edited by R. Tucker Abbott.

1839. Poe, Edgar Allan. *The Conchologist's First Book.* Philadelphia. (Poe wrote only the introduction.)

1851. Roberts, Mary. *A Popular History of the Mollusca.* London. A charming and very informative introduction.

1908. Rogers, Julie E. *The Shell Book.* New York. This was the only good popular book available at the turn of the century.

1935. Webb, Walter F. *A Handbook for Shell Collectors.* Rochester, N.Y. One of the first dealers to publish a book with prices.

1957. Johnstone, Kathleen Y. *Sea Treasure.* Boston: Houghton Mifflin Co. An excellent introduction to the hobby.

1958. Nordsieck, F. *Meeresschnecken.* Stuttgart: Gustav Fischer. Forty-four plates of shell paintings.

1961. Cameron, R. *Shells*. London: G. P. Putnam's Sons (Pleasures and Treasures series).

1966. Abbott, R. T., ed. *How to Collect Shells*. By various experts. Describes collecting techniques. Available for two dollars from the American Malacological Union, 3957 Marlow Ct., Seaford, N.Y. 11783.

1967. Wagner, R. J. L., and Abbott, R. T. *Van Nostrand's Standard Catalog of Shells*. Lists thousands of shells and gives their approximate evaluations. Shell clubs and dealers listed. New York: Van Nostrand Reinhold Co.

1970. Johnstone, Kathleen Y. *Collecting Seashells*. New York: Grosset and Dunlap.

Identification Guides

Worldwide

Abbott, R. Tucker. *Sea Shells of the World*. A Golden Nature Guide. New York: Golden Press, 1962.

Marcy, J., and Bot, J. *Les Coquillages*. Paris: N. Boubee et Cie, 1969. Gastropods only.

Shikama, T., and Horikoshi, M. *Selected Shells of the World Illustrated in Colour*. 2 vols. Tokyo, 1963. Many beautiful colorplates.

The Americas

Abbott, R. Tucker. *American Seashells*. New York: Van Nostrand Reinhold Co., 1955. Fifteen hundred Pacific and Atlantic species.

Abbott, R. Tucker. *Seashells of North America: A Golden Field Guide*. New York: Golden Press, 1968. Eight hundred fifty species.

Bousefield, E. L. *Canadian Atlantic Shells*. Ottawa: National Museum of Canada, 1960.

Keen, A. Myra and Coan, E. *Marine Molluscan Genera of Western North America*. Stanford: Stanford University Press, 1963. Illustrated keys.

Keen, A. Myra. *Marine Shells of Tropical West America*. Stanford: Stanford University Press, 1971. Excellent. Over thirty-two hundred species.

Morris, P. A. *A Field Guide to the Shells*. Boston: Houghton Mifflin, 1951. Atlantic coast, Pacific coast and Hawaii.

Rice, Tom. *Marine Shells of the Pacific Northwest*. Edmonds, Wash.: Ellison Industries, 1971.

Rios, E. de Carvalhos. *Coastal Brazilian Seashells*. North Myrtle Beach, S.C.: Richard Petit, 1970.

Warmke, G. L., and Abbott, R. T. *Caribbean Seashells*. Narbeth, Pa. Livingston Co., 1961.

Europe

Arrecogros, J. *Coquillages Marins*. Lausanne: Librairie Payot, 1958.

Dautzenberg, P. *Des Coquilles des Côtes de France*. Bibliothèque de Poche du Naturaliste, no. 6. Paris: Librarie du Muséum, 1913.

Eales, N. B. *The Littoral Fauna of Great Britain*. Cambridge: Cambridge University Press, 1929.

Grimpe, G., and Wagler, E., ed. *Tierwelt der Nord- und Ostsee*. Vol 9. Mollusk sections by Ankel, Boettger, Hoffman, Jutting and Haas. Leipzig.

McMillan, Nora F. *British Shells*. London: Frederick Warne and Co., 1968.

Nobre, A. *Moluscos Marinhos de Portugal*. Lisbon: Instituto Zoologia de Universidade do Pôrto, 1932.

Tebble, N. *British Bivalve Seashells*. London: British Museum (Natural History) Handbook, 1966.

Africa and India

Barnard, K. H. *A Beginner's Guide to South African Shells*. Cape Town: Maskew Miller, 1953.

Hornell, J. *Indian Mollusca*. Bombay: Bombay Natural History Society, 1951.

Kennelly, D. H. *Marine Shells of Southern Africa*. 2d ed. Cape Town: Books of Africa, Ltd., 1969.

Nickles, M. *Mollusques Testaces Marins de la Côte Occidentale d'Afrique*. Paris: Lechevalier, 1950.

Spry, J. F. *The Sea Shells of Dar-es-Salaam*. Dar-es-Salaam: Tanganyika Society, 1961.

Japan and the South Seas

Brost, F. B., and Coale, R. D. *A Guide to Shell Collecting in the Kwajalein Atoll.* Rutland, Vt.: C. E. Tuttle Co., 1971.

Cernohorsky, W. O. *Marine Shells of the Pacific.* Sydney: Pacific Publications, Ltd., 1967. Gastropods only.

Habe, T. *Shells of the Western Pacific in Color.* Vol. 2. Osaka: Hoikusha, 1964.

Hirase, S., and Taki, I. *A Handbook of Illustrated Shells.* Tokyo: Maruzen, 1951.

Hirase, Y. *One Thousand Shells in Colour.* 4 vols. Kyoto: Unsodo, 1914–35. The famous accordion-pleated book with colored woodcuts. Only 400 complete sets made.

Kira, T. *Shells of the Western Pacific in Color.* Osaka: Hoikusha, 1965.

Australia and New Zealand

Allan, Joyce. *Australian Shells.* Melbourne: Georgian House, 1960.

Cotton, B. C. *South Australian Mollusca.* 3 vols. Adelaide: Government Printer, 1940–61.

Macpherson, J. H., and Gabriel, C. J. *Marine Molluscs of Victoria.* Melbourne: National Museum of Victoria, 1962.

McMichael, D. F. *Shells of the Australian Seashore.* Brisbane: Jacaranda Pocket Guide, 1960.

Penniket, J. R., and Moon, G. J. H. *New Zealand Seashells in Colour.* Wellington: A. H. and A. W. Reed, 1970. Contains 150 species.

Powell, A. W. B. *Shells of New Zealand.* Auckland: Whitcombe and Tombs, Ltd., 1957.

Verco, Sir Joseph. *Combing the Southern Seas.* Edited by B. C. Cotton. Privately printed in Adelaide, 1935. Contains 1908 catalog of South Australian mollusks.

Wilson, Barry R., and Gillett, Keith. *Australian Shells.* Sydney: A. H. and A. W. Reed, 1971. Features living gastropods.

Special Families and Pearls

Allan, Joyce. *Cowry Shells of World Seas.* Melbourne: Georgian House, 1960.

Burgess, C. M. *The Living Cowries.* South Brunswick, N.J.: A. S. Barnes and Co., 1970.

Lane, Frank W. *The Kingdom of the Octopus.* New York: Sheridan House, 1957. Excellent.

Marsh, J. A., and Rippingale, O. H. *Cone Shells of the World.* 2d ed. Brisbane: Jacaranda Press, 1968. Has 258 of the 500 known species.

Ranson, G. *La Vie des Huîtres.* Paris: Librairie Gallimard, 1943.

Russell, Henry D. *Index Nudibranchia.* Greenville, Del.: Delaware Museum of Natural History, 1971. Key to the literature.

Shirai, Shohei. *The Story of Pearls.* San Francisco: Japan Publishing Trading Co., 1970.

Weaver, C. S., and du Pont, John E. *The Living Volutes.* Greenville, Del.: Delaware Museum of Natural History, 1970.

Yonge, C. M. *Oysters.* London: Collins, 1960.

Zeigler, R. F., and Porreca, H. C. *Olive Shells of the World.* North Myrtle Beach, S.C.: Richard Petit, 1969. Privately published.

Children's Books

Abbott, R. Tucker. *Quiz-Me: Seashells,* A Junior Golden Guide. New York: Golden Press, 1966. Inexpensive and informative.

Bevans, M. H. *The Book of Sea Shells.* Garden City, N.Y.: Doubleday, 1961. Excellent for ten- to fifteen-year-olds.

Clemons, Elizabeth. *Shells Are Where You Find Them.* New York: Alfred A. Knopf, 1960.

Dudley, Ruth H. *Sea Shells.* New York: Thomas Y. Crowell, 1953.

Evans, Eva K. *The Adventure Book of Shells.* New York: Golden Press, 1955.

Hutchinson, W. M. *A Child's Book of Sea Shells.* New York: Maxton, 1954. Inexpensive and excellent.

Jacobson, M. K., and Emerson, W. K. *Wonders of the World of Shells: Sea, Land and Fresh-water.* New York: Dodd, Mead and Co., 1971.

Mayo, Eileen. *Shells and How They Live.* London: Pleiades Books, 1955.

Saunders, J. R. *A Golden Stamp Book of Sea Shells.* New York: Golden Press, 1957.

Schisgall, Oscar. *That Remarkable Creature, the Snail.* New York: Julian Messner, 1970.

Tenney, Abby A. *Sea Shells and River Shells.* Boston, 1868. The first American children's book on shells.

Popular Shell Magazines

Hawaiian Shell News. 2777 Kalakaua Ave., Honolulu, Hawaii 96815. Excellent.

Keppel Bay Tidings. 65 Whitman St., Yeppoon, Queensland 4703, Australia. Quarterly on shells.

La Conchiglia [The Shell]. Via Tomacelli, 146, IV Piano, Rome 00186, Italy. Eight times a year. Color-plates.

Of Sea and Shore. P.O. Box 33, Port Gamble, Washington 98364. Quarterly on shells.

Texas Conchologist. 5238 Sanford St., Houston, Texas 77035. Nine times a year.

Index

All page numbers in boldface refer to captions and the accompanying illustrations.

250

Credits

The author and the publisher wish to thank the naturalists who generously made available their outstanding photographs—Robert Robertson, Don M. Byrne, Neville Coleman, Barry R. Wilson, Hal Lewis and Larry Harris.

All illustrations courtesy of the author except for the following.

Pages 2–3—Larry Harris; 5—Hal Lewis; 6—Barry R. Wilson.
CHAPTER ONE: 10–11—Barry R. Wilson; 13—Shell Oil Company; 14—Don M. Byrne; 15, below—Melbourne C. Carriker; 17, lower right—Robert Robertson; 18—Don M. Byrne; 19—F. H. Roberts; 21—Nina Leen; 23, lower left—Virginia Orr Maes; others—F. H. Roberts; 25—originally published in Lemche and Wingstrand, 1959, Galathea Report, vol. 3, pl. 2, fig. 7.
CHAPTER TWO: 26–27—Barry R. Wilson; 28—drawings from R. D. Purchon's *Biology of the Mullusca*, pp. 339 and 341; photo—Mary D'Aiuto; 29—Neville Coleman; 30—drawing courtesy of Gunnar Thorson; 31—all by Robert Robertson; 32—courtesy of John Nesson, M. D. and W. M. Cockerell, Artisans Custom Photolab; 33—courtesy of Sherwood W. Wise, Jr.; 34, left—Nina Leen; right—Robert Robertson; 35—Robert Robertson; 37, left—Shell Oil Company; 38, above—Barry R. Wilson; below—Don M. Byrne; 39, above—Don M. Byrne; below—Hal Lewis; 43, below—Robert Lipe; right—both Robert Robertson; 45—drawings from the Proc. Malacological Soc. London, vol. 36, and G. A. Drew, 1899; photo—Robert Robertson.
CHAPTER THREE: 46–47—Don M. Byrne; 48—Ruth D. Turner; 49—Robert Robertson; 51, above—Shell Oil Company; below—Robert Robertson; 53, above—Neville Coleman; below—Don M. Byrne; 55, above—Nina Leen; below—Robert Robertson; 57, above—Olive Schoenberg; below and right—Robert Robertson; 59—Ruth D. Turner.
CHAPTER FOUR: 60–61—Courtesy of the Delaware Museum of Natural History; 63—both Shell Oil Company; 64–65—*Manuel de Conchyliologie et de Paléontologie Conchyliologique* by J. C. Chenu, 1859; 67—both Shell Oil Company; 69, lower drawings—J. C. Chenu, 1859.
CHAPTER FIVE: 70–71—Larry Harris; 72—Nina Leen; 73—Nina Leen; 75, upper left—Neville Coleman; lower left—Don M. Byrne; upper right—Virginia Orr Maes; lower right—Don M. Byrne; 77, above—Nina Leen; lower two—Allan Mogel; 78, left—Don M. Byrne; right—Barry R. Wilson; 79—Don M. Byrne; 80—Robert Robertson; 81—drawings from J. C. Chenu, 1859; 83, above—Olive Schoenberg; below—Clifton S. Weaver; 84—Robert Robertson; 85, left—Robert Robertson; right—Larry Harris; 86—Robert Lipe; 89—Allan Mogel; 91, below and right—Nina Leen.
CHAPTER SIX: 92–93—Don M. Byrne; 94—Barry R. Wilson; 95—painting by Rudolf Freund, courtesy of Shell Oil Company; 97, above—F. H. Roberts; below—painting by Rudolf Freund, courtesy of Shell Oil Company; 98—painting by Rudolf Freund, courtesy of Shell Oil Company; 99, above—George Raeihle; below—Robert Robertson; 101, above—Mary D'Aiuto; below—Don M. Byrne; 102—Ruth D. Turner; 103—from R. T. Abbott, 1955; 105, above—Shell Oil Company; below—Ruth D. Turner; 107, above—Virginia Orr Maes; below—Nina Leen; 108—Nina Leen; 109—Don M. Byrne; 111—painting by Rudolf Freund, courtesy of Shell Oil Company; 112—both Larry Harris.
CHAPTER SEVEN: 114–115—Courtesy of Paul Leach; 116–117—all Shell Oil Company; 118—F. H. Roberts; 119, left—Robert Robertson; right—F. H. Roberts; 121, upper left—courtesy of Paul Leach; upper right—Virginia Orr Maes; lower left—Shell Oil Company; 122–127—all Shell Oil Company; 128–129—Neil Hepler; 131, left—Clifton S. Weaver; 133—Delaware Museum of Natural History.
CHAPTER EIGHT: 134–135—Hal Lewis; 139, upper right—Shell Oil Company; lower—Dennis M. Opresko; 142, upper left—Nina Leen; lower left—Neville Coleman; right—Shell Oil Company; 143—all Neville Coleman; 145, above—Barry R. Wilson; below—Dennis M. Opresko; 146, left—Nina Leen; 148, left—Hal Lewis; right—Nina Leen; 149, left—Neville Coleman; 151, above—Nina Leen; 153—Neville Coleman; 155—Don M. Byrne; 157, left—Nina Leen; upper right—courtesy of Sue Abbott; lower right—Don M. Byrne; 161, below—Robert Robertson; 162—James H. Lockwood, Jr.; 163, upper left—Shell Oil Company; 164—Olive Schoenberg; 165, above—Ruth D. Turner; below—Nina Leen; 169—courtesy of Sue Abbott; 170–171—courtesy of Thomas R. Waller.
CHAPTER NINE: 172–173—cameo from the Delaware Museum of Natural History; 174—kindness of Caroline G. Dosker of the University Museum of the University of Pennsylvania; 175, above—courtesy E. W. Andrews IV, Tulane University; below—Smithsonian Institution; 177—all University Museum of the University of Pennsylvania; 179—Smithsonian Institution; 181—University Museum of the University of Pennsylvania; 182 and 183—Shell Oil Company; 187, above—Robert Robertson; below—Shell Oil Company; 188 and 189—Shell Oil Company; 191, above—National Gallery of Art, Washington, D.C.; 192–195—Shell Oil Company.
CHAPTER TEN: 196–197—courtesy of Helen K. Krauss; 199—U.S. Bureau of Commercial Fisheries; 201—Stan LoPresto; 203—U.S. Bureau of Commercial Fisheries; 205—Stan LoPresto; 206—Mary D'Aiuto; 207—Robert Robertson; 209—Frederick A. Aldrich; 210—Mikimoto Pearl Company; 214, right—Ruth D. Turner; 217, left—Nina Leen; above—Don M. Byrne; 218—Virginia Orr Maes; 219—Natural Science Foundation of the Academy of Natural Sciences of Philadelphia; 220–221—Shell Oil Company.
CHAPTER ELEVEN: 224–225—courtesy of Hal Lewis; 228—Allan Mogel; 229—courtesy of Helen K. Krauss; 231—Allan Mogel; 232—Clifton S. Weaver; 234, left—Academy of Natural Sciences of Philadelphia; right—courtesy of W. Adam, Brussels; 237 upper three—courtesy Academy of Natural Sciences of Philadelphia; lower three—courtesy of S. Peter Dance, Wales.